Top 10 Visionaries that Changed the World

George Ilian

Cover Illustrations: Iren Flowers

Warning-Disclaimer

The purpose of this book is to educate and entertain. The author or publisher does not guarantee that anyone following the techniques, suggestions, tips, ideas, or strategies will become successful. The author and publisher shall have neither liability or responsibility to anyone with respect to any loss or damage caused or alleged to be caused, directly or indirectly by the information contained in this book.

Table of Contents

Welcome

What if you could sit down to dine with some of the world's most successful entrepreneurs and have a conversation with them? What would you ask them? What business ideas and life lessons would they give to you? Of course, it was not possible to deliver any one of these rock star entrepreneurs to your dinner table- no matter who was doing the cooking or what you were serving.

But I could be your ambassador, and I will present you in my book- *10 of the world greatest living visionaries of our time*, people who have truly changed the way we live and think, the way we work and play, the way we now see the world itself. Some might even be controversial and present us with some bad examples. The book includes a collection of 10 books. Each book has 50 Life and Business lessons from a very famous and successful person. One thing I've learned over the years of being an entrepreneur is that if you don't have passion for the business you are doing, then the probability of not making it is very high. I'm here to fuel that passion by giving you some great ideas you can depend on. The goal is to get the reader motivated and inspired to take action and succeed in life. I was really inspired to start working for myself and be my own boss when I read Richard Branson's biography, and the one on Steve Jobs really made me want to be the best at what I do, but reading these long books more than 500 pages each, is really time consuming, so I put the most important information about each person into a short and digestible form so that you can get the most value from the book in the shortest period of time. In summary, you will learn the most important things about each person; they will get you motivated, and they will save your time!

How were these ten people chosen? To a large extent by their impact. How original was their idea? How influential had it become? Did it transfer our personal lives in any significant way? Did it alter our professional lives to allow us to become more productive, more thoughtful, and better equipped to accomplish things to make our own mark in this world? Admittedly, the answers to these questions are entirely subjective. As are the choices of the people in this book, all of them are world changers whose product and services have found their way- big and small into our lives.

As important as the products and services these visionaries have brought to the world, they also have deserved reputations for creating places of work that encourage creativity, innovation, and meaning.

The goal is to bring that person's experience and wisdom to these pages for your benefit, to inspire you so you can learn and achieve. I want this book to be both a meditation on entrepreneurship and an inspiration for those who want to create something meaningful on their own. Speaking of the entrepreneurs, there is much more similarity than difference in how they think. They all start not thinking about themselves; they start to think externally, and how they can help their country (or even the world).

There are three main attributes every entrepreneur shares: opportunistic mindset, acceptance of risk and potential failure, independence, and control.

Opportunistic mindset: Where others see disruption and chaos, entrepreneurs see opportunity. It is a simple, even romantic notion of entrepreneurship, perhaps. Still, many great businesses have been created by people who were able to clearly spot an opportunity in the chaos of a crowded marketplace.

Acceptance of risk and potential failure: While entrepreneurs are far more willing to assume the necessary risk that comes with creating something new, they are just ready to allow for the possibility that they could be wrong. Dead wrong at times. Among venture capitalists, in fact, failure is viewed as something like a badge of honor, since you learn way more from your failures, rather than from your successes. As Arnold Schwarzenegger said: *"Strength does not come from winning. Your struggles develop your strengths. When you go through hardships and decide not to surrender, that is strength."*

Independence and control: Almost everyone wants to have a sense of independence and control over their life. But with entrepreneurs, having independence and control is as much a need as it is a want. Steve Jobs is a great example of this by controlling the full user experience for his customers from the buying through the packaging to the hardware and software. Make no mistake about it: The need for control is fundamental to an entrepreneur's vision. Individuals with an external focus of control typically believe that events happen as a result of circumstances that are beyond their control. By contrast, people who possess internal focus of control believe that the events in their life result directly from their own actions or behavior.

To these three core stands, entrepreneurs bring drive, tenacity, and persistence. They live what they believe, building success by a strong culture and values. They seek out niches and market gaps. They are architects of their own passionate and focused vision. An often common thought little-noticed trait among many of the most successful entrepreneurs is personal tragedy. For example, Oprah Winfrey was sexually abused from the age of nine to thirteen and Steve

Jobs was unwanted by his parents and given up for adoption at birth. But they had the will to overcome every obstacle. It comes from their trust in themselves, so many of these entrepreneurs share this fundamental adversity. If there is turmoil in their lives, there seems to be a vision to move far beyond it.

All of those traits and challenges are highly evident in the following conversations with some of the world's greatest entrepreneurs. These exceptional institution builders offer a treasure chest of insights: how to seize new opportunities, build valuable and lasting companies, lead people, think more creatively, and overcome obstacles. All of them know how to win. All of them are winners.

This book will stimulate your thinking and make the necessary adjustments needed to ensure success in your situation. I hope that these ideas will provide you with the inspiration to find out more or develop your thinking along new, creative lines and generating brilliant ideas for your life and your business.

50 Life and Business Lessons from Steve Jobs

Geniuses come in every shape and colour, and when they step into a room, we almost expect them to glow, or buzz with a special energy that sets them apart from the rest of us. To many people, the slightly-built, greying and bespectacled gentlemen in a long-sleeved black turtleneck and blue Levi jeans would never have warranted a second look. Steve Jobs was extraordinary in his apparent ordinariness.

When you peel back the layers, however, Steve Jobs was far from ordinary. His far-sightedness, persistence and absolute faith in the Apple brand and Apple products catapulted the company from nowhere in 1976, to global superstar status today: Apple is the second largest (but best-known) consumer information technology company in the world; it's the world's largest publicly traded corporation; Apple's world-wide revenue in 2014 totalled $182 billion; and at the end of 2014, Apple became the first American company ever to be valued at more than $700 billion. If you want to understand Apple, you need to think big. If you, like Jobs, want to conceive a success story like Apple in the first place, you need to have the unrestricted imagination and ambition to think even bigger than that.

The birth and re-birth of Apple were by no means his only achievements, however: Jobs also founded the pioneering NeXT, which would prove to be his segue back to Apple in 1997. He bought Pixar from Lucasfilm and made it a blockbuster success, delivering the likes of *Toy Story, Finding Nemo* and *Monsters, Inc.* to delight a generation of children (and their parents) around the world. And when he sold Pixar to Disney, he became Disney's largest shareholder and a valuable member of the board.

Collectively through his achievements, Jobs would transform the world of consumer technology, not only in computing but in music and digital animation too. He would bring lines of previously inconceivable products to the market place, sell those products direct to consumers, and make computing cooler than it had ever been before. He has quite rightly been acclaimed as the entrepreneur, and the CEO, of his generation, and one of the greatest innovators of all time.

In this book you will find an introduction to Steve Jobs, his life and work. It is by no means encyclopaedic, but it is not intended to be. The narrative is told chronology and in bite-size chunks so that you can dip in and learn about a specific period in his life, a particular project or achievement. For ease of learning, and to make you think about what Jobs can teach you in your own life and business, there are 50 short lessons, one at the end of each section, that sums up the most important points to remember. We cannot all become Steve Jobs or found a company as game changing Apple, but we can make the most of his example and become ever more successful in the things that we do.

Genius Was Born

Steve Jobs was born in San Francisco on February 24, 1955. His biological parents, Syrian-born Abdulfatah "John" Jandali, a graduate student at the University of Wisconsin, and his mother, a Swiss-American undergraduate named Joanne Carole Schieble, weren't planning on parenthood so soon, and even after Schieble fell pregnant with Jobs, her conservative father refused to let them marry. They gave Jobs up for adoption as soon as he was born, and he was adopted by Paul and Clara Jobs, who had been married since 1946 but were sadly unable to have their own children. Schieble had specified that the baby should only be adopted by college graduates, but although the Jobs both had relatively little formal education, a compromise was struck when they promised to encourage, and financially support, the child through college.

Lesson No. 1: Your start in life is not what is most important: it is where you end up that counts.

Although many adopted children describe feelings of loss, abandonment or somehow not belonging, Jobs had no such concerns: he believed he was not abandoned but rather chosen, stated that Paul and Clara Jobs "were my parents 1,000%," and in his authorised biography reiterated, "Paul and Clara are 100% my parents. And Joanna and Abdulfatah—are only a sperm and an egg bank. It's not rude, it is the truth." The Jobs lavished affection on their adopted son and provided him with a comfortable, stable childhood.

Lesson No. 2: Don't be afraid to speak the truth.

The Jobs family moved to Mountain View, which would later become the heart of Silicon Valley, when Jobs was five, and shortly after the move, they adopted a daughter, Patty. The Jobs family was complete, and Jobs' childhood was stable and unremarkable. His mother worked as an accountant for Varian Associates, one of California's first high-tech firms, and his father worked as a mechanic and carpenter.

Young Jobs was encouraged to work alongside his father in the workshop, and as a result he picked up many practical skills. Jobs learned how things work, and how to make them with his own hands. The Jobs were unpretentious, practical people, and their work ethic was passed on to both of their children.

Lesson No. 3: Practical skills and hard work underpin achievement.

Jobs was a smart child, scoring elementary school test scores two grades higher than his age, but he didn't apply himself particularly and he was often disruptive in class. He skipped a year of school, and whilst at Homestead High School in Cupertino forged a close friendship with Bill Fernandez (who later became Apple Computers' first employee), who introduced Jobs to his neighbour, Steve Wozniak. Together, Jobs and Wozniak would transform the world of technology.

Lesson No. 4: Personal relationships are vital to success.

Jobs graduated from high school in 1972 and, true to his parents' promise, they enrolled him at Reed College in Portland, Oregon, despite the fact that they could ill afford to do so. Jobs lasted just six months at Reed before dropping out. He slept on friends' dorm room floors, recycled Coca Cola bottles to earn a few cents, and ate free meals at a Hare Krishna temple. This could well have been the end of Jobs' story, but just because he had no interest in conventional education didn't mean he'd be a life-long underachiever.

Lesson No. 5: Nothing is beneath you when you're starting out.

The same year, Wozniak designed and built a new version the iconic arcade game *Pong* and he asked his friend Jobs to present it to Atari Inc. at their head office. Thinking that Jobs was the creator, Atari offered him a job as a technician. Jobs did not dissuade them of their view.

Jobs worked for the company throughout the early 1970s, but took a seven-month sabbatical to India, where he stayed at an ashram and sought spiritual enlightenment from a variety of religious teachers. He studied Zen Buddhism seriously, considered becoming a monk at the Eihei-ji temple in Japan, and remained a practising Buddhist throughout his life.

Lesson No. 6: Know yourself.

Jobs' travels in this period had a profound effect on him. When asked about the importance of gaining experience by Wired magazine in 1996, he said:

Unfortunately, that's too rare a commodity. A lot of people in our industry haven't had very diverse experiences. So they don't have enough dots to connect, and they end up with very linear solutions without a broad perspective on the problem. The broader one's understanding of the human experience, the better design we will have.

When asked by the *New York Times* for his opinion on Bill Gates, he drew parallels with his own life and implied Gates would have done better had he followed suit:

I just think he [Gates] and Microsoft are a bit narrow. He'd be a broader guy if he had dropped acid once or gone off to an ashram when he was younger.

Jobs was adamant that his cross-cultural experience as a young man in India, and his countercultural values, were essential to the development of his thinking. He believed that unless you shared those experiences and values, you would not be able to relate to him. Right from the beginning, Jobs wanted to be seen as an outsider, a rebel, and a maverick.

Lesson No. 7: Be open to new ideas and experiences.

When Jobs returned to the US after his sabbatical, Jobs and Wozniak worked on more arcade games for Atari, and also on blue box telephone dialling devices. In both cases their focus was on reducing the numbers of chips used in the circuit board design so that they were cheaper to manufacture. The two men experimented with different technologies and sold their blue boxes illegally as they circumvented long-distance call charges for phones.

Computing as a discipline was in its earliest phase in the mid-1970s, but both Jobs and Wozniak joined the Homebrew Computer Club in Menlo Park, a group of technically minded individuals who met, experimented, chatted and traded parts as a hobby. It was at the first Homebrew meeting that Jobs saw an MITS Altair, one of the earliest microcomputers, and Wozniak subsequently recalled that it was at that moment he was inspired to design the first Apple product.

Lesson No. 8: Keep abreast of new technologies.

The Birth of Apple

Steve Jobs might well be the famous face of Apple, but there's a strong case that Steve Wozniak was the brains of the outfit, at least in the company's earliest phase. Inspired by the electronics samples he and Jobs had seen at the Homebrew Computer Club, Wozniak built the Apple I personal computer kit, a pre-assembled circuit board. Users had to add their own monitor, power supply and keyboard, and the Apple I had just 4 KB of memory.

Lesson No. 9: The only way to do great work is to love what you do.

Even if Wozniak was the technical whizz kid, it was Jobs who was the one with a head for figures and who saw the commercial value of Wozniak's invention. Jobs obtained the first order, for 50 machines, from the Byte Store, a local computer store in Mountain View. The order was worth $25,000, and the parts alone cost $20,000, and as the components had been bought on 30-day credit, all 50 had to be built and delivered to Byte within 10 days. The Apple I went on sale in July 1976, and a single unit cost $666.66 (equivalent to $2,763 today when adjusted for inflation).

Lesson No. 10: Know your own strengths and those of the people around you.

Apple was incorporated as a company in January 1977, by which time the Apple I was selling well. The sole shareholders of the company at the time of incorporation were Jobs and Wozniak as they had bought out a third partner, Ronald Wayne, for $800. Wayne, who was older and, unlike his co-founders, had personal assets, thought the venture was too risky, though he'd come to rue his premature exit. In February 2015, Apple's value exceeded $700 billion, If Wayne had kept his 10% stock until then, it would have been worth approximately $60 billion.

Lesson No. 11: Be prepared to take a gamble.

To grow the company whilst allowing Wozniak to develop new products, Jobs had to take responsibility for raising substantial funding. He convinced Mike Markkula, an angel investor who had made his own fortune from stock options he acquired working at Intel, to provide an equity investment of $80,000 and an additional loan of $170,000. In exchange, Markkula took one-third of Apple's shares, and became employee No.3.

Markkula was a trained engineer, and he bought both experience and credibility to the new company. He wrote programs for Apple II, beta-tested products, introduced Michael Scott as Apple's first CEO and President, and helped Jobs obtain additional venture capital. Jobs was humble enough to recognise his own limitations, to watch what Markkula did attentively, and to learn from him. For Jobs, Markkula was both a business partner and a mentor, and this period in the late 1970s was probably Jobs' most important period of education in life.

Lesson No. 12: Choose your investors wisely as they can offer more than just funding.

Apple's second project, the not-so-imaginatively named Apple II, was launched in April 1977 and, unlike the Apple I, it had a commercial launch at the West Coast Computer Faire. It was streets ahead of its competitors for three reasons: Apple II had cell-based colour graphics; it was based on open architecture; and you could use a regular cassette tape for storage. Later versions could take a 5.5" floppy disk instead of a cassette tape, and there was a custom-built interface called Disk II. The Apple II was only one of three computers on the market released specifically for home users. Collectively these three computers were known as the 1977 Trinity, and the other two models were the Commodore PET and the Tandy Corporations TRS-80.

Lesson No. 13: Be innovative.

The first computer spreadsheet program, VisiCalc, was released in the middle of 1979 by Software Arts. It was one of the first pieces of truly user-friendly software, it retailed for under $100, and, most importantly of all, for the first 12 months it was available, it was only compatible with the Apple II. Users bought the Apple II specifically to run VisiCalc, and the Apple II ceased being a novelty item for tech geeks and became an essential part of the office furniture. Apple thus made the transition into the business market without having to make changes to their product or to spend a fortune on advertising.

Apple's growth accelerated throughout the late 1970s. Jobs ran a professional team that included both computer designers and those who worked on the production line, and together they looked how to utilise existing products and ideas in innovative ways. Jobs took his team to Xerox PARC, a research and development company in Palo Alto, in December 1979. Here they saw for the first time Xerox's graphical user interface (GUI) and Jobs was adamant that this was the future of computing. Jobs negotiated three days use of Xerox's facilities in exchange for $1,000,000 of pre-IPO stock, and that was all the time they needed to dream up the core features of the Apple Lisa, the first personal computer aimed at individual business users to have a GUI. Xerox undoubtedly did well out of this deal too: the pre-IPO price that they negotiated was just $10.

Lesson No. 14: Compatibility with related products, current and future, is important.

1980 was a bumper year for Apple - Jobs launched the Apple III in May, and the company had received attention-grabbing coverage in both *Kilobaud Microcomputing* (the leading magazine for computer hobbyists) and the *Financial Times* - and so on December 12, Apple launched its initial public offering (IPO). When Apple went public, it immediately created 300 millionaires (more than any other company in history), and it raised more capital than any US firm since the Ford Motor Company in 1956. The market was buzzing, and investors and commentators alike wanted a slice of the Apple pie. The opening price for Apple shares was $22, so Xerox instantly made a fortune, as did many other venture capitalists who had backed the company in its earliest days.

Lesson No. 15: Be generous to all your stakeholders. You can achieve success and wealth together.

Apple's first shareholder meeting as a public company took place in January 1981. Jobs took to the floor with pre-prepared speech, but a short way into the meeting he abandoned his script and spoke from the heart. Investors bought into the Jobs brand, and that of Apple, and his charisma and passion for his products spoke volumes. Jobs exuded confidence and was able to enthuse other people. Just as he had been able to entice Mike Scott to join Apple from National Superconductor in 1978, when Jobs stretched out a hand to John Sculley (then President of Pepsi Cola) to become Apple's CEO in 1983, Sculley wouldn't have dreamed of refusing. Jobs knew that having the right team at Apple was the key to its long-term success, and he wasn't afraid to tell people so:

> My model for business is The Beatles. They were four guys who kept each other's kind of negative tendencies in check. They balanced each other and the total was greater than the sum of the parts. That's how I see business: great things in business are never done by one person, they're done by a team of people.

Lesson No. 16: Surround yourself with brilliance.

The product that put Apple on the map, more than any other (at least in the company's formative years) was the Macintosh, the first mass-produced personal computer with an integral GUI and a computer mouse to control it. The Macintosh took its name from the designer Jef Raskin's favourite kind of apple (the McIntosh), but as another company (McIntosh Laboratory Inc) already owned that brand name, and refused to give Jobs a release for the name, the spelling change was necessary.

Jobs was personally emotionally attached to the Macintosh, as were many members of its development team. He told *Playboy* magazine about it in 1985:

> I don't think I've ever worked so hard on something, but working on Macintosh was the neatest experience of my life. Almost everyone who worked on it will say that. None of us wanted to release it at the end. It was as though we knew that once it was out of our hands, it wouldn't be ours anymore. When we finally presented it at the shareholders' meeting, everyone in the auditorium gave it a five-minute ovation. What was incredible to me was that I could see the Mac team in the first few rows. It was as though none of us could believe we'd actually finished it. Everyone started crying.

It was also when Jobs was working on the Macintosh that his colleague Bud Tribble first coined the phrase "reality distortion field" (RDF) to describe Jobs' ability to convince himself (and everyone else) that what seemed to be impossible was, in fact, possible. He used a mixture of charisma, bravado, hyperbole and dogged persistence to get his message through, though critics have suggested Jobs did sometimes allow the distortion of reality to run too far. Although that his colleagues were aware of it, they were easily falling into the RDF, this is how inspirational and motivational Steve Jobs was a leader of his team.

Lesson No. 17: Build and sell great products that you believe in.

The public product launch of the Macintosh was second to none, before or since. Apple spent $2.5 million buying all 39 advertising pages in a special edition of *Newsweek*; they inserted an 18-page brochure in numerous other magazines; and they ran their now-infamous *1984* commercial, directed by Ridley Scott, at the Super Bowl. That single national broadcast cost Apple $1.5 million, and the advert parodied scenes from George Orwell's dystopian novel, *Nineteen Eight-Four*. The advert's heroine wore a Macintosh emblazoned on her t-shirt, and together they saved the world from conformity. The response from Apple's shareholders was ecstatic.

Lesson No. 18: Be persistent. Be persuasive.

The Macintosh went on sale two days after the advert aired at the Super Bowl. The company ran a "Test Drive a Macintosh" promotion, a new idea whereby anyone with a credit card could borrow a computer for 24 hours to test it out at home. 200,000 consumers participated in the promotion (far in excess of Apple's predictions), and demand was so high that Apple could not not make machines fast enough to meet it. They increased the price from $1,995 to $2,495, and still consumers flocked to the stores.

The GUI on the Macintosh was completely new, and existing forms of software had to be re-written in order to be compatible with it. In order to avoid being written off as a novelty item, Apple therefore had to develop their own software that worked with their new platform. Apple bundled two programs with the computer when you bought it, MacWrite and MacPaint, encouraged Microsoft and Linux to develop Mac-compatible versions, and launched their own Macintosh Office before the end of 1985. These moves were Apple's first ventures into software, but Jobs recognised that his machines would never dominate the market unless there were sufficient, high-quality programs to run on them.

Lesson No. 19:People who are serious about software should make their own hardware.

Although Jobs was charming and persuasive, he was also disorganised and erratic in his management style. Colleagues remember Jobs running meetings into the early hours of the morning and then still expecting staff to be at their desks for seven the following morning. This inevitably caused tensions in the office, particularly with the newly-appointed Sculley. The working relationship between the two men deteriorated substantially. Jobs attempted to oust his CEO but failed. The move backfired terribly: Apple's board of directors gave Sculley the authority to remove Jobs from all posts bar that of Chairman, and then they stripped him of his management duties too. Jobs stopped coming to work and resigned completely five months later.

Lesson No. 20: Stay hungry, stay foolish.

The Next Step

Bruised from his ignominious departure from Apple, which had been the dominant feature in his life for the past decade, Jobs toyed briefly with the idea of crossing the Iron Curtain and opening a computer company in the USSR, and he also applied (unsuccessfully) to brome a civilian astronaut onboard the International Space Station. With the commercial responsibility of Apple lifted from his shoulders, Jobs became happier and more creative: in a speech at Stanford University in 2005 he would look back on his firing from Apple as the best thing that could possibly have happened to him. He reflected, "I'm pretty sure none of this would have happened if I hadn't been fired from Apple. It was awful-tasting medicine, but I guess the patient needed it."

Lesson No. 21: Look critically at yourself, know your mistakes, and work hard to fix them. No one else is going to do this for you.

Jobs had sold all bar one of his 6.5 million Apple shares, and had consequently pocketed $70 million, an eye-watering sum at any point in history, but especially in 1985. Using the experience he had gained at Apple, the first thing he did was to invest $7 million of his own money into a new venture, NeXT, and he partnered with billionaire investor Ross Perot.

Jobs used the expertise he had gained from Apple but crucially in this new company, where he alone made the decisions, he could take the products in the direction he wanted to. He had ideas about architecture he wanted to pursue, and he set off and tried them out.

Lesson No. 22: Don't be afraid to be a beginner again. There's a phrase in Buddhism, 'Beginner's mind.' It's wonderful to have a beginner's mind.

Priced at $9,999, the first NeXT computer was too expensive for home and education users it had originally been designed for. It did, however, contain experimental technologies such as digital signal processor chips, a built-in Ethernet port, and a Mach kernal, and these innovative features made it attractive to the financial, scientific, and academic communities.

Jobs identified this interest and galvanised the media to cover the lavish gala event that marked the product's launch. Jobs' hunch that the NeXT was best suited as a research machine was right: whilst he was working at CERN, Tim Berners-Lee invented his browser for the World Wide Web on his NeXT workstation.

Following his gut hunches was important to Jobs, and more often than not they proved correct. He mused on the subject:

You can't connect the dots looking forward; you can only connect them looking backward. So you have to trust that the dots will somehow connect in your future. You have to trust in something — your gut, destiny, life, karma, whatever. This approach has never let me down, and it has made all the difference in my life.

Lesson No. 23: Do what you believe is right, even if it doesn't make sense at the time.

Jobs was not satisfied with the first version of NeXT, however, and so in less than a year he released the NeXTcube. Jobs advertised the NeXTcube as the first 'interpersonal' computer: it was a personal computer that you could use to share voice files, images, graphics, and even video by email. This had never been possible before. Jobs told reporters at the *Computimes* and *New Straits Times* that this marked a revolution in computing, and in many ways this was true. The journalists picked up the message and ran with it.

Lesson No. 24: If you are not satisfied with what you have made, do it again. And this time do it better.

It is in the development of the NeXTcube that we first see Jobs' obsession with aesthetics, a major factor in the success of Apple today. He described his philosophy as follows:

When you're a carpenter making a beautiful chest of drawers, you're not going to use a piece of plywood on the back, even though it faces the wall and nobody will see it. You'll know it's there, so you're going to use a beautiful piece of wood on the back. For you to sleep well at night, the aesthetic, the quality, has to be carried all the way through.

Much to the horror of NeXT's hardware department, Jobs demanded that the NeXTcube be given a magnesium case. This was not only more expensive but more difficult to work with than earlier plastic cases. Jobs won the argument by force of personality, however, and from then on he has always been associated with developing products that are as visually appealing as they are functional.

Lesson No. 25: Functionality and design go hand in hand when you are developing a desirable product.

Jobs understood from his experience with the Macintosh that users wanted first-rate software to run on their new machines, and he encouraged software developers to design NeXT compatible programs. The machines came with *Mathematica* (a program for those working in the scientific, engineering, mathematical and computing fields) pre-installed, Tim Berners-Lee made the first web browser for NeXT platforms, and by the early 1990s there were also a number of computer games available for NeXT machines, including *Doom*, *Heretic*, and *Quake*. It was possible to install the *Meriam-Webster Dictionary* and the *Complete Works of Shakespeare* too, should you feel so inclined.

NeXT computers at first had their own, proprietary operating system, NeXTSTEP, but within a year of the launch of the first NeXT machines, Jobs realised that it was the operating system, rather than the computer hardware, that would make NeXT a fortune. He therefore took the bold step of re-orientating the company's business strategy. He oversaw the development of a PC compatible version of NeXTStep in 1991, held a demo of it at the NeXTWorld Expo in January 1992, and by the middle of 1993, the software was selling well to corporate clients. Industry trend setters such as Chrysler, First Chicago NBC and the Swiss Bank Corporation, as well as government bodies including the Central Intelligence Agency, the National Security Agency, and the Naval Research Laboratory, installed the operating system, and their belief in the software encouraged others to follow suit.

Lesson No. 26: Turn consumers into evangelists, not just customers

Under Jobs' leadership, NeXT stopped making hardware completely in 1993 and concentrated on software alone. Sun Microsystems invested $10 million in NeXT, and together Jobs and Sun's CEO, Scott McNealy, built a new operating system called OpenStep, a version of which was available for Microsoft Windows. More important than this, however, was their launch of WebObjects, a platform for building large-scale dynamic web applications. This software was adopted by the BBC, Disney, WorldCom and Dell, as well as other major international players, and it was this single product that made NeXT such a desirable acquisition target for Apple in 1996 (see *Part 4: Return to Apple*).

Lesson No. 27: Focus on your strengths.

Whilst at NeXT, Jobs experiments with original business management strategies as well as new products. He wanted to create a completely new corporate culture and to improve the sense of community at the company. Jobs emphasised the point that his staff were not employees but rather members of the company, and as such they were entitled to many benefits: until 1990s there were only two basic salary plans on offer, $75,000 to those who joined before 1986, and $50,000 to those who joined after. Performance reviews took place every six months, and if you did well, you would be offered a pay rise. Staff were paid monthly in advance (rather than bi-weekly in arrears, as was the custom in Silicon Valley at the time), and the company health insurance plan was available to unmarried and same-sex couples as well as married couples.

NeXT's offices, designed by architect I M Pei, were almost entirely open plan: only Jobs' office and the conference rooms were enclosed. This fostered a sense of oversight by and of your peers, and so encouraged staff to work harder.

Lesson No. 28: Build the right environment, to inspire creativity and hard work.

Although Jobs dedicated much of his time and effort to NeXT, it was not his only commercial interest at this time. He bought The Graphics Group from Lucasfilm in 1986 for $10 million and renamed the company Pixar. Although Jobs had no creative experience (beyond taking a calligraphy course in college), he did understand the technology behind computer graphics and believed he could take the company into a new phase in digital animation.

Pixar's first film, in 1995, was *Toy Story*, and Jobs was the executive producer. Other box office hits included *A Bug's Life* (1998), *Monsters Inc* (2001), *Finding Nemo* (2003) and *The Incredibles* (2004), and Pixar won the Academy Award for Best Animated Feature seven times. Jobs was fast becoming a force to be reckoned with in the film world as well as in the world of computers.

Lesson No. 29: Don't limit yourself. Spread your creativity into different areas.

All of these films had been distributed through Disney, and in the run-up to the expiry of this distribution contract, Jobs was responsible for renegotiating the deal with Disney's chief executive, Michael Eisner. Despite Jobs' efforts, the renegotiation efforts floundered, but Eisner was replaced by Bob Iger in late 2005, and the story took an unexpected twist. Iger offered to buy Pixar from Jobs and his partners for an all-stock transaction worth $7.4 billion. Jobs jumped at the opportunity and consequently became the largest single shareholder, owning 7% of Disney's shares. He also joined Disney's board of directors.

Lesson No. 30: Make sure you diversify your portfolio. Spreading your risk across multiple businesses can generate unexpected returns.

Return to Apple

Throughout the 1990s, under the successive leaderships of Sculley (1983 to '93), Michael Spindler (1993 to '96) and Gil Amelio (1996 to '97), Apple was struggling commercially, so much so that Amelio described the company as being, "like a ship with a hole in the bottom, leaking water." The IBM PC was dominating the computer market and had a comparable GUI; Apple's new product lines (which included Centris, Quadra and Performa) were poorly marketed and sold erratically; and in 1995 the decision was taken to license the Mac OS and Macintosh ROMs to third party manufacturers, short-sightedly removing the Macintosh's unique selling point (USP).

Lesson No. 31: With the wrong person at the helm, even a strong company can take a turn for the worse.

What Apple's directors did do, however, was realise their shortcomings, and in particular that they needed a new generation operating system to take the company forward into the 21st century. NeXT and Be Inc competed against each other in the bid process, and NeXT emerged from the battle triumphant. Apple acquired NeXT for $419 million in cash, and Jobs personally received 1.5 million shares in Apple.

Jobs was invited back to Apple, initially as a consultant in December 1996 (when Amelio was ousted) and then, seven months later, he was appointed as interim CEO, a position which would be made permanent in 2000. Way back in 1985, in an interview with *Playboy* magazine, Jobs had told the reporter:

I'll always stay connected with Apple. I hope that throughout my life I'll sort of have the thread of my life and the thread of Apple weave in and out of each other, like a tapestry. There may be a few years when I'm not there, but I'll always come back.

Unwittingly he had foretold his own future.

Lesson No. 32: Be patient, and be humble.

Jobs' return was a breath of fresh air into a company that had become increasingly stagnant in its ideas, projects and personnel. Jobs terminated research and development projects he didn't feel had long-term viability (including Cyberdog, Newton and OpenDoc); he identified a loop hole in the Mac OS licensing contracts and used it to terminate them; and he shook up the company's management structure.

Salon magazine reported that after Jobs' return, Apple employees tried to avoid stepping into a lift with him, "afraid that they might not have a job when the doors opened," but in reality only a few members of staff suffered this fate. Jobs did restructure Apple's board of directors, however, parachuting in some of the best executives from NeXT and so allowing the two companies to fully merge.

Lesson No. 33: Don't be afraid to make difficult decisions, the ones who are crazy enough to think they can change the world are usually the ones that do.

Journalists were keen to report on Jobs being the single-handed saviour of Apple, but he didn't see it that way. When asked by BusinessWeek in May 1998 if his return would reinvigorate the company with a sense of magic, Jobs replied:

You're missing it. This is not a one-man show. What's reinvigorating this company is two things: One, there's a lot of really talented people in this company who listened to the world tell them they were losers for a couple of years, and some of them were on the verge of starting to believe it themselves. But they're not losers. What they didn't have was a good set of coaches, a good plan. A good senior management team. But they have that now.

His humility over this issue won him a great deal of respect amongst his Apple colleagues and the wider tech community.

Lesson No. 34: Respect your team.

Apple's corporate recovery had begun, and Jobs was the man with both the vision and his hand on the rudder. Although he probably had only an inkling of it at the time, things for Apple were about to get very exciting indeed.

Using NeXT's WebObjects application as its basis, Jobs launched the Apple Store in November 1997. WebObjects meant that the Apple Store was quick to build - it took less than a year to design it and make it operational - and in the first month of trading, the Apple Store generated $12 million in orders. This was the first time that Apple had had a direct sales outlet: until now it had always sold products through third party agents. The direct sales model also enabled Jobs to implement his new manufacturing strategy, one where products were built to order.

The built to order model (also known as just in time, or JIT) is a concept developed in Japan by Toyota in the 1950s as part of their philosophy of Lean Management, and it was something Jobs had trialled when building the offices for NeXT. When properly implemented, it enables a company to improve its return on investment by reducing its inventory and carrying costs. JIT requires precision and organisation, but at Apple it proved very effective indeed.

The launch of the Apple Store online was the first part of this process: physical Apple Stores would open from 2001 onwards, optimising product visibility in the marketplace and ensuring it was Apple, not an intermediary, who would earn the lion's share of the profits on retail sales.

Lesson No. 35: Control the full user experience from the product itself, even to the buying experience.

Although Apple and Microsoft had a historic rivalry, Jobs took to the stage at the 1997 Macworld Expo to announce a five-year partnership with Microsoft. Microsoft agreed to release Microsoft Office for use on the Macintosh platform and make a token investment of $150 million into Apple; and in exchange, Apple settled a long-running dispute as to whether or not Microsoft Windows infringed Apple patents, and announced that Internet Explorer (a Microsoft product) would henceforth be the default web browser on Apple's machines.

Jobs was very much the public mouthpiece of Apple, and so people listened when he spoke. In reality, few people were interested in the minutiae of the partnership deal, but they did respond favourably to his over arching message:

If we want to move forward and see Apple healthy and prospering again, we have to let go of a few things here. We have to let go of this notion that for Apple to win, Microsoft has to lose. We have to embrace a notion that for Apple to win, Apple has to do a really good job. And if others are going to help us that's great, because we need all the help we can get, and if we screw up and we don't do a good job, it's not somebody else's fault, it's our fault. So I think that is a very important perspective. If we want Microsoft Office on the Mac, we better treat the company that puts it out with a little bit of gratitude; we like their software.

So, the era of setting this up as a competition between Apple and Microsoft is over as far as I'm concerned. This is about getting Apple healthy, this is about Apple being able to make incredibly great contributions to the industry and to get healthy and prosper again.

Lesson No. 36: Find an enemy! Great rivalries are the best advertisement.

With the wind in his sales, and the highly regarded reputation of Microsoft as an added boost, Jobs strode confidently into 1998 and the start of an extraordinary period of innovation for Apple. The company would transform the world of consumer electronics with the launch of the iMac, the iBook, the iPod and, of course, Mac OS.

Yet again, Jobs emphasised the importance of aesthetics in the design process for the iMac.

Design is a funny word. Some people think design means how it looks. But of course, if you dig deeper, it's really how it works. The design of the Mac wasn't what it looked like, although that was part of it. Primarily, it was how it worked. To design something really well, you have to get it. You have to really grok what it's all about. It takes a passionate commitment to really thoroughly understand something, chew it up, not just quickly swallow it. Most people don't take the time to do that.

The 'i', imaginatively, stood for Internet, individuality and innovation, and was the brainchild of Ken Segall, an employee at an LA advertising agency. Jobs had originally wanted to call the new machine MacMan, but he recognised the superiority of Segall's suggestion and adopted it.

Lesson No. 37: Call an expert when you need to.

The selling point of the iMac was its simplicity: users wanted out-of-the-box experiences, and this is exactly what Jobs gave them, even when it was hard to deliver.

That's been one of my mantras — focus and simplicity. Simple can be harder than complex: You have to work hard to get your thinking clean to make it simple. But it's worth it in the end because once you get there, you can move mountains.

It wasn't just rhetoric, however. Jobs practised what he preached. In one famous TV commercial, a seven year old and his dog were challenged to set up an iMac, racing against a Stanford University MBA student with an HP Pavilion 8250. The child and the dog were ready to go after eight minutes and 15 seconds; the MBA student was left trailing in the dust.

Lesson No. 38: Keep the design simple, and when you get there, simplify it even more.

Even more revolutionary than the iMac, however, was the iBook, the first consumer orientated laptop computer. The first model, the iBook G3, was nicknamed "the clamshell", and Jobs unveiled it during his keynote speech at the Macworld Conference and Expo in New York in June 1999.

The iBook was available in multiple bright colours (setting it apart from its cream or black competitors), and it was the first mainstream computer designed and sold with integrated wireless networking (wireless LAN). USB, Ethernet and modem ports all came as standard, as did the optical drive. The shape of the machine, which included an integral handle, was attractive and functional in equal measure, and it was also durable and very reliable. Consumers loved it and the iBook sold like hot cakes. It was the first laptop to be bought en-masse for schools.

Lesson No. 39: Don't sell products, sell dreams.

Two significant Apple product launches went hand in hand in 2001: iTunes and the iPod. Napster had already made online music sales a reality, and it was inevitable therefore that Apple would follow them into the marketplace.

Selling music was not enough for Jobs, however: he knew that people would not be satisfied sitting at home listening to music on their computers but rather would want to listen to the tracks they had purchased out and about, just as they could do with a Walkman or portable CD player. Early examples of digital music players were available to buy, but as Greg Joswiak, Apple's vice president of iPod product marketing, told *Newsweek*, "The products stank." Jobs knew that Apple could do better.

As with the iMac, the strength of the iPod lay in its combination of aesthetics and function. Jobs pulled together a team of masters in their respective arts, including hardware engineers Jon Rubinstein, Tony Fadell, and Michael Dhuey. They took inspiration wherever they could find it: Rubinstein discovered and purchased the rights to the Toshiba disk drive from Toshiba in Japan; the wheel based user interface was inspired by a Bang & Olufsen BeoCom 6000 telephone; and the shape came from a 1958 Braun T3 transistor radio. Jobs decided not to use Apple's in-house software but looked for ideas outside: he settled on PortalPlayer's reference platform and an interface developed by Pixo, whose staff he supervised directly.

Jobs had no qualms at all about taking ideas from other companies and using them in new ways. For him, such stealing didn't have negative connotations but was rather part of the creative process. He explained:

Ultimately, it comes down to taste. It comes down to trying to expose yourself to the best things that humans have done and then try to bring those things into what you're doing. Picasso had a saying: good artists copy, great artists steal. And we have always been shameless about stealing great ideas, and I think part of what made the Macintosh great was that the people working on it were musicians and poets and artists and zoologists and historians who also happened to be the best computer scientists in the world.

The first iPod was Mac compatible, had a 5GB hard drive, and could store around 1,000 songs.

Lesson No. 40: You don't have to be the first, but you have to be the best!

Jobs' launch of the iPod is important because it marks the point when Apple branched out from computers to consumer electronics. Jobs was a visionary, and he knew in his heart that the future of electronics and computers was not in desktop machines but in multi-function, portable devices, and in the computer programs to run on them. This shift in focus was made explicit in Apple's name change from Apple Computers Inc. to Apple Inc., which Jobs announced to the public during his keynote address at the January 2007 Macworld Expo.

The miniaturisation of components for the iPod of course led the way for the creation of the iPhone and the iPad. The revolutionary iPhone was, in essence, a widescreen iPod with the world's first mobile video voicemail service, and a fully-functional version of Safari, Apple's web browser. It was released to the public in July 2007 and took the mobile telecommunications market by storm, knocking market leaders Blackberry and Nokia into the dust almost overnight.

The iPad, launched in January 2010, filled the market gap between the iPhone and the iMac, and though commentators initially feared the iPad would take interest away from the iPhone and iMac, no such thing happened: consumers bought into the brand identity and wanted to own all three items. What is more, Jobs' obsession with his products' appearance meant that for the first time, electronics were cool. New iPhone models were released on a 12-month cycle, and committed fans had to have the new version immediately, every time it was released. New software functions such as Photobooth and FaceTime, and hardware features such as both front and rear-facing cameras made every new Apple product irresistible. Apple shot ahead of all its competitors, including long-term rivals Microsoft.

Lesson No. 41: Don't rely on market research, people don't know what they want until you show them.

Jobs was undoubtedly hugely successful and professionally admired by his peers and employees alike, but he wasn't always popular. He was a demanding perfectionist and always wanted to be one step ahead of the game, summarising his view as follows:

We don't get a chance to do that many things, and every one should be really excellent. Because this is our life. Life is brief, and then you die, you know? And we've all chosen to do this with our lives. So it better be damn good. It better be worth it.

The pursuit of perfection, not only for himself but for everyone else, made it incredibly difficult for his colleagues at Apple to keep up with him. In 1993, Jobs made *Fortune* magazine's list of America's Toughest Bosses, and 14 years later, the same magazine (which was, on the whole, supportive of Jobs and his endeavours), described him as, "one of Silicon Valley's leading egomaniacs."

Lesson No. 42: Don't tolerate bozos around you. Build a team of A players only.

Jobs was not afraid to tackle competition, and his detractors, head on. From the late 1980s Jobs had gone head to head with Michael Dell, CEO of Dell, and they publicly traded words. Jobs called Dell's computers "un-innovative beige boxes" and a decade later, when Apple itself was stuck in the quagmire, Dell suggested that the best thing to do to Apple was to "shut it down and give the money back to the shareholders." Dell could not possibly see into the future, however, and Jobs had the last laugh in 2006 when Apple's market capitalisation finally exceeded Dell's. He sent a two line email out to all Apple employees. It said:

Team, it turned out that Michael Dell wasn't perfect at predicting the future. Based on today's stock market close, Apple is worth more than Dell. Stocks go up and down, and things may be different tomorrow, but I thought it was worth a moment of reflection today. Steve.

Death and Legacy

In 2011, Apple had net sales of more than $108 billion and net profits of nearly $26 billion. The Apple iPhone was outselling its nearest competitor, the Samsung Galaxy S II, by seven to one, and the company shifted over 32 million units of the iPad in that year alone, contributing more than a quarter of the company's revenue. Behind the scenes, all was not so well: Jobs had been on medical leave since January, and in August 2011 he dropped the bombshell of his resignation as CEO on health grounds. He remained with the company as chairman of the board, but the markets shook with the shock: Apple's share price fell 5% in after-hours trading. For many people, Jobs' face, his unique leadership style and the commercial success of Apple had become inseparable.

The reality was that Jobs had been sick for a long time: he had first been diagnosed with a cancerous tumour in his pancreas back in 2003, and had announced the fact to his staff at Apple by the middle of 2004. Although the prognosis for pancreatic cancer is poor, and Jobs was suffering from a particularly rare form, an islet cell neuroendocrine tumour, Jobs resisted medical intervention for the first nine months, attempting to combat the disease through changes to his diet.

Jobs' reality distortion field, which had proved so effective when creating consumer products, blinded him to the seriousness of his condition, but on this occasion, force of personality and self-belief was not enough to overturn the medical reality.

Harvard researcher Ramzi Amri, writing later in the *Daily Mail*, suggested that this delay in seeking conventional medical treatment reduced Jobs' long-term survival chances to next to none. Jobs later regretted the situation, as he confided to his biographer, Walter Isaacson.

Jobs tried following a vegan diet, acupuncture, herbal remedies, juice fasts, bowel cleansings and even consulted a psychic. None of these alternative approaches worked, and he went under the knife for the first time in July 2004. The pancreaticoduodenectomy, also known as the Whipple procedure, was a major surgical operation and appeared to successfully remove the tumour.

Lesson No. 43: Sometimes you have to follow the traditional methods, especially when it is a matter of life and death.

Jobs was not afraid to speak out about illness and death, though he understandably preferred to discuss it as though it were one step removed from himself. In 2005 he gave an important address at Stanford University, which summed up his views:

No one wants to die. Even people who want to go to heaven don't want to die to get there. And yet death is the destination we all share. No one has ever escaped it. And that is as it should be, because Death is very likely the single best invention of Life. It is Life's change agent. It clears out the old to make way for the new. Right now the new is you, but someday not too long from now, you will gradually become the old and be cleared away. Sorry to be so dramatic, but it is quite true...

Your time is limited, so don't waste it living someone else's life. Don't be trapped by dogma — which is living with the results of other people's thinking. Don't let the noise of others' opinions drown out your own inner voice. And most important, have the courage to follow your heart and intuition. They somehow already know what you truly want to become. Everything else is secondary.

Lesson No. 44: Live your life to the full, personally and professionally, because no one ever knows how long they have on earth.

The honeymoon period from cancer was brief: journalists watching Jobs' keynote speech at Apple's 2006 Worldwide Developers Conference described his as looking thin, gaunt and listless, in stark contrast to his usual lively deliveries. The official Apple line was that Jobs was in good health, but rumours abounded, and shareholders started asking questions, saying that they had a right to know. *Bloomberg* inadvertently published a 2,500 word obituary of Jobs in August 2008, to which Jobs responded, tongue in cheek, "Reports of my death are greatly exaggerated." It was a line he'd taken from Mark Twain.

Jobs and his Apple colleagues tried to avoid answering questions about his health, declaring that it was a private matter for Jobs and his family, but at the start of 2009 when Jobs was too unwell to deliver the final keynote address at the Macworld Conference and Expo, he had to come clean. He initially put his problems down to a hormone imbalance, but then announced he had "learned that my health-related issues are more complex than I originally thought". Jobs announced a six-month leave of absence, appointing Tim Cook as acting CEO, and underwent a liver transplant in Memphis in April of that year. CNN reported that his prognosis was "excellent".

Lesson No. 45: When you are the face of an international company, your private business becomes everybody's business.

After his transplant, Jobs returned to Apple and worked for 18 months. He oversaw the launch of a wealth of innovative new products, from Mac OS X Snow Leopard and the Magic Trackpad, to iPads with Wi-Fi and 3G and new models of the MacBook, iPhone and Mac Mini. The buzz around new Apple products, though stimulating, was also exhausting, and again in January 2011 Jobs announced his leave of absence on medical grounds. He continued to make public appearances, including at the public launches of the iPad 2 and iCloud, but the cancer had returned aggressively and was taking its toll.

Jobs stepped down as Apple's CEO on 24 August, 2011, telling the board of directors, "I have always said if there ever came a day when I could no longer meet my duties and expectations as Apple's CEO, I would be the first to let you know. Unfortunately, that day has come." He appointed Tim Cook as his successor as CEO but continued as chairman of the board.

Lesson No. 46: Know when it is the right time to step down and let someone else take the reins.

Six weeks after Jobs stepped down, he lost consciousness and died the following day, surrounded by his wife, children and sisters. He had suffered from complications relating to a relapse in his pancreatic cancer. Apple, Microsoft and Disney all flew their flags at half mast as a mark of respect. For the next two weeks Apple's corporate home page carried a portrait of Jobs, his name and his dates of birth and death, as well as the following obituary:

Apple has lost a visionary and creative genius, and the world has lost an amazing human being. Those of us who have been fortunate enough to know and work with Steve have lost a dear friend and an inspiring mentor. Steve leaves behind a company that only he could have built, and his spirit will forever be the foundation of Apple.

Jobs was buried in his hometown of Palo Alto in a non-denominational cemetery. His grave is unmarked and his funeral was a private affairs for family and close friends. Separate memorial services were held for invited guests (including Bono, Yo Yo Ma and Jobs' former girlfriend, Joan Baez) at Stanford University, and also a few days later on the Apple Campus for Apple staff. Many of Apple's stores closed for the day so that employees could attend the service.

Lesson No. 47: Even Superman has to die sometime.

Jobs' death was front page news around the world. More than a million people left tributes. *Time* magazine and Bloomberg's *Businessweek* both published commemorative issues with Jobs on the cover. US President Barack Obama, UK Prime Minister David Cameron and Microsoft founder Bill Gates all spoke out about Jobs' contribution to society. Jobs was characterised as the Henry Ford or Thomas Edison of his time. In life, Jobs did have his detractors, but after his death these people were largely silent.

In the years running up to his death, Jobs had collected every award and accolade imaginable: he was induced into the California Hall of Fame by California Governor Arnold Schwarzenegger in 2007; *Fortune* magazine named him the most powerful person in business in 2007 and CEO of the decade in 2009; in 2010 *Forbes* magazine ranked him at No. 17 on their list, The World's Most Powerful People; and he was the *Financial Times*' person of the year 2010.

The tributes didn't stop with Jobs' death, however. When in 2012 young adults were asked to name the greatest innovator of all time, Jobs ranked second, only behind Thomas Edison. He was posthumously awarded the Grammy

Trustees Award for his services to the music industry, and a write-up in Forbes magazine described him as both the "greatest entrepreneur of our time" and "the quintessential entrepreneur of our generation".

Lesson No. 48: Be an inspiration for the next generation.

What, though, was Jobs' legacy to the world? Firstly, Jobs made technology cool in a way it had never been before. He was not only the face of Apple, but of Silicon Valley and the computer industry as a whole. The prevailing view prior to Jobs' return to Apple, in the words of Sculley, was that "High-tech could not be designed and sold as a consumer product." Jobs knew that innovation demanded people who could dream up the things others believed were impossible, and were crazy enough to act on their ideas. One of his speeches on the topic was particularly telling:

Here's to the crazy ones, the misfits, the rebels, the troublemakers, the round pegs in the square holes... The ones who see things differently — they're not fond of rules... You can quote them, disagree with them, glorify or vilify them, but the only thing you can't do is ignore them because they change things... They push the human race forward, and while some may see them as the crazy ones, we see genius, because the ones who are crazy enough to think that they can change the world, are the ones who do.

Jobs' vision of turning Apple into a consumer products company was said to be a lunatic plan, and he was completely happy about that: it confirmed that he was one of the crazy people, the rebels he admired. His plan worked because Jobs understood better than either his colleagues or his competitors what the future marketplace would look like and what the demands of consumers would be. Jobs was the man who took the tech industry out of the hands of computer geeks and catapulted it into the mainstream.

Lesson No. 49: Put a dent in the universe.

Unlike Gates at Microsoft, Jobs was not widely known for his philanthropy: he refused to sign Warren Buffet's Giving Pledge and when he returned to Apple in 1997, one of the first things he did was to terminate the company's corporate philanthropy programmes. In actual fact, it was not that Jobs wasn't generous and didn't believe in charity: like so many other things in his life, he just preferred to do it his way. It was also that unlike many other billionaires, Jobs didn't want to shout about his good works, preferring that the media concentrate their attention on Apple.

One major initiative Jobs did support through Apple was the Project Red programme, which encourages companies to create red versions of their devices and give the profits to charity. Apple has been the single largest contributor to the Project Red Global Fund since its inception, and the money goes towards fighting AIDS, malaria and tuberculosis. Project Red's chief, Bono, quotes Bono as saying that there is "nothing better than the chance to save lives".

Since his death, Jobs' personal wealth, which was estimated at around $11 billion, has been held in the Steven P. Jobs Trust, run by his widow, Laurene Powell Jobs. The transfer of wealth has made Powell the ninth richest woman in the world. She does not discuss how she spends the money, but she is known to have committed time and funding to the Emerson Collective, which makes grants and investments into education initiatives; College Track, which Powell founded in 1997 to put students from low-income families through college; the East Congo Initiative in Africa, which she has visited with Ben Affleck; and the Dream Act, a piece of proposed legislation which would provide legal status for immigrants who arrived in the US as young children. Laura Arrillaga-Andreessen, a philanthropist, lecturer on philanthropy at Stanford University and a close friend of Powell, estimates that "If you total up in your mind all of the philanthropic investments that Laurene has made that the public knows about, that is probably a fraction of 1 percent of what she actually does."

In 1993, Jobs gave an interview to the Wall Street Journal in which he said, "Being the richest man in the cemetery doesn't matter to me ... Going to bed at night saying we've done something wonderful... that's what matters to me." It seems Steve Jobs got his wish after all.

Lesson No. 50: What is important is not that we die, but the legacy we have left behind.

Final Thoughts

Steve Jobs changed the world more than any other person in his generation. He was content to be an outsider and a rebel because it gave him the freedom to dream and to try the things that other, more conventional individuals thought to be impossible. His meteoric rise from college drop out to revered multi billionaire and tech sector revolutionary took 30 years and was far from a smooth ride, but he had complete and unshakeable faith in his own abilities and was adamant that innovative thinking and hard work would pay inestimable dividends in the long-term. Jobs was right.

In this book we have learned 50 unique lessons from Jobs, his life and work. Although they do stand independently, and it is right to think about each of them in turn, there are also five important, over-arching lessons that encompass many of the smaller points.

1. Work with the best people in the business

If you want to develop the best products in the world, you need the best people in every post. However great you are, you need to delegate responsibility to others, and should ensure that appointments and promotions are given on the basis of expertise (even if it has been gained in other industries) rather than just because someone has worked with you for a long time. Trust the people you appoint, even if they are critical of you, and invest time, money and effort in your commercial relationships so that your staff are loyal and passionate ambassadors for you and your brand.

2. Always be a step ahead of the competition

In business, there is no point looking backwards: you need to look into the future and anticipate customer needs and wants. Keeping ahead requires you to have a never-ending stream of new ideas. They won't always work out, but you will always have something fresh on the drawing board. Don't let your imagination be limited by present realities: research and development can take many years, and by the time you are ready to launch (especially if you are in the driving seat of innovation), technology will more likely than not have caught up and be able to meet your requirements.

3. Believe passionately in what you do.

Passion and commitment sell products. If you don't believe 110% in what you are doing, find something else to do. To be a success, you will have to commit all your time, energy and money to your projects. We all only get one life, so if the project doesn't thrill you to the core, don't waste your life pursuing it. Stop, look around for another idea, and chase after that one instead.

4. Getting something wrong doesn't mean you have failed.

Everyone makes mistakes. It is how we deal with those set-backs that sets successful people apart from those who fail. Jobs launched some dud products. He got kicked out of his own company. He didn't let it get him down. He got back up and fought on but, and this is very important, he did so without resentment. He looked critically at himself and what he had done wrong, and he learned important lessons for the future. When Jobs returned to Apple in 1997, he wasn't the same CEO he had been when he resigned from the company years before. We all have to change, and we all have room to improve.

5. Be the change you want to see in the world.

Saying that you want to change the world is not enough.Your actions need to support your rhetoric. Jobs knew that to revolutionise the tech sector he needed not only to design and release revolutionary products, but to set the bar higher for the entire industry. He then branched out beyond computing, encouraging others sectors to prioritise innovation and quality too. The ethos he created and espoused, of always striving to be and do the best best, and then breaking your own records, will continue at Apple and in Silicon Valley as a whole long after Jobs' death.

Jobs would say that you shouldn't just aim to be an entrepreneur or an inventor. You must be a revolutionary too.

50 Life and Business Lessons from Arnold Schwarzenegger

Introduction

Everybody loves the story of an underdog, the poor immigrant who came from depressed, post-war Europe and shot to fame in the land of opportunity, the United States of America. Although it might make us green-eyed with envy, we also admire a renaissance man, someone who excels in a breadth of fields, rather than just one. These two things may explain, in part, why Arnold Schwarzenegger - world-famous bodybuilder, Hollywood movie star, Governor of California, and high profile environmental campaigner - holds such an enduring fascination for us.

In every phase of his life, in every business and profession that he has entered, Schwarzenegger has excelled. He has obtained the highest of office, won world titles, made hundreds of millions of dollars, and married for 25 years into one of the most influential political families in America, the Kennedys. He counts among his closest friends billionaire investors and presidents, rockstars, sport stars and film stars. When he writes a book, it shoots straight to the top of the best-seller list. When he makes a film, it is guaranteed to be a blockbuster. What is Schwarzenegger's recipe for success, and how can we learn from him? Surely it can't just be luck?

We can assure you, it isn't. Schwarzenegger is passionate, capable and committed. Success is not a one-off event; it is an ongoing endeavour, and Schwarzenegger has been working hard to achieve his dreams since he was a child.

In this book, a biography of Schwarzenegger, we attempt to identify and express the 50 key lessons you can learn from this Austro-American icon. Right from his childhood in Austria, through his days living above a gym in London, and bricklaying to make money on arrival in the US, to his rise to become Governor of California, the wealthiest state in America, we are going to draw out the stories and issues which have made Schwarzenegger the man he is today. Each section is briefly analysed and summarised into a memorable, bite-sized point which you can mull over. If you want to go back and read about it in more detail, you can do, but these blue points are sufficient to imprint on your mind. If you remember them, think about how to apply them in your own life, and, most importantly, act upon them, you may not become one of the wealthiest, most famous and most influential figures in the US, but you will take a significant step in that direction.

Lesson 1: Progress in life depends on action. Learn from others, think about how to apply those lessons in your own life, and then make it happen. If you don't take the initiative and act, nothing will change.

Childhood and Family

Arnold Alois Schwarzenegger was born on 30 July, 1947 in Thal, Austria. His father, Gustav Schwarzenegger, was an Austrian police chief and non-commissioned officer. He has served in the Austrian Army during the 1930s, and during the Second World War he saw action with Panzergruppe 4 in Belgium, France, Poland, Russia, and the Ukraine. Gustav Schwarzenegger was a member of the Nazi Party, having applied voluntarily to join in 1938, but in spite of quite detailed research into various European archives, no one has unearthed any links to war crimes or the SS. His service record was, it would appear, completely clean.

Gustav Schwarzenegger married Schwarzenegger's mother, a war widow named Aurelia Jadrny, just after the war in October 1945. Their first son, Meinard, was born in 1946, and Arnold followed a year later. Post-war Austria was economically deprived and depressing, and though hard working, the Schwarzeneggers were poor.

The Schwarzeneggers were a conservative Catholic family, and discipline was considered to be very important: Schwarzenegger recalls being beaten as a child for his misdemeanours, and his brother was certainly their father's favourite child. Schwarzenegger certainly suffered as a result. In a 2004 interview with *Fortune* magazine, Schwarzenegger stated:

> My hair was pulled. I was hit with belts. So was the kid next door. It was just the way it was. Many of the children I've seen were broken by their parents, which was the German-Austrian mentality. They didn't want to create an individual. It was all about conforming. I was one who did not conform, and whose will could not be broken. Therefore, I became a rebel. Every time I got hit, and every time someone said, 'you can't do this,' I said, 'this is not going to be for much longer, because I'm going to move out of here. I want to be rich. I want to be somebody.

Lesson 2: Ambition starts in childhood, and is often born out of suffering. You are never to young to have dreams, or to start working towards realising them.

> Strength does not come from winning. Your struggles develop your strengths. When you go through hardships and decide not to surrender, that is strength.

Arnold Schwarzenegger

Schwarzenegger was closer to his mother, though she was still a disciplinarian and made sure that her two sons sat through mass every Sunday morning. His father was a keen sportsman and music lover, and he instilled in both of his children an appreciation of both physical fitness and the arts.

At school, Schwarzenegger was a mediocre student, but described by his teachers as, "cheerful, good-humoured and exuberant." He was a keen footballer, and it was his football coach who first took him to a gym. Although his father wanted him to follow in his footsteps and become a police officer, and his mother had it in mind that her son would go to trade school, Schwarzenegger knew right from the age of 14 that he wanted to be a bodybuilder. It offered the chance of a more glamorous life, and an escape from Austria to the US, a land which seemed to be paved with gold.

> I knew I was a winner back in the late sixties. I knew I was destined for great things. People will say that kind of thinking is totally immodest. I agree. Modesty is not a word that applies to me in any way - I hope it never will.
>
> Arnold Schwarzenegger

Lesson 3: In determining success, personality, attitude and commitment are more important factors than academic achievement.

Schwarzenegger's brother, Meinard, was killed in a drink driving accident in 1971, when Schwarzenegger was in his early 20s. Though the two brothers had never been close - their father's unfounded belief that Schwarzenegger was not his biological son had no doubt created the rift between them - Schwarzenegger felt a sense of responsibility towards his brother's fiancee and three-year old son. In a later interview with his then girlfriend, Barbara Baker, she said that Schwarzenegger never spoke of his brother's death, and when his father died a year later, he informed her about it completely without emotion. He did, however, pay for his nephew's education, and later helped him to emigrate to the US.

> I know why you cry, but it's something I can never do.
>
> Arnold Schwarzenegger in *Terminator 2: Judgement Day*

Lesson 4: Blood creates bonds of obligation, if not of emotion. You always have a responsibility to care for those around you and to act in a responsible fashion.#

Mr. Universe

It was as a bodybuilder that Schwarzenegger first made a name for himself. In a few short years, he went from being a teenage nobody in Thal to an international sports star with money, fame and string of attractive women at his side.

Early Training Schwarzenegger officially took up weight training at the age of 15, though there is some debate as to whether he was in fact a little younger than this. His official biography claims, "At 14, he started an intensive training program with Dan Farmer, studied psychology at 15 (to learn more about the power of mind over body) and at 17, officially started his competitive career."

> Training gives us an outlet for suppressed energies created by stress and thus tones the spirit just as exercise conditions the body.
>
> Arnold Schwarzenegger

It was at this time that Schwarzenegger met a former Mr. Austria, Kurt Marnul. Marnul inspired the teenager and also invited him to train seriously at his gym in Graz. Schwarzenegger was unusually dedicated: he broke into the local gym on weekends so that he could train even when it was shut, and felt physically sick if he missed a work-out. When he wasn't training, Schwarzenegger was in the cinema watching his body-building idols - Reg Park, Steve Reeves and Johnny Weissmuller - on the big screen. By night he dreamed of becoming a bodybuilder, and by day he worked every hour to make that dream become a reality.

Lesson 5: Success takes commitment. You have to start early and work hard if you want to achieve your dreams.

As an Austrian citizen, Schwarzenegger was required to complete a year's military service at the age of 18. Although it was a physically active programme and with a great sense of camaraderie, this commitment interfered with his bodybuilding training, and so Schwarzenegger found it unacceptable. Schwarzenegger went AWOL from basic training in order to compete in the Junior Mr. Europe competition and, as he puts it, "Participating in the competition meant so much to me that I didn't carefully think through the consequences." When he returned to the army, he was punished with a week in military prison. It was, at least as far as he was concerned, a very small price to pay in order to achieve the next step in his plan.

I eat green berets for breakfast… and I am very hungry!

Arnold Schwarzenegger in *Commando*

Lesson 6: Pursuing your dreams sometimes has unpleasant short-term consequences. These are an unfortunate but necessary part of the journey to success.

Winning competitions in continental Europe did earned Schwarzenegger the chance to compete at the NABBA Mr. Universe competition. This was his way out of Austria and out of poverty. The teenage bodybuilder from Austria was about to become an international sporting star.

Mr. Universe Schwarzenegger flew to London for the 1966 NABBA Mr. Universe competition, and due to his determination and months of training, he excelled. He lacked the muscle definition of his older rival, Chester Yorton, though, and so unfortunately came in second place.

Schwarzenegger did, however, catch the eye of judge Charles "Wag" Bennett, who saw the young man's potential. Bennett invited the teenager to stay in his already crowded home above a gym in London's Forest Gate, and he devised a training programme for him which focused on improving the muscle definition and power in his legs. This would remedy the apparent weakness which had let him down against Yorton. Whilst living in London, Schwarzenegger had the opportunity to learn a few words of English, which would be essential in the competition world, and also to meet his idol (and later mentor), Reg Park.

The resistance that you fight physically in the gym and the resistance that you fight in life can only build a strong character.

Arnold Schwarzenegger

Lesson 7: You will not achieve your dreams on your own. Find older and more experienced mentors who are able and willing to help you along the way.

Bennett's investment and Schwarzenegger's commitment paid off: in 1967 Schwarzenegger again entered the Mr Universe competition, and this time he won. He was just 20 years old, the youngest ever winner of the competition. He surprised the judges and the more experienced competitors, but it was a portend of things to come.

Lesson 8: If at first you don't succeed, keep trying! Persistence pays off.

Schwarzenegger had dreamed of moving to the US since he was 10 years old: the American Dream which he had seen in the movies beckoned. In 1968, the opportunity to travel to the US finally arose. He emigrated to Los Angeles, training under Joe Weider at Gold's Gym in Venice Beach, and won the Mr. Universe title a further three times.

Mr. Olympia Schwarzenegger was always very clear that he wanted to become the greatest bodybuilder in the world, and that meant not only winning Mr. Universe, but also Mr. Olympia. My. Olympia was set up so that former winners of Mr. Universe could continue competing and making money: it was a professional (rather than amateur) competition. His first attempt, in New York in 1969, was unsuccessful, but he went on to win the title seven times, the first of which he won when he was only 23. Only one person has ever broken this record of wins.

Lesson 9: Set your ambitions sky high and don't settle for second best. Keep going until you get what you want.

The assumption was that 1975 would be Schwarzenegger's last Mr. Olympia competition: he won convincingly against Lou Ferrigno, a feat which is detailed in the documentary *Pumping Iron* (see below). Schwarzenegger had a surprise up his sleeve, however. In 1980, Schwarzenegger was training for his role as Conan in *Conan the Barbarian* (see *The Terminator*). Running, riding and sword fighting, he felt that he was in the best shape of his life, and he decided that he wanted to win the Mr. Olympia title one last time. Hired to provide the television commentary for the competition when it was broadcast, he announced his intention to compete at the 11th hour, and won with just seven weeks of preparation. He then officially retired from bodybuilding competitions, going out on an indisputable high.

> I didn't leave bodybuilding until I felt that I had gone as far as I could go. It will be the same with my film career. When I feel the time is right, I will then consider public service. I feel that the highest honor comes from serving people and your country.

Lesson 10: Sometimes opportunities arise when you are not expecting them. Seize the opportunity and you will surprise not only yourself but also others.

Pumping Iron In 1977, Robert Fiore and George Butler released *Pumping Iron*, a docudrama they had directed about the 1975 IFBB Mr. Universe and Mr. Olympia competitions. Filmed during the 100 days running up to the competitions, and during the competitions themselves, the action focused on Schwarzenegger and his primary competitor, Lou Ferrigno.

The 1975 competition was to be Schwarzenegger's last: he had been a professional body builder for a decade, and had won the Mr. Olympia competition five years running. The documentary compared the two men's training styles, personas and attitudes: it showed Schwarzenegger to be an aggressive extrovert who thrived on publicity and the attentions of beautiful women. There is a subtext of psychological warfare, and this is an area where Schwarzenegger is clearly in his element.

> The mind is the limit. As long as the mind can envision the fact that you can do something, you can do it as long as you really believe 100 percent.
>
> Arnold Schwarzenegger

Lesson 11: Even in a physical arena, your mental preparation and attitude makes the difference between success and failure. Keep focused and learn to better understand your own psychology, as well as that of your competitors.

Pumping Iron ran into financial difficulties during the final stages of production, and so was released two years late and only after Schwarzenegger had helped to raise the funds to complete it. The documentary was given a cinema release and proved unexpectedly popular: it brought the previously niche sport of bodybuilding to a national audience, resulting in a significant increase in gym usage; and the review tallying site Rotten Tomatoes reports that 22 out of the 23 press reviews for the film were positive. *Pumping Iron* was a commercial and critical success, and it was Schwarzenegger's first real taste of the silver screen. His on-screen and off-screen rival, Ferrigno, also used the documentary to kickstart his own film career: he was cast as the title role in *The Incredible Hulk*, and continued to play such roles for the next 30 years.

Lesson 12: Make use of the platforms given to you to catapult yourself onto greater things.

Arnold Classic Schwarzenegger was, and probably still is, the greatest ambassador which the sport of body building has ever had. In recognition of this fact, the International Federation of Body Buildings (IFBB) launched an annual competition, the IFBB Arnold Classic, which has run since 1989. It takes place at the same venue in Columbus, Ohio.

Part of the Arnold Sports Festival (also named after Schwarzenegger), the competition has an overall prize but also several special awards: Best Poser; Most Muscular; the Fan's Choice Award; and the Most Entertaining Routine. Competition in these subcategories is just as intense as for the main prize, though they are not held every year.

Writing Schwarzenegger published his first book, *Arnold: The Education of a Bodybuilder*, in 1977. A commercial success, the book was a combination of autobiography and weight training guide. Schwarzenegger clearly enjoyed the experience of writing, as he also signed up for English courses at Santa Monica College in California, and then graduated from the University of Wisconsin-Superior with a BA in international marketing of fitness and business administration.

Lesson 13: Education is not just for school kids. At any stage of life you can learn more and earn qualifications which will help you reach your next set of goals.

It is his writing, in part, which has kept Schwarzenegger's image at the forefront of the bodybuilding industry. For many years he wrote monthly columns for *Muscle & Fitness* and *Flex*, work which caused some accusations of conflict of interest when he first became Governor of California (see *Controversies and Challenges*), and though his relinquished his editorial role as a result in 2005, he renewed his editorial contracts in 2013.

Lesson 14: Don't ever burn your commercial bridges. Keep relationships warm in case you want or need to reignite them in the future.

Schwarzenegger's autobiography, *Total Recall* (a reference to one of his earlier films), was published in 2012. It is divided into three parts, focusing respectively on his bodybuilding, his film career, and his politics.

Terminator

Using the international platform and celebrity which he had gained as Mr. Universe and Mr. Olympia, Schwarzenegger took the opportunity to launch his Hollywood career. Casting couch directors recognised his appeal to fans in the world of sport but also realised that his incredible physique made him the ultimate action hero.

> I just use my muscles as a conversation piece, like someone walking a cheetah down 42nd Street.
>
> Arnold Schwarzenegger

Lesson 15: Identify your strengths and unique selling points, and actively promote them to others. This is how you can stand out from the crowd.

Working at first under the pseudonym Arnold Strong, Schwarzenegger made his first action film, *Hercules in New York*, in the early 1970s. Still relatively new in the US, and speaking little English, his Austrian accent was so strong that his lines had to be dubbed in post-production to make them comprehensible to American audiences. The accent, the long and unpronounceable name, and his 'weird' body type appeared to be stumbling blocks to a successful film career, and Schwarzenegger was advised time and again to change them all, but he persisted.

> The worst thing I can be is the same as everybody else. I hate that.
>
> Arnold Schwarzenegger

Lesson 16: Turn your quirks to your advantage, and don't be put off by the fact that you are different from those around you.

Schwarzenegger won a Golden Globe award from the Hollywood Foreign Press Association for his portrayal of the male lead in *Stay Hungry*, and this raised his profile sufficiently that he was cast in the title role of *Conan the Barbarian* in 1982. *Conan the Barbarian*, with its adrenalin-fuelled fight scenes and sorcery, was box office gold, and Schwarzenegger hit the big time. It was an era of film making when heroes needed muscles and great physical presence. Schwarzenegger fitted the bill perfectly.

You can scream at me, call me for a shoot at midnight, keep me waiting for hours - as long as what ends up on the screen is perfect.

Arnold Schwarzenegger

Schwarzenegger will not go down in Hollywood history as Conan, however, but as the Terminator, a cyborg assassin programmed to kill a woman whose yet-to-be-conceived son will one day save the world. A 1984 sci-fi thriller directed by James Cameron, *Terminator* was the first in a series of films, and Schwarzenegger played both heroes and villains. Films from the Terminator franchise were released in 1984, 1991 and 2003, and so Schwarzenegger had plenty of time to make other films in between.

Lesson 17: It is always easier to launch a sequel (or an update) than an original product. If you have a great idea, keep reworking it rather than trying to develop something new from scratch.

Schwarzenegger appeared in the lead role in some of the most famous action and fantasy films of the 1990s: *Total Recall* (1990), *True Lies* (1994), *Batman & Robin* (1997), and *End of Days* (1999). He also began to branch out into comedy, and films such as *Kindergarten Cop* (1990), *Junior* (1994) and *Jingle All The Way* (1996) widened his appeal to new audiences.

Lesson 18: Add variety to keep your offering fresh.

After appearing in *Around The World In 80 Days* (2004), Schwarzenegger took a break from Hollywood to concentrate on his political career (see *The Governator*). It therefore came as some surprise to his political rivals (and possibly to his allies too) that he returned to the silver screen in 2010 with *The Expendables*, the story of a team of mercenaries tasked with killing a military dictator and rogue CIA operative. A sequel, *The Expendables 2,* was released in 2012, again featuring Schwarzenegger, and he also found time in his schedule to shoot *The Last Stand* (2013), a Western-cum-action movie where Schwarzenegger portrays a sheriff fighting a dangerous drug cartel leader.

To date, Schwarzenegger's films have grossed more than $3 billion at the box office. His heroic, high-profile roles on screen made him a household name and brought him both wealth and strong connections with America's elite. Schwarzenegger capitalised on these significant assets to catapult himself into another, quite unexpected, period of his career.

The Governator

I went from being the Terminator to being the Governator.

Arnold Schwarzenegger

The Governator is Schwarzenegger's affectionate nickname, a compound created from his position as the Republican Governor of California, and the Terminator, his most famous on screen role. His successful political career began in the early 2000s, and he is now one of the most influential figures in US politics.

Lesson 19: Your name is a key part of your brand. A memorable company name or nickname will help you gain and retain visibility in the marketplace.

Political Affiliation Ever since his arrival in the US in the 1960s, Schwarzenegger has voted Republican, describing himself as fiscally conservative and socially moderate. When interviewed in 2002 about his political choices, he explained:

> I came first of all from a socialistic country, which is Austria, and when I came over here in 1968 with the presidential elections coming up in November, I came over in October, I heard a lot of the press conferences from both of the candidates Humphrey and Nixon, and Humphrey was talking about more government is the solution, protectionism, and everything he said about government involvement sounded to me more like Social Democratic Party of Austrian socialism... Then when I heard Nixon talk about it, he said open up the borders, the consumers should be represented there ultimately and strengthen the military and get the government off our backs. I said to myself, what is this guy's party affiliation? I didn't know anything at that point. So I asked my friend, what is Nixon? He's a Republican. And I said, I am a Republican. That's how I became a Republican.

Lesson 20: Be prepared to talk about your values and the reasons for them. People care what you think.

President's Council on Physical Fitness and Sports Schwarzenegger's first direct forays into the sphere of US politics occurred in the early 1990s when he was asked to chair George H. W. Bush's President's Council on Physical Fitness and Sports. As Chairman, he spent three years travelling to all 50 US states, promoting physical fitness to school children and lobbying the states' governors to support fitness programmes in schools.

Schwarzenegger travelled in his own plane, at his own expense, and had a furious work ethic, often meeting with three governors in a single day. His chief of staff, a retired marine called George Otott, recalls, "When he walked in, it wasn't about the governor, it was about Arnold... He has what we in the military call a *command presence*. He becomes the number one attention-getter."

Lesson 21: Be the person in the room who everyone else wants to talk to. Don't be cowed by power or status but rather make a place for yourself.

After President Clinton replaced Bush, Schwarzenegger took up a similar ambassadorial role as Chairman for the California Governor's Council on Physical Fitness and Sports. At this time he drafted and sponsored his first piece of legislation, Proposition 49: the After School Education and Safety Program Act of 2002, which made state grants available for after-school programmes.

Lesson 22: Commit your energy and effort to causes which you really believe in, and you are more likely to see them through to conclusion.

2003 California Recall Election For a number of years, Schwarzenegger had been considering running for elected political office in the US and had discussed it widely with friends, allies, advisors and potential donors. His political ambitions were no secret. His chance came with the 2003 California recall election.

At the time, Schwarzenegger was on tour, heavily promoting his latest film, *Terminator 3*. His mind was never far from politics, however, as his answer in a July 2003 interview with *Esquire Magazine* reveals: "Yes, I would love to be governor of California ... If the state needs me, and if there's no one I think is better, then I will run."

If you yield only to a conqueror, then prepare to be conquered.

Arnold Schwarzenegger in *Red Sonja*

Lesson 23: People don't like self-interest. If you are going to do something significant, ensure it is seen to be for the right reasons.

A petition to recall the existing governor, Democrat Gray Davis, qualified for the ballot that summer, and, ever the showman, Schwarzenegger gave a statement saying that he would announce whether he was running or not during an episode of *The Tonight Show with Jay Leno.* The public and the press held their breath, but generally leaned towards the view that he would not run as his wife (a Kennedy and a Democrat supporter) was against it.

It turns out that even Schwarzenegger wasn't sure what he was going to do until the day of the announcement:

> The recall happens and people are asking me, 'What are you going to do?' I thought about it but decided I wasn't going to do it. I told Maria I wasn't running. I told everyone I wasn't running. I wasn't running. I just thought, This will freak everyone out. It'll be so funny. I'll announce that I am running. I told Leno I was running. And two months later I was governor. What the fuck is that? All these people are asking me, 'What's your plan? Who's on your staff?' I didn't have a plan. I didn't have a staff. I wasn't running until I went on Jay Leno.

He explained his reasoning to Leno thus: "The politicians are fiddling, fumbling and failing. The man that is failing the people more than anyone is Gray Davis. He is failing them terribly, and this is why he needs to be recalled and this is why I am going to run for governor of the state of California."

Lesson 24: Sometimes you have to take a risk and follow your gut. You can think and plan for months, but eventually you are going to have to make a decision and act.

Schwarzenegger had never previously held public office and his political views were largely unknown, but he was the best-known candidate standing. The national and international press picked up on his candidacy immediately, and the news was full of predictions about the "Governator". Schwarzenegger played to his audience, giving them memorable one-liners borrowed from his most famous films, including, "I'll be back" at the end of his first press conference. The press loved it. He recruited to his campaign team actor Rob Lowe, billionaire Warren Buffet, and George Schulz, a former aide to Presidents Nixon and Reagan.

I speak directly to the people, and I know that the people of California want to have better leadership. They want to have great leadership. They want to have somebody that will represent them. And it doesn't matter if you're a Democrat or a Republican, young or old.

Lesson 25: Visibility is often more important than experience.

The recall election took place in October 2003. Gray Davis was removed from office, and 48.6% of voters chose Schwarzenegger to succeed him: he had 1.3 million more votes than his nearest competitor. When he was sworn into office alongside his wife and children, Schwarzenegger spoke briefly:

> Today is a new day in California. I did not seek this office to do things the way they've always been done. What I care about is restoring your confidence in your government... This election was not about replacing one man. It was not replacing one party. It was about changing the entire political climate of our state.

Lesson 26: Engage other people and bring them onside by speaking positively about the future and encouraging their faith in you.

Governor of California Schwarzenegger faced a line up of critics waiting for him to fail: with the exception of Reagan, when had a Hollywood movie star previously been successful in politics? But Schwarzenegger had a great deal of popular support - his approval rating hit 65% by May 2004 - and was able to bring together politicians from both sides of the house. He took a pro-active approach to reform, repealing and introducing legislation from the very start. Voters saw him as a man of action and, as importantly, as a man of his word.

> Political courage is not political suicide.
>
> Arnold Schwarzenegger

Lesson 27: You have a honeymoon period at the start of any new endeavour. Capitalise on this to make progress whilst everyone is still enthusiastic and helpful.

Schwarzenegger's first responsibility on entering office was to address California's pressing budgetary concerns, and to do this his developed and announced a three-point budget plan. This involved floating $15 billion in bonds, passing a constitutional amendment to limit spending, and overhauling workers' compensation. Public support for the measures was at first luke warm, but Schwarzenegger campaigned energetically, and the requisite legislation passed. The International Bond Market reacted particularly favourably, uprating California's projections by three points, and thus saving the state more than $20 billion in interest over the next decade.

Lesson 28: Money makes the world go round. If you don't have money to spend, you can't implement your policies and reforms, and you can't help anyone else.

Throughout Schwarzenegger's governorship, a number of issues have emerged time and again, and Schwarzenegger's leadership has been a matter of much discussion. Amongst these, LGBT rights, the death penalty, and taxation have been most talked about.

As the Republican governor of a largely left-leaning state, Schwarzenegger could have found himself in a difficult position regarding LGBT rights, but he has rightly made the law, not personal or party views, the deciding factor in campaigning and legislation. When in 2004, for example, Gavin Newsom, Mayor of San Francisco, ordered changes in certification to allow same-sex marriages, Schwarzenegger blocked the move, not because he opposed same-sex relationships but because the act was beyond the powers of the mayor. Reinforcing this position, he went on the same year to issue Executive Order S-6-04 ("All state agencies, departments, boards, and commissions shall recruit, appoint, train, evaluate and promote state personnel on the basis of merit and fitness, without regard to age, race, ethnicity, color, ancestry, national origin, gender, marital status, sexual orientation, religion, disability or other non-job-related factors."); sign into law the California Insurance Equality Act, which makes health insurance providers offer cover to employees' registered domestic partners, regardless of their sex; approve the Omnibus Labor & Employment Non-Discrimination Bill, which unified all state anti-discrimination codes; and signed SB 1193, the law which entitles the surviving spouse or designated beneficiary (including same sex partners) of a deceased serviceman or woman to a $10,000 death benefit.

Lesson 29: A strong leader is able to balance ideology and pragmatism. By treading the line between the two carefully, you can bring others along with you and implement necessary changes.

The issue of the death penalty in California has been more problematic for Schwarzenegger. As governor, he has the right to grant clemency to convicted felons on death row, though doing so is in itself a controversial act. Though Schwarzenegger has granted clemency on a number of occasions, saving men from execution, there have been occasions when he chose not to: he denied a pardon to convicted murderers Kevin Cooper and Stanley Tookie Williams, for example, and both men were therefore executed.

Lesson 30: In public office, your duty is to act in accordance with the law and with public sentiment, regardless of your own opinions and values.

Schwarzenegger's economic and fiscal policies (as briefly discussed above) have, on occasions, brought him into conflict with the Californian legislature. Though in 2004 The Cato Institute, a libertarian policy research foundation, rated him #1 amongst US state governors for his taxation and spending policies, he's often found it difficult to get budgets approved by the state legislature. When deadlock has occurred, Schwarzenegger has spoken critically of his opponents, comparing them to children in kindergarten.

Schwarzenegger won his second term as governor in autumn 2005. It was the most expensive election in California's history - the total election spending for both sides was in excess of $300 million - and it had not actually gone well for Schwarzenegger: he lost all four of the reform initiatives he had proposed at the ballot. He no longer had the political leverage he had enjoyed during his first term, and was forced to move towards the centre in order to get legislation through.

> Learned helplessness is the giving-up reaction, the quitting response that follows from the belief that whatever you do doesn't matter.
>
> Arnold Schwarzenegger

Lesson 31: Success does not come cheaply. There are times when it doesn't matter how good you are, you just have to outspend the competition.

In his second term as governor, Schwarzenegger focused on attracting investment into California to improve the state's finances and the perceived standard of living of voters. In defiance of President George W. Bush's moratorium on state funding for stem cell research, he allocated a further $150 million in funding, stimulating the nascent industry in California. He formed the Climate Action Board and worked with Democrats to agree a bill to agree the Global Warming Solutions Act of 2006 (both in line with his role as an environmental campaigner), and he agreed to increase the minimum wage in California to $8.50 per hour. Such acts angered conservative Republicans but were popular with mainstream and left-leaning voters.

And now, of course this is another thing I didn't count on, that now as the governor of the state of California, I am selling California worldwide. You see that? Selling.

Arnold Schwarzenegger

Lesson 32: Political ideology and allegiances should be but guiding forces. You still have to do what is right, and what meets with the approval of voters.

The global economic crisis, beginning in 2009, hit California hard, and with a debt of $42 billion, Schwarzenegger struggled to fulfil his spending commitments. He suggested Proposition 1A to increase tax revenues to $16 billion, there were moves to replenish the California General Fund, and two Fridays a month were declared as furloughs: state employees could not come into work and were not paid.

Lesson 33: Whether or not you succeed is not always within your control. External factors cannot always be compensated for.

Schwarzenegger's second term as governor ended in January 2011, and he was not eligible to seek re-election. He has, however, continued to have an active role in politics and debate.

Environmental Campaigner Schwarzenegger isn't the most obvious choice to front the clean energy and sustainability campaigns in the US, but that is perhaps why he is so effective. Making use of his high-profile public position, his political influence and business ties, and possibly also the surprise factor that it is a Republican heavyweight using his voice to advocate for renewable energy, Schwarzenegger has become a key ally for environmentalists and reformers.

The future is green energy, sustainability, renewable energy.

Arnold Schwarzenegger

Lesson 34: Use your public platform to add your voice to issues you care about.

Typically mild mannered and conservative, Schwarzenegger opened a recent public statement with the line, "I don't give a **** if we agree about climate change." By taking the debate away from the traditional front line between those who are concerned about the environmental and social impact of climate change, and those who believe global warming is a hoax, he went on to force both sides to identify points that they can agree on: 7 million people a year die from fossil fuel pollution, which is unacceptable; fossil fuels will not be the preferred energy sources of the future because they will run out; and given the choice between being stuck in a sealed room with an electric car and a diesel or petrol-fuelled car belching fumes, we would all opt for the former. To do otherwise would result in certain, painful death. These aren't politically charged points, they are practical ones. Schwarzenegger advocates, in his own words, for, "a smarter, cleaner, healthier, more profitable energy future."

Lesson 35: Regardless of your politics, everyone has a responsibility to create a safer, healthier future for our planet.

In 2010, Schwarzenegger founded R20 Regions of Climate Action, a non-profit organisation which works to promote and implement projects that produce economic and environmental benefits by reducing energy consumption and greenhouse gas emissions, improve public health and create new, green jobs to strengthen local economies. Working in cooperation with the United Nations, R20 produces reports, brings regional governments together, and implements projects as diverse as LED street lighting in Brazil, waste management in Algeria, and solar bakeries in Burundi.

In his personal life, Schwarzenegger appears to practise, at least part, what he preaches. He has adapted his two Hummers to run on hydrogen and biofuels, and installed solar panels to heat his house.

I have a private plane. But I fly commercial when I go to environmental conferences.

Arnold Schwarzenegger

President Schwarzenegger? In her unofficial biography of Schwarzenegger, journalist Wendy Leigh quotes Schwarzenegger as saying, "I wanted to be part of the small percentage of people who were leaders, not the large mass of followers. I think it is because I saw leaders use 100% of their potential – I was always fascinated by people in control of other people." Having married into a political family (his mother-in-law, Eunice Kennedy Shriver, was the sister of President John F. Kennedy), perhaps it is natural that Schwarzenegger should have the highest levels of political ambition. But could an Austrian bodybuilding film star actually become president of the United States of America?

At first glance, the answer is no: currently only those born in the US are eligible to run for the presidency, as it outlined in Article II, Section 1, Clause V of the US constitution. Although *The Simpson's Movie* (2007) does show Schwarzenegger as the president, it is fantasy. A constitutional amendment would have to be passed (as was the case in the 1993 Sylvester Stallone film, *Demolition Man*) for Schwarzenegger to be able to take the top job. Schwarzenegger has reportedly been lobbying legislators about a possible constitutional change, and if he were to file a legal challenge to the provision, some legal commentators believe the law suit could ultimately win him the right to run for office.

Lesson 36: Just because something isn't possible now doesn't mean that it won't ever be possible. Stay positive, look to the future, and lobby for change.

Schwarzenegger's support is considered highly valuable to candidates in the Republican primaries, in any case. He was close friends with both Rudy Guiliani and John McCain, the two main Republican contenders in the run up to the 2008 presidential elections, and thus remained publicly neutral until Giuliani dropped out of the race. McCain and Schwarzenegger shared concerns about the US economy and the environment.

Business Interests

Schwarzenegger made his first million before he was 30, and before he hit the big time in Hollywood. He is a serial entrepreneur, forward looking, organised and with exceptional marketing skills.

Lesson 37: You don't have to pigeonhole yourself into any one field: it is fine to be a renaissance man (or woman) with interests in many fields.

Schwarzenegger's first business was brick building. He set up a company with Franco Columbu, another bodybuilder, and the combination of effective marketing and timing (the company was launched just before the 1971 San Fernando earthquake increased demand in the construction industry) brought them quickly into profit. They invested this money in turn in a mail order business selling fitness products and VHS training tapes.

Lesson 38: No kind of business is too simple, or too humble. There is money to be made everywhere.

Money from the mail order business, plus his bodybuilding competition winnings, were used to buy Schwarzenegger's first apartment building. It cost Schwarzenegger $10,000 and gave him a taste for real estate investment. Along with fellow celebrity investors Bruce Willis, Demi Moore and Sylvester Stallone, he put money into Plant Hollywood (a competitor to Hard Rock Cafe) and also into shopping malls and residential developments. He took guidance from a raft of successful investors, including Donald Trump, Warren Buffett and Milton Friedman, and used his contacts to make inroads into the film, publishing and sports industries.

Lesson 39: Take advice from people you admire, and learn from them. Success is a joint endeavour!

Schwarzenegger's business reputation and profile is such that he will replace Donald Trump as the host of the popular TV show, *The Celebrity Apprentice*.

Philanthropy and Outreach

Help others and give something back. I guarantee you will discover that while public service improves the lives and the world around you, its greatest reward is the enrichment and new emanating it will bring your own life.

Arnold Schwarzenegger

Stop the Madness Schwarzenegger made use of his public profile as early as the mid-1980s to campaign on issues he believes to be important. An early such project was *Stop the Madness*, an anti-drug music video endorsed by President Ronald Reagan and featuring a number of celebrities of the day, including Whitney Houston, David Hasselhoff, and La Toya Jackson. The video was broadcast for a six-month period in 1985 and '86, and it sparked anti-drug campaigns in Europe, as well as being adopted for public service announcements in the US.

The USC Schwarzenegger Institute Though Schwarzenegger is proud to call himself a Republican and to represent that political party in elections, he does not toe the party political line to the determinant of common sense. Indeed, Schwarzenegger is intelligent enough to realise that some of the challenges we face cannot be surmounted by partisan groups, and a long-term, co-ordinated effort from multiple parties is required. For this reason, he has founded, and dedicates significant time to, the USC Schwarzenegger Institute at the University of Southern California.

Lesson 40: The biggest problems we face will only be solved if we work together. Find like-minded people, regardless of where they sit on the political spectrum, and commit to finding solutions.

I welcome and seek your ideas, but do not bring me small ideas; bring me big ideas to match our future.

Arnold Schwarzenegger

The USC Schwarzenegger Institute for State and Global Policy, to give it its full name, was founded to advance post-partisanship. It encourages political and business leaders, regardless of their political ideologies or affiliations, to work together to find the best solutions to benefit the wider population. A think tank and lobbying organisation of

63

sorts, the institute draws upon the work of academics and entrepreneurs, business leaders and scientists, and seeks to influence public policy and debate.

Schwarzenegger has laid down four guiding principles for the institute, which are:

- Science and evidence have an important role to play in finding solutions;

- Local solutions are often the best means to solve global problems;

- Great innovation and great solutions rarely come from government, but rather from individuals, entrepreneurs, and the community;

- Future leaders, including students and young people, must help shape the solutions for our future.

Clean energy and the environment (see *Environmental Campaigner*) is a key area of the institute's work, but education, fiscal and economic policy, health and human wellness, and political reform are also of significant interest.

After-School All-Stars The mission of the After School All-Stars (ASAS) is to provide comprehensive after-school programmes that keep school children safe and help them to succeed not only in the school environment, but also in life. Participants should be taught life skills to keep themselves safe and healthy, to graduate from high school and go on to college, to have fulfilled careers, and to be able to give something back to their communities.

As it stands, ASA serves more than 72,000 at-risk youth from low-income families. The vast majority of these students are African America, hispanic or from ethnic minority groups, and 85% of them qualify for free lunches. Schwarzenegger sees the programme, and in particular its use of sport, as a way to give these students a senses of purpose and value, to teach them discipline and team work, and to instil in them aspiration.

> You know, nothing is more important that education, because nowhere are our stakes higher; our future depends on the quality of education of our children today.
>
> Arnold Schwarzenegger

Lesson 41: The children of today are the decision makers and business leaders of tomorrow. We must invest in them so that they become disciplined, productive adults.

Sport and Fitness Ambassador A pin up for small boys and teenagers around the world, Schwarzenegger has positioned himself as an ambassador for sport and physical fitness. In addition to the After School All-Stars (see above), he is active as a coach and international torch bearer for the Special Olympics (founded by his former mother-in-law, Eunice Kennedy Shriver), and also served terms as Chairman on George H. W. Bush's President's Council on Physical Fitness and Sports.

Wealth, Awards and Accolades

Schwarzenegger's exact wealth is unknown: conservative estimates range from $100 million to $200 million, though his 2006 tax return has been used to produce an estimate as high as $800 million. The breadth of his investments, and the recent instability of international real estate prices, make an accurate figure hard to calculate. What we do know, however, is that Schwarzenegger doesn't have to clip coupons: he spent $38 million of his own money on a Gulfstream jet in 1997, and took no salary whilst he was Governor of California as he was making more than enough elsewhere. Having more money in the bank doesn't make him happier, as a 2003 interview in *The Guardian* reveals: "Money doesn't make you happy. I now have $50 million, but I was just as happy when I had $48 million."

Lesson 42: After a certain point, you don't need to know how much you earn or how much you are worth. It doesn't matter. Instead, commit to using your money for good, and enjoy it.

The awards and accolades given to Schwarzenegger are, as one might expect, as varied as his interests and experiences. In film, he received a Golden Globe Award in 1977 for *Stay Hungry*, and he has a star on the Hollywood Walk of Fame. The WWF declared him to be their Heavyweight Box Office Champion in 1999, and the WWE inducted Schwarzengger into their Hall of Fame in 2015. The Schwarzenegger Institute for State and Global Policy, the Arnold Sport Festival and Arnold's Classic bodybuilding competition, and Arnold's Run ski trail at Sun Valley are all named in his honour, and on the occasion of his 60th birthday, the mayor of Thal (Schwarzenegger's birthplace in Austria) declared it to be "A Day for Arnold".

Controversies and Challenges

Citizenship Schwarzenegger took US citizenship in September 1983, and normally this would have annulled his former citizenship (Austrian) as Austria does not permit dual citizenship. Schwarzenegger requested special permission, however, and was allowed to become a dual national. His subsequent actions as Governor of California have caused some controversy back in Austria.

> As long as I live, I will never forget that day 21 years ago when I raised my hand and took the oath of citizenship. Do you know how proud I was? I was so proud that I walked around with an American flag around my shoulders all day long.
>
> Arnold Schwarzenegger

Lesson 43: Have pride in where you come from and where you live. Your environment, past and present, have created the person you are today.

Austria does not permit the death penalty, as the country outlawed the death penalty in 1968. A second piece of legislation, Article 33 of the Austrian Citizenship Act, states that, "A citizen, who is in the public service of a foreign country, shall be deprived of his citizenship, if he heavily damages the reputation or the interests of the Austrian Republic." As Schwarzenegger has not always used his right as governor to grant clemency to prisoners on death row, Austrian MP Peter Pilz has demanded that his Austrian citizenship be revoked. Schwarzenegger's support for the death penalty contravenes Protocol 13 of the European Convention of Human Rights and, Pilz argues, therefore damages the reputation of Austria. To date, the Austrian government has ignored Pilz's demands.

Lesson 44: If you become a public figure, expect to be challenged and held to account for your actions, even if you had no choice but to act in a certain way.

Conflicts of Interest As a high-profile public figure with diverse business and personal interests, it should come as no surprise that Schwarzenegger has often been accused of having a conflict of interests. These allegations have been made both in regard to financial interests, but also that by spreading his time and energy too widely, he cannot possibly give his job as Governor of California (see *The Governator*) his full attention.

The first major such accusations were made in summer 2005 when the press reported that Schwarzenegger continued to hold a position of executive editor for two American

Media magazines. Schwarzenegger had a long association with he publications and continued to write regular bodybuilding columns. He announced that his salary from the work - $250,000 a year - would be donated to charity.

Lesson 45: Philanthropy is a good way to detract attention when you are being criticised for something you have done wrong.

More and more such arrangements came to light, however. The *Los Angeles Times* reported he had a consulting contract which would earn him $8 million over the next five years, and *The New York Times* revealed another arrangement with Weider Publications worth in excess of $1 million a year, plus phantom equity.

Though not illegal, such relationships did call into question Schwarzenegger's voting on policies regarding the advertising and sale of performance enhancing dietary supplements, the companies behind which often advertised in American Media publications. In 2005 the *Washington Post* also reported that American Media had paid $20,000 to actress Gigi Goyette not to discuss her affair with Schwarzenegger.

Gropegate During his first campaign for governor, a number of allegations of sexual and personal misconduct were levied against Schwarzenegger. Though he admitted to having "behaved badly sometimes" and apologised to those involved, the accusations lingered.

The first allegations date back to 1977 when Schwarzenegger gave an interview to *Oui* magazine. He discussed his sexual orgies and smoking cannabis, which he is also seen doing after winning Mr. Olympia in *Pumping Iron*.

> Oh, you tho k you're bad, huh? You're a choirboy compared to me! A f*cking choirboy!
>
> Arnold Schwarzenegger in *End of Days*

Six women have also alleged sexual assault and harassment, reports of which appeared in the *Los Angeles Times* in 2003. The accusations were all physical: three women claimed that Schwarzenegger had grabbed their breasts, and hence the scandal was dubbed "Gropegate". The other women alleged Schwarzenegger had also touched them inappropriately. No prosecutions have ever been made, however, and the allegations do not seem to have had an adverse impact on Schwarzenegger's career trajectory, or his standing with voters.

Lesson 46: Sexual misconduct will come back to haunt you. Think of the long-term impact of your actions so that you can mitigate any fall-out.

Steroid Use Schwarzenegger has been unusually candid about his use of performance-enhancing anabolic steroids during his bodybuilding career. The drugs were not illegal at the time, and he described them as,"helpful to me in maintaining muscle size while on a strict diet in preparation for a contest. I did not use them for muscle growth, but rather for muscle maintenance when cutting up."

Although he has spoken about his drug use, Schwarzenegger has been rather more defensive when the topic is raised by others. In 1999, Dr William Heepe predicted his early death, stating that there was a link between his steroid use and later heart problems. *The Globe*, a US tabloid, made similar assertions, and Schwarzenegger sued both of them for libel. Heepe was forced to pay $10,000 in damages for libel by a German court, and the tabloid settled too.

Lesson 47: Protect your reputation, image and business interests through whatever means are necessary.

Personal Life

The best activities for your health are pumping and humping.

Arnold Schwarzenegger

Schwarzenegger's first love was Barbara Outland, an English teacher who he met in 1968, shortly after arriving in the US. Initially the couple got on well, and they lived together, but they were very different people, and not at all compatible: Schwarzenegger summarised the problem as, "Basically it came down to this: she was a well-balanced woman who wanted an ordinary, solid life, and I was not a well-balanced man, and hated the very idea of ordinary life." Their love life was passionate but turbulent. Schwarzenegger has a number of affairs, and though at first Outland found him to be a joyful personality, totally charismatic, adventurous, and athletic, she later described him as "insufferable".

Lesson 48: The nature and values of two people must be in sync if they are to enjoy a mutually satisfying relationship.

In 1977, Schwarzenegger attended a charity tennis match, where he was introduced to Maria Shriver by their mutual friend, Tom Brokaw. Although Schwarzenegger was in a relationship at the time with a Venice Beach hairdresser named Sue Moray, he was very much open to Shriver's advances. She was, after all, the niece of former President John F. Kennedy, rich, well-connected, and beautiful.

The couple married in April 1986 and had four children, Katherine, Christina, Patrick, and Christopher. Shriver worked throughout their marriage as a news anchor and was a popular First Lady of California after Schwarzenegger took office (see *The Governator*). Shriver championed the role of women in public life, encouraged community service, and in 2005 launched the WE Connect Program to give support to families who were struggling economically.

In our society, the women who break down barriers are those who ignore limits.

Arnold Schwarzenegger

In the mid 1990s, Schwarzenegger had an extra marital affair with a member of his household staff, Mildred Baena, and fathered her child. Schwarzenegger managed to keep the affair, and the child, secret for 14 years, but he was forced to confess when Shriver discovered the truth and confronted him. Shriver made a public statement that her husband's admission was, "painful and heartbreaking," and she asked for privacy.

Lesson 49: Relationships of all kind - personal and professional - depend on trust. Once that trust is broken, there is little hope for the relationship's survival.

Consider that a divorce!

Arnold Scwarzenegger in *Total Recall*

Shriver filed for divorce in July 2011, citing irreconcilable differences. The divorce lawyers were hired before news of the affair was released to the public, and the financial details of the settlement were also laid out at this time. Custody of the two younger children is shared between Shriver and Schwarzenegger, who live near to one another, as does Baena and her son.

Conclusion

The length of Schwarzenegger's career, and the breath of his activities, is quite mind boggling, and it can be too much to take in all at once. In a bid to understand the essential qualities of the man, and what has driven him to such lengths, it is therefore distilling his lessons down further into three over-arching points, and explaining them in this conclusion.

#1 You need to have drive to succeed

People do not become successful by accident: making your goals a reality requires sustained effort, often over many years. Your state of mind - notably your focus, your determination and your persistence - are integral factors to whether or not you will achieve your goals. Schwarzenegger knew, right from childhood, that he wanted to achieve great things, and that through discipline and hard work he could make it happen. He has never lost sight of the fact that even when by luck opportunities do come his way, he must still be the driving force behind his career if he wants to succeed.

#2 Decide what you are going to do, and give it your all

There is no point in making a half-arsed attempt at something. If it is worth your while doing, it is worth doing properly. If you focus your attention and effort, and put in the hours, you will achieve far more. This applies whether you are developing a skill (bodybuilding, acting, learning a foreign language), or trying to gain experience, contacts, or a promotion at work. Nobody remembers the guy who came second in the competition, or who lost the election. Give what you do 100%, and you then stand a far greater chance of making it to #1.

#3 Be open to opportunities, and capitalise on them

When Schwarzenegger became Mr. Universe, he could never have foreseen that one day he would be Governor of California: he had never even been to the USA! What he did know, however, is that throughout your life, doors open to you, and they are not always the ones you are expecting. You have to keep your mind open to new ideas and possibilities, and make use of your existing platforms, skills, contacts and experiences to pursue them.

Lesson 50: I'll be back! Terminator's most famous catch phrase reminds us that we can always reinvent ourselves, and that success is the result of repetition and persistence.

There is no doubt that Arnold Schwarzenegger has more achievements to come, more surprises up his sleeve, and that he will continue to be a prominent figure in American politics, business, sport, and the entertainment industry for many years to come. Although he has had a number of hurdles to overcome in his life to date, and his personal and professional lives have not been without controversy, he remains a strong and, on the whole, positive role model for ambitious individuals in all walks of life.

The Life and Business Lessons of Bill Gates

Introduction

Few leaders in the business world are as revered or renowned as Bill Gates. His name has become synonymous with innovation and leadership in the software industry, enormous success, and of course, "The Richest Man in the World". Many look to Gates' story as both an inspiration and a blueprint for pursuing their own entrepreneurial dreams. This eBook has been written with these people in mind, or those who are simply curious about the life of one of the most interesting businessmen of the last century. It is also deliberately brief, for those who hope to learn the most they can from the story of Bill Gates, but have little time on their hands to do so.

This book offers an introduction to Gates, his business success and the lessons that we can learn from him. It is not a text book nor a biography, but more of a cheat sheet for reading on the bus or in the bathroom, so that you can pick out the most significant points without having to carry around a bag of weighty tomes. You can read it all in one sitting, or look up specific case studies as and when you are looking for inspiration or direction. The key lessons outlined here are drawn from interviews Gates has given over the past 40 years, from the numerous blogs and articles written about him, and, most importantly, from the successes and failures on his road to the "Richest Man in the World".

On October 28th 1955, William Henry Gates III was born into an upper-middle class Seattle family. Gates was the middle child in his family, with one older sister, Kristi, and one younger sister, Libby. Gates' father, William H. Gates, Sr., was a prominent Washington lawyer, while his mother, Mary Maxwell Gates, was a well-respected teacher and local business figure, and held positions on a number of different company boards throughout her long career. Gates was affectionately known in his family as "Trey", a nickname that he earned from being the fourth to take the paternal name William H. Gates in his family, and thus the III-suffix with his name (Trey is a term commonly used in card games – a popular pastime in the Gates household - to denote a three). His childhood was a happy and carefree one, and Bill enjoyed a healthy and active social life that many parents dream of for their children. He participated regularly in various sporting activities, was a member of the Cub Scouts, and would spend summers with his family surrounded by nature in Bremerton, Washington.

When Gates was 13, he was enrolled by his parents at the exclusive Seattle Lakeside School, which was the perfect environment to nurture his creative and competitive spirit. Before this move, Bill had experienced some difficulties with 'fitting in' – he lacked direction, and was seemingly developing behavioral problems at the transition to becoming a teenager. At age 11, Gates developed rather rapidly intellectually, and begin to also display a high level of emotional independence and rebellion from authority. He began to rebel against the control of his parents, particularly his mother. According to an anecdote told by his father, during a family dinner, Bill Gates Sr. threw a glass of cold water in Bill Gates Jr's face as a result of a particularly heated and bitter fight with his mother. By the age of 12, he was sent to counselling by his parents to address some of these issues. As a very clearly intelligent child, he was in need of the greater focus and discipline that a school like Lakeside could provide. There, in 1968, he was introduced to his love of computers when the school fortuitously purchased a computer link terminal for use by its students. Although computers were still too prohibitively expensive for the school to own outright at the time, this method allowed the school to lease computer time for its students on a machine owned by General Electric via the link-up terminal. Interestingly, Lakeside didn't just permit their students to use the machine in a tightly controlled environment, but allowed them a degree of relative freedom – an approach which Gates attributes to being responsible for his exploding interest in computers as a teenager. It was also at Lakeside that Bill met and developed a relationship with longtime friend and future business partner, Paul Allen. During this time, the pair got their first taste of business collaboration, working together to create a traffic counting program called 'Traf-O-Data'. Although this particular scheme wasn't remarkably successful, it laid the foundations for future cooperation between the two young entrepreneurs.

After doing particularly well on his SATs (achieving an almost perfect score of 1590), Gates was accepted to study at Harvard University. Although he was set on the road to becoming a lawyer – a path that his parents had actively encouraged from very early on in his academic career – his true interests laid elsewhere. He was particularly gifted at mathematics; however, upon discovering that he was not Harvard's best math student, he quickly lost interest in pursuing this as his major. Instead, he diverted a lot of his efforts into the field of computer science. While at Harvard, he reconnected with his schoolmate Paul Allen, who dropped out of university in Washington and moved to Boston, where he began work for tech conglomerate Honeywell as a programmer. United again, the pair eventually collaborated and conspired to form their own company: Microsoft. Following Allen's lead, Gates soon made the call to drop out of college and pursue his business venture with Microsoft full-time. He moved to Albuquerque, New Mexico and worked with Allen to establish the company there.

He later explained the sense of urgency that he and Allen felt in needing to pursue their business dreams, and his justification for leaving college in his final year:

"I loved college. It was so exciting to have conversations with lots of really smart people my age and to learn from great professors. But in December of 1974, when my friend Paul Allen showed me the issue of Popular Electronics that had the Altair 8800 on the cover, we knew it was the beginning of a major change. The Altair was the first minicomputer kit that came with Intel's 8080 microprocessor chip.

For a while, Paul and I had been talking about how that chip would make computers affordable for the average person someday. We had the idea that this would create huge opportunities to write really interesting software that lots of people would buy. Once the Altair 8800 came out, we wanted to be among first to start a business to write software for this new generation of computers. We were afraid if we waited, someone else would beat us to it.

It was a hard decision and I know my parents had their concerns. And while I would never encourage anyone to drop out of school, for me, it turned out to be the right choice."

Microsoft's big break came when the small start-up was commissioned by IBM to develop the software that was to be used on its machines. Gates and Allen arranged this by purchasing the rights to the third-party software that was to form the basis of the soon to be ubiquitous operating system, MS-DOS, and then selling the licenses to run the software to IBM, while retaining ownership rights. By doing so, Microsoft not only profited from the initial deal with IBM, but also earned royalty fees for each machine that the software was installed on. And when the personal computing industry really took off in the early to mid-80s, Gates and Allen were able to offer the same licensing deal for the same software to IBM's competitors, as the company held no ownership rights or patents to the operating system that they originally commissioned. This business-minded stroke of genius was ultimately the deal that led to Gates making his early fortune.

After this episode, Gates became the sole representative of Microsoft when Paul Allen fell ill with Hodgkin's disease in 1982. In 1985, Gates launched the first edition of Microsoft Windows, which was to become the almost universal basis on which personal computers would be operated for at least the next 20 years. The following year, Microsoft went public on March 13th 1986 – a move which was incredibly well received by investors. The initial public offering (IPO) saw the company's stocks valued at a price of

$21 per share. While the actual sale of Microsoft shares at its IPO made Gates his first million (specifically, a total of around $1.6 million), it was the 45 percent share of the company that he retained following the IPO that made him the bulk of his fortune. By July 1986, Gates' share in Microsoft was worth around $350 million dollars. In 1987, Gates became the world's youngest ever billionaire at the age of 31, and by age 39, Gates was officially the world's richest man with a total net wealth of $12.9 billion.

Gates continued at Microsoft in the positon of CEO, which he held until stepping down from the post in 2000. He was replaced in this role by Harvard friend and room-mate Steve Ballmer, while Gates continued at the company in the position of Chief Software Architect. In 2006, it was announced that Gates would be stepping down as an executive at Microsoft in order to focus his efforts on philanthropy through The Bill & Melinda Gates Foundation. Gates transitioned from a full-time to a part-time role at Microsoft by 2008, but retained his position as a non-executive chairman at the company. With the recent promotion of Satya Nadella to the chief executive position in 2014, Gates relinquished his post as chairman, and now holds the title 'Founder and Technology Adviser' at Microsoft. Gates' priority nowadays is clearly philanthropy, on which he spends at least two thirds of his time. He has funneled a huge chunk of his personal fortune through The Bill & Melinda Gates Foundation, which is dedicated to fighting "extreme poverty and poor health in developing countries, and the failures of America's education system", and is estimated to have donated around $28 billion to the foundation. Through his work in this area, Bill Gates is now not only known as the world's richest man, but also one of its most generous.

With the basic outline of the life of Bill Gates to date in mind, the rest of this eBook will explore the individual characteristics that helped to shape Bill in his youth and young adulthood, and would carry on to be an influence as he led Microsoft towards the position of being the world's foremost software company. Each chapter of this book will take a look at one of the eight key traits and influences that have helped shape Gates' success all throughout life: from college, through to his early entrepreneurial years, to the multibillion dollar success story he has become most famous for.

Risk

"Business is a money game with few rules and a lot of risk" – *Bill Gates.*

Even from an early age, Gates seemed to be aware of the need to take risks in life to enjoy rewards. Despite knowing that there could be severe consequences for such an abuse, Gates and his fellow computer enthusiasts at Lakeside School in Seattle spent their time researching and exploiting bugs that would allow them to enjoy more computer time via the school's exclusive computer link terminal. At the time, the school purchased 'time' to use the General Electric owned computer through a special uplink, which was itself an expensive endeavor. Although this crafty strategy was eventually found out and Gates and the other implicated students were punished with restrictions on using the school's computer link during that summer, this was early evidence of an individual who had developed an appetite for calculated risk. As a young boy, Bill reportedly loved playing board games, his favorite of which was the aptly named *Risk*. The objective of this popular game is to move your 'armies' across a world map, attacking your competitors and defending your own territories, and ultimately pursuing the final goal of world domination. The 'risk' in the game comes in deciding where to attack and how to spread your armies throughout your controlled territories. Of course, this risk is magnified by the fact that the outcome of battles is not necessarily decided by skill or strategy, but by the roll of the dice. Much like the board game that he loved as a child, Gates' life was one that has been heavily guided by calculated risk, as well as the invisible hand of lady luck.

Perhaps the first real major personal risk that Gates took in life was his decision to drop out of Harvard to pursue his business aspirations with school friend Paul Allen. Education was a value that was always prized and revered by the Gates family. From his early childhood, Gates' parents encouraged the natural curiosity within Bill to flourish. He was the kind of child who asked a lot of questions, a trait which his patient parents helped to nurture and develop with their emphasis on the importance of reading and self-learning. At the age of 13, despite being great advocates of the public education system, Gates was enrolled at the private Seattle Lakeside School as his parents wanted to provide their son with the most optimal learning environment based on his personality. There was little surprise, therefore, when Gates was accepted to study at Harvard – a course which seemed to be predestined thanks to his natural ability and the encouragement of his parents. So when Bill took the decision to take a leave of absence from Harvard to found and run Microsoft, it was obviously a serious decision. He knew that his parents would be unhappy with such a course of action and, although they were taken aback by his decision, when they saw how much he wanted to pursue the dream of running his own company they offered him their full support. According to Gates, he told his father when he decided to drop out that he would be going back to Harvard. It took 32 years, but Gates indeed returned to Harvard in 2007 when he was invited to receive an honorary doctorate degree from the university.

Much of the innovation required for a business to develop involves a good deal of risk, and this was certainly also the case at Microsoft. From the inception of the company in 1975, through to the mid-2000s, Gates directed much of the product conception at Microsoft and oversaw some significant projects. Some of these were particularly successful, such as the company's famous contract with IBM that led to the creation of MS-DOS and the launch and reception of Microsoft Windows 95. However, others were less so, such as the poorly received Windows Vista and the company's lackluster success with its early foray into the world of smartphone software. What is important to remember, however, is that had Gates not driven the company to take risks with new products, Microsoft and its legacy would be a relic of the technological past, much like the Commodore 64 gaming console, or the floppy disk. Instead, thanks to the risks that were exemplified by Microsoft's changing focus in a dynamic tech world, it has managed to stay incredibly relevant by today's standards and is even continuing to innovate in certain areas ahead of its competitors. Interestingly, some of the reputational damage to Microsoft over time has been a result of the lack of risks it has taken on certain concepts. A clear example of this is the development of internet browsing software and related technologies. In an infamous quote from 1993 (of which the official attribution is unclear), Gates is rumored to have bluntly stated that Microsoft was "not interested" in the internet. Later in 1998, he admitted: "Sometimes we do get taken by surprise. For example, when the internet came along, we had it as a fifth or sixth priority". This was arguably a valuable learning experience for Gates and his company. By isolating itself from the initial buzz of the internet and not taking risks to embrace the new medium, Microsoft paid in the long run. It will be surprising to see either Gates or the company making a similar such mistake in the near future.

What can we learn from the risks that Bill Gates has taken throughout his life? First, his risks were *always* calculated. Whether it was leaving Harvard to pursue his start-up dreams, or taking risks on products and innovation, Gates was never reckless with the risks he took. There was always a clear goal in sight and there was always limited exposure. Microsoft's endeavors have often been hugely impactful but rarely radical (which perhaps best typified by the MS-DOS origin story, discussed further in the next chapter). Although many of Gates' critics cite this as evidence of a lack of creativity rather than a careful risk management, it is a method that has proved incredibly successful for him and his company. Even when he enjoyed huge success soon after he left Harvard to pursue his Microsoft dream, he could have easily returned to college had the venture fallen through. Before an audience of 1700 students at the University of Chicago, however, Gates reiterated the importance of education. He emphasized that students thinking of following his early exit example should only do so if they have a "very unique" idea that they are eager to work on and are supremely confident of their success. To paraphrase this idea and apply it as a general strategy in life, always analyze the size of the risk and the potential for return – if either of these factors point to an unpalatable outcome, then re-think your strategy.

Lateral thinking

"I choose a lazy person to do a hard job, because a lazy person will find an easy way to do it." – *Bill Gates.*

Lateral thinking is a quality that has been highly valued throughout history, and has led to some of the most famous solutions to history's greatest quandaries and answers to some of the most perplexing riddles. For the average individual, lateral thinking can help us to achieve solutions to problems in day to day life, or in the longer term, and is an actively sought after quality that is often tested in job interviews for competitive positions. When it comes to thinking outside the box, there are few who have applied this as successfully to the business world as Bill Gates. While there are several examples of Gates' applying this style of logic to achieve his business aims, perhaps his most famous exhibition of this characteristic could be seen when he and then business partner Paul Allen were commissioned by computing industry behemoth IBM to supply the operating system for their machines.

Following Gates and Allen's creation of the company in 1975, Microsoft enjoyed some early success with Altair BASIC, which was the foundation product of the company. This was the first high-level programming language available for the Altair 8800, a microcomputer that heralded the beginning of the personal computing age. Altair BASIC was the first in a range of programming language systems known as Microsoft BASIC, which became a common feature in personal computers throughout the late 1970s and early 1980s. At this time, Microsoft's debut project enjoyed hundreds of thousands of users. The success of Microsoft BASIC attracted the attention of the many in the fledgling industry, including the world's biggest name in computing, IBM. In July 1980, after IBM's efforts to obtain an operating system deal with the more established company Digital Research fell through, they solicited Gates and Allen to provide the proprietary software for their range of personal computers. The pair agreed to the deal, however they had one small problem – they didn't have an operating system to sell.

On July 27th, 1981, Microsoft acquired 'QDOS '('Quick and Dirty Operating System', later known as '86-DOS') from Seattle Computer Products for the tidy sum of $50,000. This was to become the basis of 'MS-DOS' ('Micro-Soft Disk Operating System'), which Microsoft modified according to IBM's specifications before delivering the final product. Despite being more than competent software programmers, both Gates and Allen knew that the real opportunity of their deal with IBM had nothing to do with creating an original or revolutionary piece of software. This would have taken years of development and testing, and cost an enormous amount of money in terms of dollars and man hours. Such a feat was beyond Microsoft's capabilities at the time. What's more, IBM needed fast results; having to wait years for a final product from Microsoft could have killed the deal. Though IBM was typically fastidious in its product research and development, it had come to release that PC design and rollout depended heavily on quick turnaround times in order for the technology inside a machine to remain relevant. With this in mind, Gates and Allen saw the value of purchasing the rights to an off the shelf operating system which had already been thoroughly developed and tested for bugs, and had all the makings of a functional piece of software, for use on IBM machines after some minor tweaking. The real genius in the Microsoft/IBM deal, however, had nothing to do with the functionality of the operating system, but everything to do with the concept of software ownership.

In negotiating to charge licensing fee for MS-DOS to IBM rather than selling the rights outright, Gates and Allen had gotten a hold of 'the goose that laid the golden egg'. The arrangement meant that instead of handing over direct ownership of the rights to MS-DOS to IBM, Microsoft was paid a royalty fee for each machine that the operating system was installed on. With this move, Microsoft also wrote a non-exclusivity clause into the deal with IBM, which meant that the company could sell the software directly to IBM's competitors. During the following decade, dozens of competitors to IBM sprang up in the field of personal computing, and almost all of their machines ran MS-DOS. The decision to push for this deal displayed an incredible amount of foresight and lateral thinking. Many in the fledgling PC industry, including IBM, firmly believed that the real business potential in the field lay in proprietary hardware. Microsoft, on the other hand, saw the money making potential of software and, through the establishment of MS-DOS, was able to dominate the industry in this area, and reap unprecedented financial benefits. This deal made the pair their fortunes, and catapulted Microsoft into the spotlight as the single most important software company in existence.

Many of the truly great minds in history have evidenced a high capability for lateral thinking, a talent which is particularly well-received in the business world. There is a fundamental advantage for those who are able to think laterally in such situations; this is because when we think laterally, we are able to think in a way that most people cannot. And when we can think in a truly unique way in order to arrive at solutions to complex problems, we have a greater chance of enjoying gains based on our ability to act in a unique and rewarding way. Gates, reported to be a deep thinker from an early age, has proven to be a master of lateral thinking, and offers in this trait another example that we should strive to emulate.

83

Competition

"I can buy 20 percent of you or I can buy all of you. Or I can go into this business myself and bury you." - *Bill Gates to AOL chief executive, Steve Case on Microsoft's potential for acquisition of the company.*

The spirit of competitiveness was actively fostered during Gates' childhood in a family environment that encouraged and rewarded healthy competition. Whatever game the Gates children were playing, "there was always a reward for winning and there was always a penalty for losing." His parents encouraged his participation in sports and always rewarded victories, however small they were. According to his mother, Mary, Gates was "competitive in cards with his sister, races to see who could do jigsaw puzzles faster, ski racing, sailing – whatever. He wanted to do it well, and as good as the other folks that he was with." During summers spent with his family in a rented cabin on the Hood Canal in Bremerton, WA, Gates' spirit competitiveness was again nurtured when he, along with family and friends, participated in their own 'Olympic Games'. Here, like always, this spirit of competitiveness was again obvious and actively encouraged in the Gates family. When Bill was enrolled at Seattle's elite Lakeside School at the age of 13, his spirit of competitiveness was further developed. According to Gates:

Rigor absolutely defined my Lakeside experience. Lakeside had the kind of teachers who would come to me, even when I was getting straight As, and say: "When are you going to start applying yourself?" Teachers like Ann…One day, she said: "Bill, you're just coasting. Here are my ten favorite books; read these. Here's my college thesis; you should read it." She challenged me to do more. I never would have come to enjoy literature as much as I do if she hadn't pushed me.

At the helm of Microsoft, Gates was fiercely and famously competitive. He had a borderline obsession with being the best in the business and aimed to shut out any competitors. However, Microsoft's most famous rivalry was perhaps with fellow PC heavyweight Apple, and carried over on a personal level between Gates and Apple co-founder Steve Jobs. The history of the relationship between two of personal computing's biggest companies is long and complex. The two companies enjoyed a close relationship at first, when Microsoft worked to provide the productivity software that Apple's machine required to be competitive in the business world. Gates even recommended to However, the rivalry really began when Microsoft launched its first GUI-based (Graphical User Interface – as opposed to the text based MS-DOS) operating system in 1985, Microsoft Windows. Prior to this, Apple had the only GUI computer on the market with the Apple Macintosh. As Microsoft improved its Windows OS over time, it began to adopt more features that seemed to have a number of parallels with the Apple system. In 1988, Microsoft released Windows 2.0 which saw Apple launch a copyright suit against Gates' company, which went on unresolved for many years. Eventually, GUI-interface computing came to be seen as the only way to complete many personal computing tasks, which meant that it couldn't be copyrighted. Furthermore, Gates had persuaded Apple to license its 'virtual displays' found in its GUI operating system to Microsoft for the purpose of developing Windows 1.0. In 1992, Apples claim was dismissed, with Judge W. Schwarzer ruling that each of the above conditions nullified all of Apple's 189 contestations. In the long run, this ultimately meant that Microsoft and other competitors would be able to continue Apple's GUI-based platform as a model for the development of future operating systems. Microsoft and Apple had gone head to head, with the former coming out the clear winner.

Although, Gates won out in his fight against Apple, his desire to crush his competition landed him and his company in hot water when, in 1998, Microsoft was charged by the Department of Justice with anti-competitive behavior. The company was accused of becoming a monopoly and engaging in abusive practices contrary to existing anti-trust laws. These charges were filed on the basis of the argument that its handling of operating system and web browser sales. Specifically, this was to do with the fact that Microsoft, in its apparent efforts to snuff out internet browser provider Netscape Navigator, had bundled its flagship Internet Explorer web browser as a free piece of software with the Microsoft Windows operating system. In 1999, the presiding judge ruled that Microsoft was indeed guilty of monopolistic behavior and had exhibited attempts to crush its competition. As a result, it was demanded that Microsoft be broken up into two parts to remedy this issue, with one arms to produce the operating system, and the other arm, other software. Although this decision was overturned on appeal, this ordeal did a lot of damage to both Gates' image and that of his company. The former came to be seen as an industry bully, and the latter was viewed as the monopolistic giant in control of the personal computing world.

Gates' experience with Microsoft has shown both the good and bad sides of competition. On the one hand, his persistence in going head to head with Apple resulted in the creation and development of one of its most successful pieces of software in Microsoft Windows. On the other hand, however, Gates' dogged pursuit of his competition very nearly led his company to the brink of disaster. From this we can observe that there are indeed limits to the benefit of competition. While it is the very spirit of competition that drives us to innovate and succeed, it can also become a consuming force which may work in our detriment if pursued to excess. Fortunately for Gates, he appeared to have learned his lesson from this experience without paying too high a price.

Branding

"If I were down to my last dollar, I'd spend it on PR." – *Bill Gates.*

When it comes to business and everyday life, paying close attention to branding is an indisputable key to success. Public perception is one of the driving influences of popularity, and Gates' experience with this – both in terms of his own branding and Microsoft's – has indicated just how important this can be. Gates is a man with a healthy respect for the importance of good marketing, once stating in an absolutist fashion "if you can't make it good, at least make it look good." During his time at the helm of Microsoft, Gates was closely involved with the company's marketing strategy, including right from the company's inception. In the early days of Microsoft, Gates would personally spend hours planning and delivering the company's PR strategy. Initially, this involved spending a great deal of his time travelling long distances to pitch Microsoft products to potential buyers. Later, this role was expanded as Gates became the face of Microsoft by participating in a large number of interviews as the company began to enjoy early success. He went on to appear personally in print advertisements for various Microsoft products, and at the height of the company's success, in high budget television commercials. In 2008, Gates appeared alongside comedian Jerry Seinfeld in a series of Microsoft commercials, which were seen as a direct response by Gates' company to the 'anti-Microsoft' Apple campaign from around the same period. Although the $300 million campaign received mixed reviews, it nonetheless highlighted Gates' own personal commitment to the value of marketing.

A more clearly successful instance of Gates' personally driven marketing approach can be seen in the official launch of Windows 95. Long before the black turtleneck and Levi 501 jeans-wearing Steve Jobs' made Apple product launches the annual must see tech event, Gates poured huge resources into launching Microsoft's groundbreaking operating system with a huge amount of fanfare. Microsoft spent $300 million on the marketing campaign for Windows 95, and roped in celebrities like Jay Leno and the Rolling Stones to aid in its promotion. Following its launch, Windows 95 was a huge and unprecedented success. It has been purchased by hundreds of millions of consumers and has been run on billions of terminals. Perhaps most importantly, the operating system brought in billions of dollars in revenue for Microsoft. How much of its success was due to its accompanying marketing campaign is hard to quantify, however, it is certainly reasonable to suppose that it had a significant effect in making it perhaps the single most popular operating system ever. What's more, Microsoft's Windows 95 campaign was perhaps the first major example of making the previously unexciting concept of tech release dates and carnival of entertainment of sorts. It set a model which many, including Steve Jobs and Apple, would later emulate as a core part of their own companies' marketing strategies.

Despite his readiness to embrace and exploit the great marketing machine, Gates has also been on the negative end of public perception, and in a very personal way indeed. Over time Gates came to be viewed as the face of corporate greed and establishment wealth, which, as a figure who was named the world's richest man 12 years in a row, was a hard image to avoid. To make matters worse, there were several instances of public interaction where Gates was not portrayed as the most humble of characters. When he was called to testify as part of the United States vs. Microsoft Corporation antitrust lawsuit, he was perceived as being very uncooperative during the entire process. Gates gave terse answers to most questions, and displayed a lack of humility and a high degree of petulance, combativeness and entitlement in his behavior. This was also repeated when Microsoft was ruled by the European Commission to have violated competitiveness standards, and was ordered to pay the single biggest fine in the history of the commission (and equivalent of $794 million) as a result. This episode of Gates' life yielded valuable a valuable lesson – sometimes good branding involves not only active engagement through deliberate marketing campaigns, but also through the management of the public image during unforeseen events. Though Gates and Microsoft were certainly entitled to object to the anti-competiveness accusations that they were charged with, the manner in which this was done was arguably harmful to both the image of Gates and his company. Gates, however, did appear to learn from this experience, and took great efforts to appear as more of a relatable 'every man' following this episode.

In an era of unprecedented levels of branding and public relations, we can all learn a valuable lesson from Gates' experiences. Though he has displayed a clear passion and vision for marketing his company's products, he has not been infallible in this area. Furthermore, while his efforts to directly coordinate and participate in Microsoft's planned PR campaigns have been particularly enthusiastic, Gates has experienced some difficulties with the more impromptu moments that come with being a public figure under intense scrutiny. While a somewhat cynical view, some have suggested that his engagement in the world of philanthropy was part of an effort to redeem his and Microsoft's reputation following its anti-competitiveness lawsuit. That Microsoft began to decline from its apex of immense popularity shortly after its antitrust trials is perhaps no coincidence. However, in any event, Gates' up and down experience with image perception highlights just how important branding can be. Often, life is a popularity contest for many, from individuals to corporations. Those who can present themselves and their interests in the best light possible will often have a competitive advantage in winning the support of their audience.

Focus

"If I'd had some set idea of a finish line, don't you think I would have crossed it years ago?" – *Bill Gates.*

One of the common misconceptions of being successful in the business world – or simply enjoying a decent amount of success through any venture – is the role of good fortune. Many people seem to place an excessive amount of emphasis in the belief that others have succeeded where they haven't, because others have had more than their fair share of luck. This is, in fact, a toxic attitude that breeds complacency and encourages laziness. Indeed, the story of Bill Gates is one that is often touted as a 'right place, right time' success story – the kind where the stars aligned and the universe was in perfect harmony, and just so happened to generate the kind of luck that made Gates a very wealthy man. While there was indeed an element of this in Gates' success, it was also his dedication, hunger and focus that made his success possible, and is one of the reasons why he and his company profited so immensely from the personal computing boom rather than a rival company. Though he came from a well off, upper-middle class family, this was of no importance to Gates when it came to his motivation. According to his father, Gates had an appreciation for the value of money from an early age. Even after Microsoft became a roaring success, he famously would fly coach rather than first class when traveling for business to spare the company's travel budget. He also exhibited a great deal of focus in his childhood when it came to learning. Gates was a gifted student with passions in many different areas aside from computers.

Perhaps the best example of Gates' focus is in the attitude he demonstrated in building and improving Microsoft, even after the company achieved monumental success. Gates was not content with a Harvard degree, nor a moderately successful business. He displayed no apparent urge to relax his fiery ambition, not even after earning his first million dollars, nor his first billion. Instead, Gates is a man who apparently works to dynamic and shifting goals – for him, there is no finish line, only the next objective. Gates' work ethic is famous, and was a quality that was instilled in him by his parents from a young age. In a recent interview, he claimed: "I never took a day off in my twenties. Not one. And I'm still fanatical, but now I'm a little less fanatical." He was constantly working away at his prized project in building his company to be the biggest and the best, and was simultaneously responsible for many different arms of the business in the early days, from research, to business development, to marketing. Whether it was developing new program ideas, negotiating business contracts or traveling long distances in to

91

market the company to prospective clients, Gates' focus and ambition was evident in so many ways.

The hunger that drove Bill Gates' to become the world's most successful and iconic businessman is also the same hunger that compels him to work towards solving some of the world's most complex problems. Commendably, he appears to have brought the same level of intensity to this work that he exhibited in developing Microsoft. He regularly travels to regions of the world to raise awareness for various global health issues and to oversee and implement programs sponsored by The Bill & Melinda Gates Foundation. Gates also campaigns relentlessly for causes that the foundation targets, from vaccinations, to poverty, to education. He conducts this work in tandem with his current part-time role at Microsoft, which he approaches today with no less vigor than in the company's early years.

As one of the most obvious traits that can lead to success in any area, focus is also perhaps one of the most often overlooked. For a person to have a great vision or idea is typically not enough; though this can certainly provide the initial spark required for an endeavor to succeed, focus is the fuel that gets you to the finish line. One of the unique attributes of Gates is that his source of focus and hunger is seemingly inexhaustible. Success with MS-DOS was not enough, nor was Windows; indeed, he has carried the same attitude across to his work in philanthropy, from which many in the developing world may benefit immensely. Focus is a rather difficult trait to create out of nothing. However, it is most likely to be exhibited in the pursuit of a goal for which you care deeply. If you feel that you are lacking focus in pursuing your goals, it is perhaps time to reassess your objectives and question whether you are pursuing what truly matters to you.

Adversity

"Life is not fair; get used to it." – *Bill Gates.*

Though Gates life is not exactly the kind that has been peppered with tragedy, he has nonetheless had to deal with his share of adversity, the trials of which he had to overcome to enjoy his success. Indeed, Gates has shown from his life that adversity isn't just something that we must overcome; instead we can use some of the more difficult experiences in life to help direct our future. For Gates, this was apparently one of the main factors that drove him to become one of the world's leading advocates for philanthropy and investment in solving the problems of the developing world.

All throughout his life, Gates was particularly close to his mother, Mary. Of their parents, she was the most constantly involved with rearing Gates and his siblings during their childhood. When she passed away in 1994 following a short battle with breast cancer, Gates was devastated. In a television interview, Gates' father recounted an anecdote of his son being pulled over by traffic police when speeding to the hospital where his mother died. However, instead of wallowing in his own grief at the sudden loss of his beloved mother, Gates made a positive out of the sadness of her passing in stepping up his work in the area of philanthropy. His mother had always taught Gates and his siblings about the importance of civic duty and the value of 'giving back'. Mary Gates' philanthropic spirit was further emphasized in a letter she gave to her daughter-in-law on the day of her wedding, a mere 6 months before she died. In it, she reminded Melinda, "from those to whom much is given, much is expected". Following his mother's death, Gates donated $10 million dollars to the University of Washington to establish a scholarship in her name, as a tribute to her memory, her passion for education and her own spirit of philanthropy.

Microsoft also faced a significant challenge when Gates' friend and business partner, Paul Allen, was diagnosed with Hodgkin's lymphoma in 1982. Though Allen received radiation treatment and completely recovered from the illness, the experience reportedly affected Gates and helped to lend him some perspective in life. His friend's diagnosis also seemed to have the effect of focusing Gates, making him even more determined to drive Microsoft's success to new heights.

Gates also experienced several challenges when at the helm of Microsoft, particularly with regards to the anti-competitiveness cases that were brought before the company. Possibly the most testing experiences of his professional career, he navigated these hearings somewhat clumsily, as discussed above. However, despite this, Gates soon recovered from this experience and urged his company along a new path with a corporate restructure, and refocused much of his energy in his philanthropic work. It would certainly have been easy in such a situation to become bogged down by adversity, but Gates showed an ability to bounce back and take a new direction after the difficulties associated with his company's antitrust lawsuits.

Though, Gates life is one that was not one of significant adversity, no life is without its personal challenges. It is important, therefore, to be able to deal with any adversity that might rear its head, whether that comes in the form of a personal loss or a professional challenge. Perhaps the most important lesson we can learn from Gates is that although we may experience challenges in life, our ability to use these experiences to create positives and draw new focus is possible. That is, out of darkness it is still possible to find some hope.

Adaptability

"People always fear change. People feared electricity when it was invented, didn't they?" *– Bill Gates.*

With Microsoft, Bill Gates was in the fortunate position of enjoying great success and making big money relatively early in the company's history. From very near to the beginning, Microsoft was a behemoth in the world of personal computing. However, one of the difficulties of early success is being able to sustain this over time. For Microsoft, this has been possible thanks to the spirit of adaptability of the company that has very often been driven by Gates himself. Perhaps some of Gates' ability to adapt came from the fact that, as a child, he was encouraged to participate in a broad range of activities. During his time at Lakeside School, Gates excelled at a wide array of subjects including Math, Science, English, and was even a talented Drama student. His parents emphasized the importance of a broad and varied education, which was perhaps also shown in Gates' change in career aspirations while at college: from law, to math, to computer programming.

Microsoft's most famous early success was born from its adaptability when it was effectively drawn into the business of making operating systems. Before it was approached by IBM, who commissioned Microsoft to provide the basis of the proprietary software for its machines, the company had no experience in operating systems. It had created computer language programs such as Altair BASIC and its successors; however, this was a vastly different exercise from creating the software required for a personal computer's operating system. When Microsoft was in early discussions with IBM about the provision of ancillary software for its machines, Gates referred the company to Digital Research, a company that was already well-established in the provision of operating systems. However, when it became apparent the Digital Research were not willing to do business with IBM, Gates and Allen adapted the direction of their company, and seized the opportunity to take up the contract with IBM that Digital Research had rejected.

At times, Microsoft has shown somewhat of a tardiness in adapting to changes in the tech industry, and it has certainly paid dearly on these occasions. The first example of this can be seen in Microsoft's approach to internet technology. As stated above, Gates and his company were rather slow off the mark when it came to fully embracing the potential for engaging with this now omnipresent aspect of personal computing. When Microsoft decided to finally go down the path of assimilating its services with internet-based software, it was already too late. While it was somewhat successful in shutting out its main early competitor, Netscape Navigator, by including Microsoft's Internet Explorer with every copy of Windows 95 (a move which led to the anti-competitiveness lawsuit, discussed above), it did not take enough steps to embrace the internet's full capital potential. This complacent attitude allowed competitors such as Google to step in and dominate the internet sector. Despite spending billions on its online arm with services such as Windows Live (which pales in comparison in terms of internet traffic from services provided by Google), and recently purchasing Yahoo! for the significant sum of $44 billion, Microsoft's online presence has been rather underwhelming to say the least.

However, one area where Microsoft has exhibited a good level of adaptability is in its entry into the console gaming market. Though it would have been entirely plausible for Gates' company to rest on its laurels and isolate its success to the realm of personal computing, Microsoft's experience with the XBOX has been a resounding success. When the product was launched in 2001, it was a bold incursion into a field that was then dominated by the Sony Playstation. Since then, the XBOX has come to hold its own, carving out a loyal following of gamers and enjoying great success with the release of several generations and, in particular, the uniquely interactive XBOX Kinect. The Kinect broke sales records wide open for the volume and speed of sales of a consumer electronics item – 10 million units in just 60 days. Although this success came during the leadership of Steve Ballmer, Gates' nonetheless played an important role in guiding Microsoft's product development strategy during this period.

Through his company, Gates has enjoyed varying levels of success when it comes to adaptability. Although adaptability has proven to be a game changer for Microsoft, particularly in terms of its early success with entering the world of producing operating systems, and the transition to the manufacture of gaming consoles from its traditional PC orientation, it has also lagged behind in key areas of development, particularly in the field of internet services. Perhaps one of the best lessons we can learn from Gates and Microsoft with regards to adaptability, however, is that is decidedly easier to adapt when things are on a smaller, less defined scale. This is one of the reasons that it was so easy for Gates and Allen to make the switch to producing operating systems early in the peace. One of the challenges of running such a large and established company such as Microsoft, is indeed the burden of previous success. Of course, it is a little too easy to judge the mistakes of Gates and Microsoft with the benefit of hindsight – Gates may be the world's richest man, but all the money in the world can't buy a crystal ball.

Humility

"We all need people who will give us feedback. That's how we improve." – *Bill Gates.*

One of the things that marks a truly great leader is a healthy dose of humility. This all too infrequently exhibited trait can be misinterpreted by some as a weakness; however, true humility is in fact both a sign of immense power and consideration of that power. However, in the early part of his career, Gates is not exactly the kind of person who could be easily described as humble. It was rather apparent that he had immense faith in his company, his ideas, and his potential to succeed, something that he did not shy away from showing. Of course, given the then unprecedented level of achievement he attained from such a young age, it is surprising that Gates was a grounded as he was. Yet, despite the apparent brashness and self-confidence that he exhibited in his early days, Gates has evolved into a much more balanced individual in this regard, an attribute which is often accompanied by age and life experience. Although he certainly could have continued at the helm of Microsoft unchallenged, Gates stepped down as CEO in 2000, and relinquished control of the company even further over the following decade to spend more time focusing on philanthropic work through The Bill & Melinda Gates Foundation. One can only imagine how difficult this move must have been to make. Although some have questioned the extent to which Gates relinquished control of Microsoft during the tenure of his successor, Steve Ballmer, it is easy to empathize with the decision to give up executive control of the company that defined his success being rather difficult. While Gates' ability to hand over the reins of the company was itself admirable in its display of groundedness and perspective, the fact that he did so to go on and focus on philanthropic work displays an even greater level of humility.

Although Gates was dogged with the reputation of being the face of corporate greed for much of his career as the head of Microsoft (particularly during the late 90s and early 2000s), he has more than redeemed his reputation with his philanthropic work through The Bill & Melinda Gates Foundation. The foundation was created in 2000 as a channel through which the couple could coordinate their philanthropic giving. Today, it is one of the world's largest private foundations, with an endowment of over $42 billion as of November 2014. The Foundation is "driven by the passions and interests of the Gates family"; namely, "alleviating poverty, hunger and disease in the developing world, and improving the state of America's education system." In 2010, Gates joined with long-time friend and fellow multibillionaire Warren Buffett to create 'The Giving Pledge', a drive which encouraged other billionaires to commit to giving away at least half their wealth in the name of philanthropy. So far, Mark Zuckerberg, Paul Allen, Steve

Case and Larry Ellison are among those who have signed the pledge. To date, Gates has given away a significant proportion of his wealth through the foundation, at around $28 billion dollars and counting. Gates is incredibly active in championing the goals of the fund and working to raise awareness surrounding the issues that it tackles.

Looking back to the time before he was consumed by work for the foundation, Gates learned how an apparent lack of humility can be incredibly damaging to one's image. The Bill Gates of today is generally viewed more sympathetically, perhaps due to his move away from Microsoft and his commitment to spending his fortune helping to make the world a better place. But when he was viewed primarily as 'the face of corporate greed', Gates was in fact reviled by many. Indeed, he did little to help improve this reputation when he acted with very little apparent humility when he testified before the hearing into Microsoft's anti-competitive practices, discussed above.

This final lesson from Gates – on humility – is perhaps the one that has shaped him the most into the man that he is today. On the one hand, we can see from Gates' life how an apparent lack of humility can be a boon. Perhaps enormous success and complete humility aren't truly compatible, and Gates wouldn't have achieved what he did with Microsoft if he had have been more humble in the beginning. However, we can also see from Gates' example that there are limits to this, and that a lack of humility can ultimately be damaging to one's reputation. Eventually, it seems, true humility is something that even the smartest individuals learn the benefit of with experience, and can become one of the most truly rewarding influences in life.

Conclusion

It is fitting, though perhaps unsurprising, that the world's richest man is also one from whom we have so much to learn. Thanks to the encouragements and values instilled by his parents, his own instinctive personality, and the people and events that came to influence him at various stages of his life, the eight traits and elements discussed above help to shape Gates' success. From the above exploration of how some of these key concepts, we can see that the outcomes that Gates achieved aren't entirely down to luck. A range of qualities, from openness to risk, to focus, to the ability to think laterally were all instrumental in his success. Gates' ability to utilize these traits and characteristics in combination helped to drive much of his personal success.

From the above analysis of the influences on Gates' life, what were the most important? First, it seems that a solid family life formed an excellent basis for him to become successful as an adult. Gates was very close to his mother, who instilled many of her core values and beliefs in Gates, including a dedication to philanthropy and a healthy respect for education. Gates' father has also been a profound influence in his life. Although he didn't follow through with a career as a lawyer, his decision to take the pre-law path shows that his father was a significant role model in his life. William H. Gates, Sr. was tasked with running the William H. Gates Foundation, the precursor to The Bill & Melinda Gates Foundation, which had the objective of putting laptops in every classroom in America. Furthermore, the fact that Gates' father continues to work closely with his son in an advisory executive capacity at The Bill & Melinda Gates Foundation highlights the respect that Gates has for his father, and vice versa. Gates' wife, Melinda, is also inseparable from the list of influential people in his life. On meeting his future wife, then a Microsoft employee, in 1986, he was quickly enamoured by her forthrightness, intelligence and independence. Shortly after they married in 1994, she helped to spur the couples move into philanthropy and has continued to play a central role in driving this objective, now the most consuming element of the pair's lives.

Outside of family, Gates has also had a few other key figures that have provided significant influence in his life. Warren Buffett, Gates' long-time friend and fellow multibillionaire, is counted well among them. The two have rotated between the top spot of 'world's richest man' in recent years, and have also shared a commitment to 'giving back' much of their enormous wealth to help others. Aside from this common link between the pair, they are in fact close friends. Gates and Buffett first met in 1991 through a mutual connection, although both parties were initially apprehensive about the meeting. However, they eventually hit it off, and Gates had soon discovered that he had found a valued mentor in Buffett. In setting up The Bill & Melinda Gates Foundation, Buffett proved instrumental in offering Gates guidance. On this, Bill noted:

> "When Melinda and I started our foundation, I turned to him for advice. We talked a lot about the idea that philanthropy could be just as impactful in its own way as software had been. It turns out that Warren's brilliant way of looking at the world is just as useful in attacking poverty and disease as it is in building a business. He's one of a kind."

It is also clear that, while Gates has certainly had key influential figures in his life, much of his success appears to have been self-driven. This is particularly evident when you consider how early Gates achieved the bulk of his success, as well as the fact that even as a child, Gates displayed many characteristics that formed the basis of his later success. Indeed, many of the inherent personality traits exhibited by Gates have been viewed as the driving force behind his entrepreneurial achievements, and something that many budding entrepreneurs have attempted to emulate. His appetite for both risk and competition, his naturally brilliant intellect and inclination towards lateral thinking, and his impressive dedication and focus all appeared in Gates' from a young age, and carried through into his later years to help fuel much of his business success. However, we also know that Gates developed many qualities along the way that helped make him a much more well-rounded individual, and one who was able to carry that initial success forward. His adaptability to change, handling of adversity and ability to act with humility despite his enormous success, have all helped to make Gates a much more nuanced individual with both more to offer and gain from the world.

Meanwhile, Gates' individual achievements have been some of the most remarkable of the last century. No entrepreneur before Gates had ever been as successful in the sheer speed with which his business empire was built. His remarkable foresight (along with that of business partner, Paul Allen) to fill a gap in the market before that market even existed, resulted in one of the fastest accumulations of personal wealth in history, even to this day. Gates also helped to drive the change that has altered, in a very fundamental way, how we all live our lives. Though not directly behind the technology boom that occurred from the latter part of the 20th century to today, the enormous success of Microsoft helped the industry explode in terms of investment, innovation and accessibility. Finally, Gates has done more than anyone before or since in terms of philanthropy. His commitment to spending a vast amount of his fortune helping the world's most disadvantaged overcome sickness and poverty is exemplary, as is his drive to encourage other 'mega-rich' individuals to do the same. In this regard, much of his impact is still yet to be felt and will no doubt affect the lives of just as many, if not more, than in his significant life so far.

However, despite his enormous success and legacy, both from early and later in life, we know that Gates is not infallible. He has made mistakes and bad decisions just like everyone else; he is, after all, human, despite his seemingly superhuman achievements. Indeed, good fortune did play a significant role in securing the quantifiable success that Gates has secured in his life. A person with exactly the same characteristics may well have failed in their entrepreneurial aspirations where Gates excelled, were it not for the crucial element of luck. Although we may not necessarily be able to emulate the same level of success as Bill Gates, we can take lessons from his achievements and apply them to ourselves and the pursuit of our goals – both in the world of entrepreneurship, and beyond. And though it is very unlikely that any one of us will scale the same great heights as a result, we may still be richer for it – simply by understanding the factors that shaped a most unusual life in that of Bill Gates.

50 Life and Business Lessons from Donald Trump

Introduction

Donald Trump is to business as the Russian President Vladimir Putin is to world politics: no one can quite understand his meteoric rise to power, his methods are questionable, he is exceptionally wealthy, and he has made plenty of influential enemies at every step of the way. However, even if you the thought of inviting him to dinner fills you with dread (and you would certainly want to keep him away from your daughter), at the same time you cannot help but respect what he has been able to achieve. If Trump does realise his ultimate ambition of becoming Republican presidential candidate and then President of the United States in 2016, the parallels between these two exceptionally powerful, determined men might become even starker still.

This book is more than a biography of one of the most controversial figures in US public life today: it is also an educational tool for those who wish to better understand the man, to learn about his strengths and weaknesses, and to apply some of his lessons in their own business lives and careers. There are perhaps even lessons you can take away for your private life: Trump has a great track record of attracting beautiful women, though maintaining a meaningful relationship with them appears to pose more of a challenge. You can learn from his mistakes and failings just as you can from his successes.

We have subdivided the content of this book to make it easily accessible to the casual reader: you can read it all in one go, or dip in and out of the sections of most interest to you. The book begins with an overview of Trump's early life and education so that you can situate the man and his work in an appropriate context. We then examine his core business, The Trump Organization, and the way he was able to develop it from a relatively modest (though profitable) family-run company into a major player in the US real estate market, and with property assets around the world. Moving on, the next chapter explores Trump's additional business interests, and specifically the roller coaster ride that is the ups and downs of Trump Entertainment Resorts, Trump's hotel and casino empire.

In the middle part of the book you can read about three areas of Trump's life that, whilst not central to his business activities, certainly help to promote the man and his brand. These are his media forays (*The Apprentice* and Miss Universe chief amongst them); his interest in American football, golf and wrestling; and, perhaps most interesting of all, his recent political manoeuvrings. If you are keen to learn about his run to become the Republican party's presidential candidate for 2016, his policies, rhetoric and approach, this is the section to look at.

There are ups and downs in everyone's lives, and so the third part of this book examines Trump's awards and accolades, but also the many challenges and criticisms he has faced. Not all of Trump's business endeavours have succeeded - there have been some fairly epic failures that would have toppled smaller companies and discouraged less confident men - and he has also been mired in numerous legal cases, criminal investigations, and serious, apparently well-founded allegations that he is far too close to the mob.

The fourth and final part of this book looks, we hope, at the most intimate sides of Trump: his personal life, including his marriages and other significant relationships; and his personality. Here you can read three psychologists' analysis of what makes Trump tick and how his character is expressed, and we have also made a few comments on the personality cult he has created, deliberately or otherwise, around himself. The parallels with other narcissists, as defined by Sigmund Freud and Michael Maccoby, are especially enlightening.

The book ends with a short conclusion, summing up some of the most important points. Whether or not he realises his political ambitions in 2016, no one can doubt that we will see far more than Mr. Trump, and sooner or later he usually gets what he wants.

The title of this book is *50 Lessons You Can Learn From Donald Trump*, and we want to make these lessons explicit, even if you have so far had little opportunity to reflect on the man, his work and what they might mean for you. We have therefore highlighted in blue what we feel to be the key lessons in each chapter, drawing them from the wider text. If you have little time to read the entire book, but still want bite sized tips to take away, you can simply read these lessons. It is time to get stuck in now to the lessons of Donald Trump.

Life and Education

Donald John Trump burst forth into this world on 14 June, 1946, the fourth of five children. The family were well off, and Trump had a fortunate childhood. His mother, Mary Anne, was a Scottish immigrant from the Isle of Lewis who had arrived in the United States in the 1930s, where she met and married Fred Trump in 1938. Trump Senior was of German descent: his ancestors had arrived in the US and made their money as restauranteurs in the Klondike Gold Rush, profiting from the population influx rather than the core business of mining gold. The family name was in fact Drump, not Trump, but Trump's grandfather anglicised it in order to fit in better in his new homeland. He knew the importance of a name, which is in any case a family's brand, dictating in no small way how that family is seen by others.

Lesson 1: Those who are drawn to the sources of money are in the best position to make money.

The earliest years of Trump's life were spent in the New York borough of Queens. He was privately educated, as were all of his siblings, first of all at Kew-Forest School in Forest Hills, and then, as it became apparent to his father that he was quite a handful, at the New York Military Academy. He he studied at NYMA from the age of 13 and, in his own words, the military school gave him "more training militarily than a lot of the guys that go into the military". The education he received, though exceptionally strict, gave Trump a strong work ethic and discipline, which would stand him in good stead throughout his career. He was a popular student, academically gifted, a student leader and a star athlete. NYMA bought out these characteristics in him.

Lesson 2: Success requires a disciplined approach, which is best instilled at a young age.

Having graduated successfully from High School, Trump entered Fordham University in the Bronx. He studied there for two years before transferring to the University of Pennsylvania, where there was a specialist course in real estate at the Wharton School, one of very few such programmes in the country. Trump graduated with a BSc in economics in 1968, not top of his year, but with a solid academic grounding.

Whilst Trump was studying, the Vietnam War was in full fight and he should have been drafted, particularly given his military training. However, despite being found fit for service in 1966, Trump was able to defer four times in order to continue his education, and he was given a final medical deferment in 1968. Their is some question as to whether the latter was a legitimate deferment: when asked on the campaign trail in Iowa which foot suffered from the supposed foot spur, Trump could not remember. One sense an aversion to the military and to military service in some of Trump's most recent speeches, especially in his ridicule of John Kerry for having been captured whilst fighting, and his apparently deliberate avoidance of the draft suggests he felt this way from a relatively early age.

The Trump Organisation

The Trump Organization began its life as Elizabeth Trump & Son, and it was the Trump family business, founded by his father. Donald Trump worked for the firm whilst studying at the University of Pennsylvania, and officially took up his position there upon graduating in 1968. Elizabeth Trump & Son was primarily a real estate business, with interests not only in real estate development but also in property sales and marketing, brokerage and management. In the late 1960s the company was already a multi-million dollar business: Fred Trump had purchased a foreclosed apartment complex in Cincinnati 1962 for $5.7 million, and he also had significant stakes in property projects in Brooklyn, Queens and Staten Island. The company was doing well, making money, and growing in size, but that was not enough for young Trump.

Lesson 3: It is easier to become a "self-made man" if you and your family already have access to capital, and an established means of making money.

Right from the start, Trump had big ambitions for Elizabeth Trump & Son, encouraging his father to make liberal use of loans in order to expand. Fred Trump quickly identified his son's business acumen, let him try out his ideas, and saw that they were successful. He therefore decided to hand him complete control of the company in 1971, just three years after he had graduated. Trump's first move now that he was in charge was to rename the company as The Trump Organization, and it has traded under that name ever since. This rebrand meant that the company no longer looked and sounded like a Mom and Pop enterprise: it was something altogether more impressive.

Lesson 4: Don't underestimate the importance of branding.

As the head of The Trump Organization, Trump swiftly came to public attention, though not in the most positive of ways. New York city's Justice Department accused him of violating the Fair Housing Act, a piece of legislation designed to protect tenants, in 39 of the building he managed. Trump felt that The Trump Organization, as a large company, was being unfairly victimised by the Justice Department, and it took him two years to settle the charges. In the meantime, the case was in the local press, and it made for dinner table chatter.

Trump had a nose for opportunities that would make money, however, and he was not to be deterred by idle gossip or harassment by the law. He moved the company's offices into the centre of Manhattan, networked with everyone he met there intensively, and made full use of the personal and professional relationships he formed, leveraging them for profit. If he did create genuine friendships during this period, they were secondary to strategic alliances. He made two key real estate purchases in this early phase of his commercial career: the Pennsylvania Central Railroad's yards on the west side of Manhattan; and the Commodore Hotel adjacent to Grand Central Station.

Lesson 5: Always be on the look out for opportunities, and position yourself quickly to be able to take full advantage of them.

To the traditional investor, both of these properties looked (at least on the face of it) to be poor investment prospects. The company behind Pennsylvania Central Railroad had entered bankruptcy, and initial plans to redevelop the yards as apartments were unfeasible due to the depressed economic climate. Similarly, the Commodore was unprofitable as a hotel, and had been for some time. There was a substantial risk that whoever took on the properties would simply be burning their money with no prospect of making it back.

But Trump was prepared to take a gamble and to think outside the box. He knew that the land where the Pennsylvania Central Railroad yard stood was valuable, and the same was true for the Commodore. Trump bought the option to purchase the railway yards, and decided to market them as the site for a convention centre. His bid beat those of two other firms, and was approved by the government in 1978. Trump also bid for the construction contract, though this was given to someone with greater experience. The railway yard site became the Javits Convention Center, and Trump realised a profit.

Over at Grand Central Station, Trump acquired the Commodore Hotel site for $60 million with no cash payable up front. This credit line was invaluable as it deferred the risk. He was able to enter into a business partnership with the Hyatt Hotel Corporation, and to completely renovate the hotel, replete with an impressive new glass facade. Trump arranged the financing and a 40-year tax break, making him a particularly attractive business partner. His wife Ivana (see Personal Life) had a flair for design and played a key role in the hotel's renovation. The improved appearance of the building coincided with the rejuvenation of the area around Grand Central Station, and the value of Trump's initial investment soared. He could then repay the $60 million debt from his profits.

Lesson 6: If you are too risk averse, you cannot make money. You need to gamble something to be in with a chance of winning.

Confident now of his ability to regenerate major city sites and turn a substantial profit, Trump leased the land for what would become Trump Towers. Adjacent to Tiffany & Company on Fifth Avenue, this retail and apartment complex cost Trump $200 million to build. It was designed with Der Scutt, the same architect Trump had worked with for the redevelopment of the Commodore. The 58-storey tower included a six-storey atrium lined in pink marble, as well as an indoor waterfall, and its ostentatious appearance attracted celebrity tenants and famous brands alike. Trump had begun to make a physical mark on New York.

The development of Trump Towers was somewhat controversial, however. In a rush to demolish the old building on the site, the Bonwit Teller flagship store, valuable Art Deco bas-relief sculptures were destroyed. Not only did this anger art lovers, but they had also already been promised to the Metropolitan Museum of Art, putting Trump in a potentially awkward situation. Actually, he didn't care. More serious from a legal point of view, though, Trump's demolition workforce included 200 undocumented Polish workers, some of whom were never paid, yet were expected to work 12 hour shifts. Some of them lived on site, and they appeared to have been given the jobs ahead of US labourers. Trump claims to have been completely unaware of this debacle, and to have rarely visited the site, but this doesn't ring entirely true. It took until 1999 to resolve the lawsuit brought against him by his workforce, and the findings of that case are sealed. It is likely that Trump made a substantial settlement but demanded a gagging clause in exchange.

Lesson 7: If you cut corners to do something quickly or on the cheap, expect the repercussions to catch up with you sooner or later.

The Trump Organization ran into severe financial difficulties in the early 1990s, and you can read more about this under *Additional Business Interests*. Although the banks and bondholders had lost millions of dollars, they did agree to allow Trump to restructure his companies and their debts. He was forced to decrease his personal stake in the companies, however, and to sell off the beleaguered Trump Shuttle airline and his private yacht, Trump Princess. Trump and his businesses were saved towards the end of the decade by two factors: an up-tick in the US economy, and consequently also in real estate prices; and the death of his father, after of which he inherited a quarter share in his father's estate. This was valued somewhere between $250 and $300 million and abled him to settle many of his most pressing business debts. Yes, Trump is a self-made man, but with an exceptionally favourable starting position and a subsequent timely injection of capital in the form of his inheritance.

Lesson 8: No rise to the top is without its hurdles. Sometimes you have to make sacrifices along the way.

One of The Trump Organization's later successful development projects, also in New York, is the Trump World Tower on United Nations Plaza. Completed in 2001, and the work of Greek architect Costas Kondylis, it stands at 861 feet high and was briefly the tallest all-residential tower in the world before being overtaken two years later by the 21st Century Tower in Dubai. The 20,000 square feet penthouse suite, which comprises the top two floors of the building, was on the market for a long time for $58 million (despite the fact that the entire building cost Trump just $300 million to construct), but it failed to sell and hence was subdivided into four smaller living units. This tower too was controversial on account of its height - it dwarfs surrounding buildings, including the adjacent United Nations headquarters - and, as far as many people were concerned, its lack of distinguishing architectural features. Trump secured planning permission nevertheless, and rents in the building are consistently high. It seems that there is demand to live here regardless of the building's unremarkable facade.

Lessons 9: If you want to do something on a massive scale, not everyone is going to approve.

Trump has been shrewd in that a major arm of The Trump Organization now focuses not on developing real estate projects from scratch, and investing Trump's own capital in them, but on licensing the Trump name for use by other companies. The Trump Organization's branding and licensing division is run by Trump's three eldest children, Donald Junior, Ivanka and Eric, and its value is somewhere between $562 million (*Forbes*' valuation) and $3 billion (Trump's own, most likely excessive, valuation). It may well be the most valuable part of the Trump empire.

Lesson 10: Your business' brand is one of its greatest assets. Use it to your full commercial and personal advantage.

The strength of this approach is that it enables Trump to widen his exposure and explore multiple industries without risking his capital. Someone else always carries the risk, and pays Trump to use his name. Some of these businesses, including Trump Magazine, Trump Mortgage, Trump Steaks and GoTrump (a travel website) have been commercial failures for their owners, but Trump has made money regardless. Trump Restaurants, Trump Sales and Leasing, and the Donald J. Trump Signature Collection of men's wear and accessories have enjoyed greater success, benefitting no doubt from their association with the Trump name. Such is the perceived value of the Trump name, in fact, that as far back as 2005 The Learning Annex was paying him $1.5 million for every one-hour lecture that he gave.

Additional Business Interests

The Trump Organization owned a significant stake in Trump Entertainment Resorts, a hotel and casino company, but ever since the company's creation, it has been far from plain sailing in business. A succession of four bankruptcies (1991, 2004, 2009 and 2014) has meant that the company has had to be reconstructed on multiple occasions, and it is still not on a rosy financial footing.

Lesson 11: If at first you don't succeed, try, try again! Don't be afraid to fail.

With his real estate hat on, Trump began buying properties in Atlantic City in the early 1980s. He received a gaming license and initially planned to build his own casino there, but he was then asked to manage the construction of a hotel and casino for Holiday Inn, also in Atlantic City. Trump cut his teeth in the casino business on Holiday Inn's time, then bought out their shares in the property in 1986, renaming it the Trump Plaza Hotel and Casino. He took the same approach with the Atlantic City Hilton, acquiring the nearly complete hotel from Hilton Hotels for $325 million. He called this one Trump's Castle Hotel Casino.

It was in attempting a hat trick that Trump came unstuck. He bought the unfinished Taj Mahal for for $230 million, but it ended up costing him $1 billion before he could open it for business in 1990. The project had been irresponsibly financed with a number of junk bonds and short-term loans, and the combination of soaring interest rates and lower than expected returns (the result of an economic recession) meant that the company had to file for bankruptcy.

Lesson 12: Just because something appears to be cheap, doesn't mean that it doesn't come with hidden costs.

Being overly optimistic about a business' prospects, combined with an inability to restructure debt, is an ongoing theme in the history of Trump Entertainment Resorts, and should be a sobering lesson to us all. Trump was forced to cut his stake in the company to just 27% in 2004 so that bondholders could take stock in exchange for relinquishing debt. Debts continued to rise, however, and by 2009 the company owed creditors $1.2 billion.

Lesson 13: *Part of being a winner is knowing when enough is enough. Sometimes you have to give up the fight and walk away, and move on to something that's more productive. - Donald Trump*

Trump had to accept a further reduction in his stake, this time to 5% of the reorganised company and a further 5% for use of his name and likeness. The company was back in the bankruptcy courts in September 2014, a month after Trump filed a lawsuit asking for his name to be removed from the group's hotel and casino properties.

Lesson 14: *Sometimes by losing a battle you find a new way to win the war. - Donald Trump*

Trump has always preferred to make his money from bricks and mortar investment rather than investing in other companies' stocks and shares, but between 2011 and 2014 he made an exception to this rule. The global real estate market was depressed, and especially so in the US, and the interest to be earned from bank deposits was on the floor. He decided to take a gamble and bought stocks in 45 companies including Facebook, Citigroup, Bank of America, Procter & Gamble and Johnson & Johnson. This move paid off, and of the 45 companies Trump invested in, 40 of them returned him a profit. He claimed his total gains on the investments amounted to $27 million.

Lesson 15: *Be prepared to make sacrifices in order to increase your business' chances of long-term survival.*

Media Forays

Lesson 16: *I could never have imagined that firing 67 people on national television would actually make me more popular, especially with the younger generation. - Donald Trump*

Donald Trump transformed himself from successful though unpopular business tycoon to household name with one reality TV series: *The Apprentice*. Trump hosted the series, broadcast on NBC, for 14 seasons from 2004 onwards, and the final prize in each case was a one-year, $250,000 contract to run a company within the Trump empire.

Lesson 17: *Always be on the look-out for opportunities to raise your public profile, even if it is in areas not core to your business.*

The Apprentice's boardroom and accommodation suites are all purpose-built sets within Trump Towers, not quite the penthouse suites that viewers were initially led to believe. Trump's three eldest children, Donald Junior, Ivanka and Eric, often accompanied him as advisors on the show, as did senior figures from within his company.

Lesson 18: *Success is a team effort, and your family, friends and colleagues all have important roles to play.*

Trump hosted *The Apprentice* and *The Celebrity Apprentice* (a spin off series), and he was also the face of *Donald J. Trump Presents The Ultimate Merger*, a reality dating show on TV One. Season one of *The Apprentice* peaked at 28.1 million viewers during the finale episode, but this success was never matched by subsequent seasons or the dating show. The reason that the series was so important in Trump's rise is that it put him regularly in front of television viewers. The viewing public felt they got to know him. They saw his charisma, his leadership, and his decisiveness, all qualities which they admired.

Although *The Apprentice* has done wonders for Trump's public image, his real delight (and source of girlfriends and wives) seems to have been his association with the Miss Universe Organization, the annual Miss USA and Miss Universe beauty pageants. Trump and NBC took control of the contest in 2002, each with a 50% stake, and this relationship continued until September 2015 when NBC cancelled all business relationships with Trump: his controversial comments about illegal immigrants in a public speech made him an unattractive business partner for the channel. Trump bought out NBC's stake, and immediately resold the entire company to WME/IMG.

Lesson 19: Sex and glamour will always sell.

Part of the Miss Universe prize was use of an apartment in Trump Place for the duration of the winner's reign. The competition seemingly had a symbiotic relationship with Trump's own modelling agency, Trump Model Management, which has several high profile faces, including Jodie Kidd, Isabella Rossellini and Paris Hilton, on its books. Trump appeared regularly with Miss Universe contestants on his arm, savouring the glamour and attention that the competition brought. It remains to be seen whether this association will continue now that he has sold the company.

Trump is admirable in that he is prepared to poke fun at himself, allowing himself to be caricatured on screen, and making cameo appearances. He appeared as a character in *The Little Rascals*, *Home Alone 2*, *The Fresh Prince of Bel-Air*, *Days of Our Lives*, and *Wall Street: Money Never Sleeps*, and has twice been nominated for an Emmy Award.

Sports Interests

Trump was a keen athlete in school and college, but as he grew older his interest was primarily in investing in sports teams and facilities rather than playing sports himself. His first major purchase, back in 1983, was the New Jersey Generals football team, and this coincided with Trump's formation of the United States Football League (USFL), a major competitor to the well-established National Football League (NFL). By going head to head with the NFL, Trump was hoping to ultimately force a buy-out and to double his investment, but that never happened: the USFL struggled to gain traction and the 1986 season was cancelled.

Lesson 20: Know your market inside out before you try to take on the big players.

Trump has had greater success with golf, investing heavily in golf courses around the world. Internationally he has acquired the Menie Estate and the Turnberry Hotel and Golf Resort, both of which are in Scotland, and Doonbeg Golf Club in the Republic of Ireland (to be renamed Trump International Golf Links, Ireland).

Although more of a personal interest than a commercial one, Trump is a huge fan of World Wrestling Entertainment and a close friend of WWE's owner, Vince McMahon. The 1991 WBF Championship was hosted at Trump Plaza, and so too were two WrestleMania events. In WrestleMania's The Battle of the Billionaires, Trump backed wrestler Bobby Lashley against McMahon's Umaga. The stakes were high: the loser's backer would be shaved bald, and Trump is rather proud of his hair. Fortunately for him, Lashley won the match, and Trump's barnet thus remained in tact. In 2013 Trump was inducted into the celebrity wing of the WWE Hall of Fame at Madison Square Garden for his promotion of wrestling as a sport.

Lesson 21: If you want to be seen as a man of the people, build rapport by participating in sports they love.

Political Aspirations

Lesson 22: *One of the key problems today is that politics is such a disgrace, good people don't go into government. - Donald Trump*

Make America Great Again! Trump's election slogan certainly has a ring to it. His desire to enter the top level of American politics has been long-held: in 1988, 2004, and 2012 he mooted the idea of running for President, and he also considered running as governor of New York in 2006 and 2014, but in the end he bided his time. This was probably a good move, because in the late 1990s a New York Times/CBS News poll found that 70% of Americans held an unfavourable opinion of Trump. It was not until his role on *The Apprentice* (see *Media Forays*) that the tide of public opinion turned in his favour.

Lesson 23: *If you have something large that you want to achieve, and which is important to you, bid your time until you are in the best possible position to make it happen.*

Trump's politics have been based primarily on opportunism rather than ideological conviction, and as such his allegiance has swung in all directions. Prior to 1999 he was a supporter of the Republican party. He then threw his weight behind the Reform party (1999-2001) and the Democrats (2001-2009) before returning to the political right, which is probably his natural home.

Having rejoined the Republican Party in 2009, declaring himself anti gun control and pro-life, he set about being a thorn in President Obama's side, questioning his birth certificate and right to take office. The allegations he made were proved to be unfounded when the Democrats presented Obama's long form birth certificate from Hawaii. Riding high on his increased profile generated by his television appearances, however, Trump decided that the time had come to go public with his ambitions for President. Early in 2015 he decided not to renew his contract on *The Apprentice*, freeing up time to campaign.

Lesson 24: *Belonging to a tribe, and being seen to share their values, is important if you want to raise support.*

Trump announced his candidacy on 16 June, 2015 at Trump Towers in New York. His announcement speech lasted 45 minutes and focused on his pledge to restore the

American Dream. He took a negative stance on Iran, ridiculing John Kerry for negotiating with Tehran to improve diplomatic relations. There were allegations that Trump's campaign team paid actors to cheer as he spoke (allegations which Trump denies, though leaked emails seem to support). Most controversial were Trump's comments about Mexican immigrants, however. His stated, "When Mexico sends its people, they're not sending their best...They're sending people that have lots of problems, and they're bringing those problems with [them]. They're bringing drugs. They're bringing crime. They're rapists. And some, I assume, are good people." This sent shockwaves through the liberal establishment, and through Trump's business associates, all of whom immediately wanted to distance themselves from such a firebrand. NBC, Macy's, Univision, and NASCAR cut ties with Trump almost immediately, and the speech created a media storm. There was a major backlash against Trump on social media, but he stuck to his guns, and numerous other Republican heavyweights, including Rudy Giuliani, spoke out in his defence. Trump did file a $500 million lawsuit against NBC saying that his comments had been taken out of context and distorted by the media, but he is unlikely to get far with the case.

Lesson 25: If you want to be the centre of attention, regardless of the cost, don't be afraid to court controversy.

Although the popular press (and the foreign media in particular) initially laughed at the suggestion that Trump might actually win the Republication nomination - the *Huffington Post* and the *Wall Street Journal* in particular covered his run as an entertainment story rather than as a serious news item - within three months, no one was laughing. Over the course of the summer, having campaigned especially hard in Iowa, New Hampshire, California and Nevada, YouGov and similar polls showed him surging ahead of the other Republican nominees, including Jeb Bush. In the swing states of Florida, Ohio and Pennsylvania, approval polls showed him neck and neck with the Democrats' Hilary Clinton.

Lesson 26: Don't underestimate the power of determination.

Trump was one of 10 Republican candidates invited to participate in Fox News' television debate in August 2015. He was the only candidate to refuse to pledge not to run as an independent if he lost the Republican nomination (though he did sign the pledge later on), and then set another fox amongst the chickens with his apparently misogynist attack on presenter Megyn Kelly. Women viewers were outraged, and Trump's decency was questioned, but it was Kelly who suffered most from the fallout, receiving death threats from Trump's supporters.

Lesson 27: *I have made the tough decisions, always with an eye toward the bottom line. Perhaps it's time America was run like a business. - Donald Trump*

Trump's official position is that he is a conservative Republican, and he certainly has some sympathies with the right wing Tea Party movement. He supports traditional marriage (in spite of his own multiple divorces and affairs). His views on the economy are relatively conventional: Trump wants to eliminate corporation tax, reduce income tax, and abolish inheritance tax. To compensate for these losses of income, he'd increase import tariffs and also apply a 15% tax on outsourcing.

It is when it comes to other matters that Trump's political views raise eyebrows. He's an avowed climate change denier, believing global warming is a "total hoax" cooked up by the Chinese to make US manufacturing non-competitive. He advocates "bombing the hell" out of Iraqi oil fields as a solution to the Middle East crisis, stating, "I wouldn't send many troops because you won't need 'em by the time I'm done." He would ban abortion save in cases of incest, rape, or health, and his comments on immigration are particularly vitriolic (see above).

Lesson 28: *In politics, sometimes personality and infamy are more important than coherent policies and diplomacy.*

No one knows what 2015-16 will bring for Trump. He may well secure the Republican nomination, but whether the country as a whole is ready to elect a President who, though successful in business, lacks diplomatic finesse, remains to be seen. We shall watch and wait with interest.

Awards and Accolades

At all stages of his career, Donald Trump has courted admirers, recognising that the best way to raise your profile is to get others to do it for you. The awards and accolades he has received fall into multiple fields.

First of all, and possibly most admirably, Trump has been given two honorary doctorates in business, one from Robert Gordon University (2010) and the other by Liberty University (2012). He has his own star on the Hollywood Walk of Fame, and also appears in the Gaming Hall of Fame, the WWE Hall of Fame, and the NY Ride of Fame. 2015 has been a particularly successful year for Trump and those who idolise him: The Republican Party of Sarasota voted him Statesman of the Year; he was given the Commandant of the Marine Corps Leadership Award by the Marine Corps–Law Enforcement Foundation; and last but not least he was granted the Key to the City of Doral, Florida.

Lesson 29: Making others sing your virtues will save you the time, effort and cost of doing it for yourself, and it often has a bigger impact.

Though not exactly an award, but certainly a recognition of his achievements, Trump appears year in, year out on America's rich lists. But how much is he actually worth? No one seems quite sure. In a July 2015 press release, just after announcing he would run for president, Trump claimed that he was worth "in excess of TEN BILLION DOLLARS," but this is likely to be an exaggeration: *Forbes'* estimated his wealth at $4 billion, and the Bloomberg Billionaires Index has it pegged at $2.9 billion. Federal election regulators, who must disclose the wealth and financial holdings of any presidential candidate, reported in July 2015 that he has assets of at least $1.4 billion.

Challenges and Controversies

Lesson 32: *What separates the winners from the losers is how a person reacts to each new twist of fate. - Donald Trump*

Not everything that Donald Trump touches turns to gold: he has had his fair share of business failures, bankruptcies and legal challenges, as well as allegations that haven't made it to court. Some of these failures can no doubt be put down to not keeping up with fast changing markets, and to factors beyond Trump's control, but there is also some evidence to suggest that he is sometimes carried away with his own self belief, gambling beyond his capacity, and not willing to accept that he lacks omnipotence.

One product that failed to hold its own in the marketplace, despite having the Trump name and marketing machine behind it, was Trump Ice. This bottled water brand was promoted by Trump himself during the first season of *The Apprentice*, and the series' winner, Kelly Perdew, was employed as the company's project manager and Executive Vice President. In spite of the hype and publicity, however, Trump Ice was a flop. The supermarket chains and specialist grocery stores that were its prime outlets struggled to make sales, and by early 2010 Trump Ice was defunct. Its demise was no doubt hastened by Sylvester Stallone, who tried it during a blind test on the TV show *Entertainment Tonight* and declared he wouldn't even wash his socks in it.

Lesson 33: *Promotion alone cannot save a poor product in a competitive marketplace.*

Trump Shuttle (trading as Trump Airlines) ran into difficulties in the early 1990s when it failed to adapt to changes in the airline business. Trump created the airline in 1989 out of part of an already foundering Eastern Air Lines using a $380 million loan. Trump Shuttle ran hourly services between New York, Boston and Washington DC, and Trump promoted it as a luxury service. He gave his planes upmarket interiors, his taste in which was questionable: gold coloured toilets made an appearance onboard. Trump had misunderstood his market. Passengers wanted affordable convenience, not costly extras. Many of them defected to competitors, and this coincided with the sharp spike in aviation fuel prices caused by the first Gulf War. Trump Shuttle never made a profit. Trump defaulted on the loans he'd taken to finance the acquisition, and his creditors ran scared. He was forced to admit defeat, and Trump Shuttle ceased to exist in April 1992.

***Lesson 34: Not all events are within your control, and you need to have contin-
gency plans for the worst-case economic scenarios.***

Errors of judgement have crept into Trump's personal spending too. Sometimes greed
just got the better of him. When the Kingdom 5KR super yacht came up for sale in the
late 1980s, Trump couldn't resist buying it from the Sultan of Brunei. The yacht had
been built in 1980 for Saudi billionaire Adnan Khashoggi, and it was one of the largest in
the world, with 11 suites, a helipad, private cinema, disco and swimming pool on board.
To crown its celebrity cache, the yacht had also appeared in the James Bond film *Never
Say Never Again*. Trump retrofitted the yacht and renamed it Trump Princess. He'd
overstretched himself financially, however, and was forced to sell the yacht in 1991 for
just two-thirds of what he had paid for it.

***Lesson 35: It is better to invest in things that are likely to make you more mon-
ey than in the costly trappings of ostentatious wealth.***

More troubling, however, are the string of lawsuits brought continually against Trump,
and the allegations of his links to organised crime. Although all major corporations in
the US are likely to run up against the law now and then, for Trump, fighting it out in
court seems to be business as usual. Sometimes he wins, and sometimes he loses: perhaps he just enjoys playing the game.

The first major court case against Trump took place in 1973 when the Justice Department unsuccessfully sued Trump Management Corporation for racial discrimination.
The company was accused of discriminating against potential black renters, and although Trump never admitted to this, he did settle out of court.

Time and again, Trump has been accused of sharp practice, of misrepresentation, and
of defrauding investors and customers. This is one of the most unsavoury sides of his
business. Investors who had paid up to $300,000 for condos in the failed Trump Ocean
Resort Baja Mexico alleged Trump has misrepresented his role in the project: billboards
featuring his face were used to advertise the project, and an article in the San Diego
Union-Tribune quoted Trump as saying he was a significant equity investor in the development. When the case came to court, Trump disavowed any financial responsibility for
the project's failure, saying he was only a spokesperson. He was advised to settle with
more than 100 of the development's investors for an undisclosed amount, and did so in
2013.

Lesson 36: Even if you are not going to admit to being in the wrong, be prepared to be held accountable for your actions, to pay up and move on.

New York Attorney General Eric Schneiderman filed another law suit against Trump in 2013, alleging Trump had defrauded more than 5,000 customers of Trump University of $40 million. Trump University was supposed to teach its students real estate investment techniques but was never licensed as an educational institution. Additionally, the courses advocated the use of false advertising, bait-and-switch tactics, intentional misrepresentation and other fraudulent practices. A a New York Superior Court upheld part of the case in 2014, finding Trump guilty of not obtaining a license to operate his for-profit school, and a separate class action civil suit brought by former students was allowed to proceed. In response, Trump filed a $1 million defamation suit against one former student, Tarla Makaeff, who had joined the class action suit, in a bid to intimate other participants in the action. Trump lost and was ordered to pay Makaeff and her legal team $798,774.24 in legal fees and costs.

Lesson 37: If you do business in the greyer areas of legality, expect now and then to get caught out.

Some of the legal cases that Trump has been involved in have been quite entertaining, at least for bystanders. The American comedian Bill Maher joked on *The Tonight Show with Jay Leno* that he would give $5 million to charity if Trump produced his birth certificate to confirm his mother had not mated with a orangutan (this coming shortly after Trump's own demands to see Obama's birth certificate, passport records and college transcripts). Playing along initially, Trump duly produced his own birth certificate, then sued Maher when no donation was forthcoming, claiming that the commitment was legally binding. Maher was understandably furious, replying that Trump needed to learn the difference between a joke and a contract, that it was obvious humans and orangutans can't reproduce. He described Trump publicly as a "rich idiot" which understandably didn't go down too well either, though Trump did drop the lawsuit.

Moving now to allegations of Trump's links with organised crime, it must first be said that these have never been proved in court. However, the mafia is known to have a significant involvement in the US construction industry and in the hotel trade anywhere in the world, and the allegations made against Trump have come from credible sources.

Lesson 38: Choose your business associates and friends wisely. Their actions, good or bad, will reflect back on you.

Wayne Barrett, a New York based investigative journalist and co-author of the unauthorised biography *Trump: The Deals and the Downfall* drew upon government records and interviews to conclude that Trump's life "intertwines with the underworld... There was a certain amount of mob association during which the father and he were building, which was very difficult to avoid in the New York construction world," Barrett said. "He went out of his way not to avoid them, but to increase them."

Barrett's assertions, supported by the findings of another journalist, David Marcus, are based on the fact that Trump bought the property where Trump Plaza in Atlantic City now stands for more than twice the market price: $220 per square foot. He acquired it from Salvatore Testa, an infamous Philadelphia mobster, and the Trump Plaza's casino, Harrah's, was then constructed by companies owned and controlled by Nicademo "Little Nicky" Scarfo and his nephew Phillip "Crazy Phil" Leonetti, two other known mob bosses. This is recorded in a report on organised crime compiled by a New Jersey state commission in 1986.

In his book *Blood and Honor*, George Anastasia describes Scarfo's reign as head of the Philly mob as one of the bloodiest in the mob's history, and claims he also controlled the bar tenders union, which represented Trump's workers in Atlantic City. There is one more link between Scarfo and Trump: they shared the same investment banker, Kenny Shapiro, the man responsible bribing Atlantic City Mayor Michael J. Matthews.

Trump worked extensively with mob controlled companies, including the S&A Concrete Co., in Manhattan. S&A was owned by Anthony "Fat Tony" Salerno, the boss of the Genovese crime family, and Salerno and Trump shared the same lawyer, Roy Cohn. Though Trump has always denied it, anonymous sources claim that Salerno and Trump met privately in an apartment on at least one occasion, and due to their mutual association with Cohn, it is likely that they had a reasonable understanding of each other's business and connections. To be fair to Trump, few construction companies in 1980s New York were untarnished by mob associations, so he may have had no choice. He was investigated in 1979 for bribery, and again two years later during a racketeering probe, but on neither occasion did the federal investigation lead to criminal charges. He may have been clean, but it is equally possible that he was able to pull in favours at a high level, and to silence those who might talk.

Lesson 39: Doing your due diligence is vital. If you don't like what you find, step away else it comes back to haunt you.

The allegations of criminal associations did not stop in the 1980s, however. Another business partner, Felix Slater, is a convicted fraudster with close ties to the Costra Nostra. The *New York Times* and the BBC have gone to some lengths to prove Slater's involvement in money laundering schemes in the 1990s, and the New York Times also alleged that in 1995 he used a "soldier in the Genovese crime family" to resolve a conflict with the rival Gambinos. In 2009 he was found guilty of stock fraud and money-laundering and agreed to pay $60 million in restitution to his victims, but in the end he was let off with a $25,000 fine in exchange for his cooperation on other federal government enquiries.

In spite of Sater's murky dealings, it seems that Trump had no compunction about working closely with him. The two men have collaborated on a number of high profile projects including Trump SoHo, Trump International Hotel and Residence Phoenix, and Trump International Hotel and Residence Ft. Lauderdale. As late as 2011, well after Sater's fraud conviction, Sater was still listed as a senior advisor at The Trump Organization, though since them Trump has attempted to distance himself from his erstwhile friend.

Lesson 40: Just because you have gotten away with something once doesn't mean you should keep risking it time and again.

It should be noted that the mob allegations are not targeted at Trump directly, but rather at his associates. There are, however, political commentators who believe that he can turn his ties to the mob into better poll numbers: the mob retains strong influence over certain unions, for example. Ford O'Connell, a GOP strategist and veteran of Senator John McCain's 2008 presidential campaign, believes that Trump might even leverage his mob connections to gain the GOP nomination: he can prove he has a track record of dealing with unsavoury types and is able to get things done.

Personal Life

Donald Trump's personal life has been colourful to say the least: he has been married three times, had numerous affairs, and is said to have bombarded even Princess Diana with flowers and unwanted affection.

Trump first married in 1977 to a Czech model, Ivana Zelníčková Winklmayr. Together they had three children, Donald Junior, Ivanka and Eric, but it was an unhappy marriage, a problem which was exacerbated by Trump's infidelity. Trump had a long-running affair with actress Marla Maples, who he is said to have met in church during a Sunday service, and he married her in 1993, shortly after ending another relationship with model Carla Bruni (now the wife of former French President Sarkozy). Maples and Trump had a daughter, Tiffany, but that marriage had also foundered by the mid 1990s. Maples was awarded alimony of just $2 million, an amount specified in their pre nuptial agreement.

Lesson 41: If you date a woman solely for her beauty, and she dates you only for your money, don't be surprised if it doesn't work out too well.

Here Trump's personal life story takes an interesting twist: he became infatuated with the newly divorced Princess Diana. He sent endless flowers, wrote to her and, by some accounts, made quite a nuisance of himself, embarrassing the princess, who wisely kept her distance. In his book, *The Art of the Comeback*, Trump admits, "I only have one regret in the women department — that I never had the opportunity to court Lady Diana Spencer." That really would have been a coup for the boy from Queens, but alas it was not to come to pass. Diana died in an infamous Parisian car crash 1997, Trump's desires unmet.

And so, Donald Trump turned his affections back to a ready supply of models. He proposed to Slovenian model Melania Knauss in 2004, and married her a year later. The couple had a son, Barron William Trump, in 2006, the fifth and last of Trump's children.

Lesson 42: Professional success does not automatically translate into success in your personal life.

Personality Cult

Like him or loathe him (Trump is, after all, the Marmite of the business world), it cannot be denied that Donald Trump has a personality that grabs attention. His political policies might be incoherent and all over the place, but this isn't standing in the way of his political rise, nor his business success, because Trump is all about personality.

The interesting thing about this is that it's not that people actually have to like Trump: as Robert Tracinski, a journalist at *The Federalist*, explains, "the paradox is that the more unpleasant his personality is revealed to be, the greater his appeal to his core group of supporters." Trump is seen to have balls, to be prepared to tackle challenges head on. No one believes that he has special skill or tact, but they're not looking for that. They see him as a man with a certain charisma, a strong man who is not afraid to anger others to get what he wants: the parallel with Vladimir Putin is again apt, though in both cases granting such a personality free rein has its significant costs.

Lesson 43: You don't have to be nice to get ahead.

It would be fair to say that a vote for Trump, and vocal support for him, is a protest vote: unlike those he stands against in the presidential race, he has no political experience, no voting record in the Senate or Congress. People turn to Trump because he is prepared to shout louder to get his views noticed. Again, Tracinski makes an interesting observation:

> Support for Trump is a protest vote, but not a rationally considered protest vote in favor of a specific cause. It's an expression of general, unfocused rage. Trump supporters just want someone who's willing to turn over the tables and call people names and burn the place down. And that's why the more unpleasant Trump is—the more he insults lady reporters and boasts about how rich he is, the more he thumps his chest about how sexy he is and calls everybody else a loser—the more they love him.

There are certainly precedents for personality cults around charismatic, though deeply flawed, national leaders: Stalin, Mao and, latterly Venezuela's Hugo Chavez do all spring to mind. In each of these cases, morals, responsible behaviour and logic took a back seat when delivering the tough guy image. When people want change, when they are bored of a staid society and frustrated at entrenched interests, they are prepared to gamble. Evolution through a democratic process is slow; shouting about your issues, losing patience and even being reckless certainly gets attention, and people feel that change is possible and forthcoming, even if the reality of the situation is quite different, or the change that results rather worse than what was there before.

Lesson 44: Effective leaders, good and bad, share certain personality traits.

Moving beyond the idea of a personality cult, however, serious analysis of Trump's personality traits are already underway by psychologists. Writing in *Psychology Today* in September 2015, Dr. Ryne A. Sherman, Dr. Tomas Chamorro-Premuzic and Dr. Robert Hogan came to some interesting conclusions having watched and analysed Trump's behaviour.

When Trump is at his best, Trump is highly adjusted. He doesn't suffer from nerves and is confident about his own attributes. Consequently, though he is not phased by criticism, he also does not listen or respond terribly well to feedback, howsoever it is delivered. In fact, when criticised he is likely to go on the offensive, fighting back with venomous insults.

Trump is highly competitive: he thrives on the thrill of the chase, and has to come out on top. For him, coming second is just not good enough. He is results focused, which tends to be a positive thing, but he can alienate his allies by trying to compete with (and, more often than not, dominate) them too. He lacks interpersonal sensitivity, trampling on the feelings of others when it suits him to do so. His decisiveness, whilst being a strength, can be hurtful to those around him.

Lesson 45: Properly managed, a competitive spirit, both with yourself and with those around you, can drive you forward.

Trump undoubtedly has a very sociable side: he loves a good party and to be the centre of everyone else's attention. Perhaps this is another aspect of his competitive nature. The problem with the me, me, me approach is that he doesn't listen and tends to talk loudly without thinking first about the potential impact of his words. He doesn't care for other people's rules, thinking they don't apply to him, and consequently strays into some quite grey areas, personally and professionally. While this can get things done, it can also make him vulnerable to legitimate criticism.

The darker side of Trump, that which has fuelled his notoriety, is that his boldness - the characteristic which defines him most - comes across as arrogance. Although he can make a good first impression, his sense of entitlement can start to grate. He believes his own copy and hence overestimates his capabilities, ignoring those who question his judgement or who have alternative opinions. When people do not hold him in the same high esteem that he holds himself, he is quick to anger, and often vindictive in his language and actions. Even the *Harvard Business Review* is happy to call him a narcissist, guilty of "outbursts that would not be tolerated in a schoolroom".

Lesson 46: There is a fine line between self confidence and arrogance. The first is a requisite for success; the second might be your downfall.

Trump undoubtedly has a mischievous side: he likes to play devil's advocate and to sail close to the wind. He is an impulsive risk taker and because he has no sense of regret when he gets something wrong, he doesn't always learn from his mistakes for the future.

Last but not least, Trump is low on dutifulness: he feels no sense of responsibility towards others, personally or professionally, but does what suits Trump. He won't take orders or advice and doesn't care about how others feel. Though these attributes might stand him in good stead in the cut-throat business that is US real estate, his succession of failed personal relationships tell a different story, one of someone who struggles to make personal connections, to empathise, and to show compassion.

There is some argument that Trump's personality traits, though not endearing to many ordinary people, may in fact serve him well. Sigmund Freud called men like Trump "normal narcissists": they have large amounts of aggressive energy, and are biased towards action. Normal narcissists are independently minded, cannot be intimidated or otherwise deterred from their chosen course of action and indeed can be very charming too.

In 2000, Michael Maccoby wrote an article entitled 'Narcissistic Leaders: The Incredible Pros, the Inevitable Cons' for the *Harvard Business Review*. In this article he developed Freud's concept further, suggesting that there were also "productive narcissists", often captains of industry, whose self-confidence spurred them to achieve great things. Maccoby listed Bill Gates, Steve Jobs and Andrew Carnegie as exhibiting this trait, and Trump certainly has it too.

The warning to Trump, if there is one, is that productive narcissists, like Shakespearean heroes, often have fatal flaws. They become obsessed with their own vision to the detriment of all else, losing touch with reality. When questioned by subordinates, they lash out, leading to situations where they are entirely surrounded by yes-men. If productive narcissists want to remain at the top of their game, especially in politics, they should at least pretend to be humble, and trust their colleagues. Success has to be a team effort.

Lesson 47: We all have our flaws. What sets some people apart from others is their sensitivity to that fact and willingness to do something about it.

Conclusion

Lesson 48: *Anyone who thinks my story is anywhere near over is sadly mistaken. - Donald Trump*

Donald Trump is at a crossroads in his career. If he wins the Republican nomination and becomes President of the United States in 2016, however unlikely that possibility might seem, he will have won the ultimate award, a prize that so few men have ever held that even the most competitive side of his personality could not help but be delighted by it. There is no doubt in Trump's mind that he is the man for the job, that he has what it takes, and even that he deserves it. The only sticking point is whether or not he can create enough hype as to carry public opinion along with him. People know that he is bold, they know that he is brash, and they know that he has no track record in politics. The last of those things may not matter if Trump can make them believe, as he does, that it is time for someone strong to shake things up, to do it the Trump way.

Trump's story, which we have barely touched the surface of in this book, teaches us that a man's success is dictated by three things: good fortune; who he is; and what he does. We'll think about each of these points in turn.

You should never underestimate the importance of being born into a family and society that can give you a financial, social and educational advantage, nor of simply being in the right place at the right time to capitalise on opportunity (or to avoid disaster). That said, there is no point in being fatalistic: we can all choose to improve our lot, or just be content with what we have. If like Trump you have a fiercely competitive streak and aspire to be on top in every aspect of your life, it isn't just going to fall conveniently into your lap. You do have to study and work hard. You do have to network aggressively and build alliances with all manner of people, including some who you may not like. And you do need to be prepared to make sacrifices, including in your personal life, and from time to time give up your indulgences and say goodbye to failing projects and frivolous assets in order to shore up your chances of realising your long term goals. You need to always keep your eye on the bigger picture.

Who is Trump? He, just like anyone else is the sum of his genetic make-up, of course, and his experiences. Both of these aspects are exhibited in his personality, his emotions, his values, and his ambitions. Not everyone is born to be a leader, and not everyone wants to rise to the top of a hierarchy, but we can still develop our character traits to help us move in the direction we want to go. Trump may naturally be independently

132

minded, charming, energetic and biased towards action; if you are not, you can work at developing these skills and characteristics until they become second nature for you too.

Last but not least, Trump's success is determined by what he does, by his behaviour. There are, undoubtedly, occasions when he has strayed perilously close to the edge, risking his businesses, his freedom, and his reputation, but by raising the stakes high and being prepared to gamble, he's also earned whopping returns. Although Trump's behaviour does sometimes seem erratic, on the whole each action is part of his wider business strategy. He is no fool and knows the importance of both planning and game play, when to chance his luck, and when to play it safe or retreat and nurse his wounds.

Lesson 49: Though not everything in life is within your control, what you do and say, and how you present yourself, can make it better or worse.

Trump has cut his teeth in business, and in a cut-throat business at that, and he deploys the lessons he has learned there in all aspects of his life. You can do the same. What is more, you have an advantage over Trump: you can learn from the things he has done right, but you can also see, perhaps in a way he cannot, where his weaknesses lie. By understanding his shortcomings, you can ensure that you do not make the same mistakes that he has, and consequently you can leapfrog beyond him.

Lesson 50: Experience taught me a few things. One is to listen to your gut, no matter how good something sounds on paper. The second is that you're generally better off sticking with what you know. And the third is that sometimes your best investments are the ones you don't make. - Donald Trump

50 Life and Business Lessons from Elon Musk

Introduction

Whatever skeptics have said can't be done, Elon has gone out and made real. Remember in the 1990s, when we would call strangers and give them our credit-card numbers? Elon dreamed up a little thing called PayPal. His Tesla Motors and SolarCity companies are making a clean, renewable-energy future a reality...his SpaceX [is] reopening space for exploration...it's a paradox that Elon is working to improve our planet at the same time he's building spacecraft to help us leave it.

Richard Branson

It wouldn't be too much of a stretch to describe Elon Musk - one of the most imaginative entrepreneurs of the 21st century - as a living legend. Richard Branson has espoused his virtues, he has been favourably compared to visionary American industrialists such Henry Ford and John D. Rockefeller, and when Jon Favreau, the producer of *Iron Man*, was making the film, he even sent Robert Downey, Jr. to spend time with Musk in the SpaceX factory so that he could get some inspiration for his character.

But for Musk, at least, it is not all about him. The estimated $12.9 billion he has made in business are almost a side show: he is bored of journalists taking an interest in him, and wants to talk far more about his work, his companies, and what they are doing to change the world. In order to get under the skin of his success (and, one hopes, to be able to replicate it), you need to be able to understand two things: WHY Musk is doing what he is doing; and HOW he is able to do these things. He thinks, and does, things differently to everyone else, and that's why studying his lessons is invaluable.

This book - part biography, part self-help tool - is intended to inform you about the life, ideas, approach and work of Elon Musk to date. There is, after all, likely to be much more to come from this extraordinarily innovative entrepreneur. We have endeavoured to analyse his actions, strengths and weaknesses, and to summarise them into 50 short, memorable lessons that you can action in your own personal and commercial life. We can't guarantee that you will be as successful as Musk, but you will gain a level of insight. The book is designed to be easily digestible by a layman reader, but also to have sufficient detail that those with a specific interest in one or more of Musk's business, or in his unique style of leadership, will also be able to take away something of value.

The first section of this book examines Musk's family background and education. This is to help you understand where the man is coming from, what it is that makes him the man he is. There are certainly a few indications of his early precocity and, indeed, virtuosity, and you will recognise the names of several key characters who have remained with him into adulthood, contributing notably to his success.

Lesson 1: Success is not about an individual. It is also about the team that has got them into the position where they can succeed.

We then look at Musk's business endeavours in turn, starting with Zip2 and x.com (later PayPal), the two internet start-ups that catapulted Musk from being an ordinary geek in Silicon Valley to being a multi millionaire who everyone else wanted to work with. There is substantial coverage of SpaceX and Tesla Motors, probably the two most exciting and groundbreaking of Musk's enterprises, but also of SolarCity and the Hyperloop, an idea that seems to have had its origins in the science fiction obsession of Musk's early childhood.

In the final section of the book we examine the rewards and accolades that Musk has received, his politics and beliefs, and his private life. Although the public persona is one of great confidence and success, Musk has known pain and tragedy too. His personal relationships have been scrutinised by the press, and have at a times fallen victim to his complete addiction to his work, to his wealth, and to his ego. Musk has his challenges in that regard, and so here the lessons you can learn might well be about what not to do, rather than simply emulating his behaviour.

Background and Education

Born on 28 June, 1971, Elon Musk is one of the youngest, and most dynamic, of the world's self-made billionaires. He is of mixed ancestry - his father, though born in South Africa, is of British and Pennsylvania Dutch origin, and his mother is a Canadian - and he was born in Pretoria, South Africa, the eldest of three children. His siblings are his brother, fellow entrepreneur Kimbal Musk, and a sister, Tosca Musk. Their parents, Errol and Maye Musk, divorced in 1980, after which Musk lived mostly with his father.

In South Africa Musk was privately educated, first at Waterkloof House Preparatory School in Pretoria, where fellow alumni include the professional golfer Richard Stearne and international cricketer Eddie Barlow. The young Musk was bullied throughout his childhood, including on one particularly serious occasion when he was thrown down a flight of stairs and beaten unconscious. He was an academic child, always buried in a book, sometimes for up to 10 hours a day according to his brother. He was addicted to science fiction but also heavy-weight non-fiction books such as the *Encyclopaedia Britannica*.

He goes into his brain, and then you just see he is in another world. He still does that. Now I just leave him be because I know he is designing a new rocket or something.

Maye Musk

As far as Musk was concerned, education was simply "downloading data and algorithms into your brain," and hence he found conventional classroom learning exceptionally slow and frustrating. Almost everything he did learn was from his own reading, not from the classroom.

Lesson 2: A conventional education isn't for everyone. Sometimes the most important lessons are those we can teach ourselves.

Musk got his first computer when he was nine years old. The *How to Program guide* was supposed to take the user six months to complete, but Musk mastered it in three days. He developed a basic video game, Blastar, using BASIC. He describes it as "a trivial game...but better than Flappy Bird." The precocious teen sold this game to *PC and Office Technology* magazine for $500, equivalent to around $1,200 today. You can still find the game online and play it.

Lesson 3: You are never too young to start being an entrepreneur. Have faith in your ideas, and encourage your children to develop theirs too.

Leaving school, Musk decided not to stay in South Africa: he didn't relate well to the culture and felt that his entrepreneurial skills would be far better deployed across the pond. And so he emigrated to Canada, where his mother's nationality gave him citizenship rights. He enrolled at Queen's University in summer 1989 (where he would meet his first wife, Justine), and after four years (the second half of which was spent at the University of Pennsylvania), Musk graduated with a BSc in physics and a BA in economics. Showing his entrepreneurial streak early, Musk and fellow student Adeo Ressi (who went on to become the founder and CEO of TheFunded and The Founder Institute, as well as a board member of the X Prize Foundation) purchased a 10-bedroom frat house at the university and ran it as a nightclub.

Lesson 4: The relationships - personal and professional - that you establish in college might well be some of the most important you ever have. Maintain your friendships and associations, and support one another.

If you go back a few hundred years, what we take for granted today would seem like magic – being able to talk to people over long distances, to transmit images, flying, accessing vast amounts of data like an oracle. These are all things that would have been considered magic a few hundred years ago.

Elon Musk

From Pennsylvania, Musk moved across the US to California to take up a PhD offer at Stanford University. The lure of neighbouring Silicon Valley proved irresistible to the 24-year old Musk, however, and he lasted just two days on the course. Even as a student, there was a pressing question on his mind: What will most affect the future of humanity? The five answers that he came up with, the internet; sustainable energy; space exploration, in particular the permanent extension of life beyond Earth; artificial intelligence; and reprogramming the human genetic code, would determine his future direction as an entrepreneur.

Lesson 5: As an entrepreneur you have to know what is important to you. Once you have established this, it will dictate the direction you and your businesses follow.

Getting Started

Fresh out of college, Musk knew he had to get onto the Internet bandwagon or forever be left behind. He marched into the lobby of Netscape, uninvited, but was too nervous to talk to anyone or ask for a job, so he turned tail and walked out again. Starting his own business seemed less nerve-wracking, and Musk decided to keep it in the family. He joined forces with his younger brother Kimbal (also a successful entrepreneur, and now with business interests in technology, health and food sectors) to create a software company called Zip2. The first $28,000 of start-up capital came from their father, Errol Musk.

Lesson 6: Take advantage of the capital - human and financial - that is available to you. Be grateful for it and deploy it in such away that everyone who contributes will benefit.

Zip2 has been described as, "a primitive combination of Yelp and Google Maps, far before anything like either of those existed". The Musks worked around the clock, sleeping in the office and showering at the local YMCA.

Work like hell. I mean you just have to put in 80 to 100 hour weeks every week. [This] improves the odds of success. If other people are putting in 40 hour workweeks and you're putting in 100 hour workweeks, then even if you're doing the same thing, you know that you will achieve in four months what it takes them a year to achieve.

Elon Musk

Zip2 developed, hosted and maintained consumer websites for media companies and enabled those companies to target their services at specific groups of online customers. Many companies couldn't see the appeal of the Internet - what was wrong with a listing in the Yellow Pages? - but as recognition of the potential of the internet increased, so too did the appeal of Zip2's offering. Simply but professionally designed, the software was bought by more than 200 media clients including the *New York Times* and the *Chicago Tribune*. Musk was client facing and a strong salesman, gaining the company new contacts and business relationships, but his own board had concerns about his management technique and they blocked his bids to become CEO.

Lesson 7: However great your idea, there is no substitute for hard graft and the right timing. All three of these things need to be in place if your business is going to be a success.

Compaq (now a division of HP) acquired Zip2 from the Musk brothers in 1999, just four years after they had founded the company. Compaq paid $307 million in cash, plus a further $34 million in stock options, and so overnight both Elon and Kimbal became multi millionaires. Elon alone is thought to have made $22 million from the deal.

Financial Services

Musk took $10 million of his earnings from Zip2 and reinvested it straight away into a venture called x.com. This was an online banking and email payments company, and Musk was confident that the internet banking and money transfer was a business about to explode. He was right.

Lesson 8: If you have a gut hunch about the potential of an emerging market, be prepared to put your money where your mouth is. Only then can you test the waters and benefit from the upswing.

X.com wasn't the only start-up operating in this field, however: Confinity, trading as PayPal, had also recently been launched as a payment platform for handheld devices. The two companies were operating out of the same building, and recognising that there was no point in going head to head if they could work together and dominate the market, they merged in 2000.

Lesson 9: You won't always be the only person to have come up with a great idea. Sometimes you'll have to weigh up the pros and cons of competition v joining forces.

The merger didn't go especially smoothly. There were a lot of big egos in the room, all of them successful internet entrepreneurs in their own rights. Whilst Musk was on a fund-raising trip / honeymoon with his first wife, his partners staged a coup and re-placed Musk as CEO with Peter Thiel. Musk disagreed with the decision, but had to accept it. At the same time, Musk wanted the joint company to continue trading as x.com, thinking that the names Confinity and PayPal would quickly date. Customer surveys showed, however, that the general public equated the name x.com with something that was x-rated, which was a serious stumbling block for the brand. Musk was therefore forced to admit defeat and reverted to using the name PayPal in 2001.

In hindsight, this was the right decision: PayPal was clear about what it did in a way that x.com was not. The company focused exclusively on online payments, with x.com terminating its other banking services.

Lesson 10: We are all learning throughout our careers. Everyone needs to be humble and to be able to bounce back when they have made a mistake.

PayPal grew rapidly on the back of a viral marketing campaign: new subscribers were automatically recruited when they received funds using the software. It was simple to use, free for buyers, affordable for sellers, and answered growing needs for better financial security online. The company went public in October 2002 and Musk alone (who was PayPal's largest shareholder) netted $165 million in eBay stock. The total value of PayPal at the time of the acquisition was $1.5 billion. Musk had been catapulted into the big time.

Space: The Final Frontier?

Going from PayPal, I thought: 'Well, what are some of the other problems that are likely to most affect the future of humanity?' Not from the perspective, 'What's the best way to make money?'

Elon Musk

Before the ink was even dry on the sale of PayPal to eBay, Musk was already looking at his options for the future. He had always been fascinated by space and space technology, and he wanted to both reinvigorate our interest in space exploration and get increased funding for NASA, both of which had largely fallen by the wayside since the end of the Cold War. His first idea was to create a Mars Oasis, a miniature greenhouse project on the red planet where he could experiment with growing food crops.

Lesson 11: Sometimes even the sky isn't the limit. If you have a dream, however hard it might be to realise it, that doesn't mean you shouldn't try to make it happen. Giant leaps forward demand giant dreams!

Musk travelled to Russia with Jim Cantrell, a well-established fixer in the aerospace industry, and his old business partner Adeo Ressi. The three men planned to buy refurbished Dnepr-1 rockets, converted intercontinental ballistic missiles (ICBMs) that can be used to launch artificial satellites into space. They met with some major Russian aerospace companies, including NPO Lavochkin and Kosmotras, but the Russians didn't take them seriously: they had no experience in satellites or other areas of space technology, and look just to be wealthy time wasters. They returned home empty handed.

Lesson 12: Money alone doesn't buy you credibility. You need to do your research, plan, and bring in the right level of expertise if you want to be respected in new fields and markets.

They returned a year later, this time with Mike Griffin, formerly of NASA's Jet Propulsion Laboratory, who was at that time working with spacecraft and satellite manufacturer Orbital Sciences. On this occasion the group had more professional credibility, and Kosmotras therefore offered Musk one rocket for $8 million. Believing (probably quite rightly) that he was being screwed over, Musk stormed out of the meeting and headed for home. On the flight home he calculated that he could build his own rockets for the Mars Oasis far more cost effectively, estimating that the raw materials needed were only 3% of the total sales price of a rocket. Even enjoying a 70% gross margin, Musk reckoned he could cut the launch price by a factor of 10. Vertical integration and and a modular approach would be the keys. The seeds of SpaceX were sown.

Lesson 13: Applying models and strategies from different industries can make you huge savings in your own industry, particularly if you have the capacity and inclination to do things in house.

Musk's aim with SpaceX was to create a simple, inexpensive and reusable space rocket which would reduce the cost of space transportation and, ultimately, make viable the human colonisation of Mars.

Musk was determined to work with the best in the business from the word go, and so he approached Tom Mueller, an employee of aerospace conglomerate TRW Inc. and the inventor of the world's largest amateur liquid-fuel rocket engine, which was capable of producing 13,000 lbf (58 kN) of thrust. The two men founded SpaceX in El Segundo, California, and they immediately got to work. Their first rocket, Falcon 1 (named in ho-nour of *Star Wars*' Millennium Falcon) was developed and manufactured between 2006 and 2009 and became the first privately developed launch vehicle to go into orbit.

I think it is a mistake to hire huge numbers of people to get a complicated job done. Numbers will never compensate for talent in getting the right answer (two people who don't know something are no better than one), will tend to slow down progress, and will make the task incredibly expensive.

Elon Musk

Lesson 14: If you want to make the very best products, you have to hire the very best people in their field.

The Falcon 1 was a two-stage-to-orbit rocket completely designed by SpaceX. It had two engines, a Merlin engine and a Kestrel engine, and it was launched five times. On the last of these occasions it successfully delivered into orbit the Malaysian RazakSAT satel-lite. The rocket was then retired, making way for subsequent models (the Falcon 9, the Falcon Heavy and the Dragon) which utilised improved design features.

Lesson 15: Never rest on your laurels. You have to constantly be thinking of - and actioning - the next big idea if you want to keep ahead and ensure your offering is fresh.

Failure is an option here. If things are not failing, you are not innovating enough.

Elon Musk

The trajectory of SpaceX has not always been smooth: the first three test rockets all exploded before reaching orbit, leaving Musk with just enough money for one more try. It was fourth time lucky or that was it: no one was going to invest in the company until they had at least one successful launch. Luckily for Musk, the Falcon made it up into orbit on that fourth occasion.

Lesson 16: Make sure that you have sufficient cash reserves to carry you through your product development phase comfortably. You don't want to run out of money at the final hurdle and be left with nothing to show for your effort and expenditure.

In June 2015 a SpaceX rocket resupplying the International Space Station exploded just two minutes after launch. The likely cause was a failed steel strut holding down a canister of helium. In theory, the strut in question was designed to withstand 10,000 pounds of force, but it failed with just 20% of that force. This meant that the bottle shot to the top of the tank in the rocket's upper stage, causing helium to spew into the oxygen tank and over pressurise it. The rocket broke up into thousands of small parts and the Dragon cargo capsule it was carrying fell into the sea, along with its 4,000 pounds of supplies. Had the Dragon capsule been programmed with software to deploy its parachute, it may have survived, and so the next-generation version (which is expected eventually to carry crew members into orbit) will have that software as well as its own thrusters. SpaceX is sending its own, autonomous underwater vehicle to search for debris in a bid to better understand the cause of the accident and its impact on other parts of the craft. Remarkably, in spite of seven years of launches, this was the first such mishap SpaceX suffered. To give engineers time to learn lessons from the incident, the first Falcon Heavy launch will be pushed back until spring 2015, but it is not expected to have long-term detrimental impact on the company and its plans.

Lesson 17: One relatively small oversight or error can have dramatic consequences. Don't overlook the small things.

It is worth considering at this point the funding model for SpaceX. Although Musk did invest substantial amounts of his own fortune (an estimated $100 million by March 2006), he was by no means the only stakeholder. In 2008, $20 million in investment came from the Founders Fund (the venture capital fund behind PayPal, Spotify and Airbnb). The total budget of the company over the past 10 years has been in the region of $1 billion, of which the majority has come as income from development contracts. NASA alone has paid SpaceX somewhere in the region of $500 million. SpaceX has contracts for more than 40 space launches, and therefore gains revenue both from down payments and ongoing progress payments as each stage of a project is completed. Musk has retained approximately two-thirds of the company's shares, an eye watering sum given that after SpaceX's successful COTS 2+ flight in May 2012, the company was valued at $2.8 billion.

Lesson 18: Cash flow problems kill companies. You need to understand clearly exactly how much money will be needed at each stage of your business' growth, and where that money is going to come from.

Although there has been much discussion in the marketplace as to if and when SpaceX will have an IPO, Musk has personally stated that he plans to hold off on this until the Mars Colonial Transporter is flying regularly. In his own words, "I just don't want [SpaceX] to be controlled by some private equity firm that would milk it for near-term revenue". In practical terms, Musk has no need to make a public offering of shares: SpaceX is a cash cow, and there are plenty of private customers eager to lap up shares without having them publicly traded. In January 2015 Google and Fidelity (the venture capital arm of Fidelity Investments) spent $1 billion buying 8.333% of SpaceX, giving the entirety of SpaceX a valuation of $12 billion.

For Musk, SpaceX is not just about the money: he has plenty of that, and it is the challenge he has set himself that really excited him. We will talk more about his beliefs about life in outer space in *Politics and Beliefs*, but it warrants mention here that Musk believes it is feasible to put the first man on Mars by 2021. He made this claim in an interview with the *Wall Street Journal* in 2011. What is more, he doesn't expect this to be a one-off achievement: in June 2015 he went one stage further, telling etv.com that by 2035 thousands of rockets will be flying to Mars each year, enabling us to establish a self-sustaining space colony with more than one million inhabitants.

Lesson 19: You will put your best efforts into pursuing an idea if it excites you. Yes, there has to be a business case for the idea too, but it is far more rewarding (and more likely to succeed) if your business is also a passion.

SpaceX's low cost launch model has put significant pressure on its competitors to lower their prices, something which can only please Musk. An orbital launch from the Falcon Heavy costs just $1,000 per pound, spurring Arianespace (a European competitor) to request subsidies from the European Union to be able to compete. In 2014 SpaceX won nine out of 20 worldwide bids for commercial launch services, more than any other company. SpaceX has signed contracts with the United States Air Force, NASA and the United States Department of Defense in addition to its conventional commercial contracts.

Lesson 20: If you can provide a high-quality product or service at a competitive rate, customers will come to you and you will dominate your marketplace.

Transport and Energy

Tesla Motors takes its name and inspiration from the Serbian American physicist, electrical engineer and inventor, Nikola Tesla (1856-1943), who worked with Thomas Edison in New York and who in his own right made major contributions to the modern alternating current (AC) electricity supply system. Clearly a pin-up of Musk's (who himself has a BSc in physics, see *Background and Education*), the motor in the Tesla Roadstar is based almost entirely on Tesla's original 1882 design.

Lesson 21: The best ideas aren't necessarily new ideas. Be prepared to take products or services that already exist and rework and improve them for the modern world.

As with PayPal, Musk was not the founder of Tesla Motors: that credit falls to two men, engineer Martin Eberhard and his business partner Marc Tarpenning. Eberhard and Tarpenning founded Tesla Motors in summer 2003 with the principal aim of commercialising electric vehicles. They wanted to create first an aspirational sports car model which would show off the capabilities of the their technology, and then diversify into more mainstream, affordable models for ordinary families. Musk invested in Tesla Motors in February 2004 and joined the company as the Chairman of the board. He took an active interest in product development (though not in the day to day running of the business), and Eberhanrd credits Musk with the insistence on a carbon fibre reinforced polymer body, as well as the design of the power electronics module to the headlamps.

Lesson 22: If you find someone else who has a great idea, and you have the skills, connections and capital to make it happen, work together. You don't have to be the inventor!

Musk's investment in Tesla Motors was in the region of $7.5 million (which came from his personal funds), and this relatively modest investment made him the controlling investor in Tesla's first funding round. To any onlooker, Musk's investment was completely crazy, however much you like cars. The last successful automotive start-up in the US was Chrysler in 1925, and no one had ever made money out of electric cars. It looked like a bottomless pit for money, with little or no chance of a financial return. Surely Musk wasn't just going to throw away everything he'd worked so hard to earn? Was he delusional?

When Henry Ford made cheap, reliable cars, people said, 'Nah, what's wrong with a horse?' That was a huge bet he made, and it worked.

Elon Musk

Lesson 23: If you want to make really big bucks, there will always be an element of risk involved. You need to do your homework and decide if the gamble is worth it, ignoring detractors if you think that the odds are indeed in your favour.

There's a tremendous bias against taking risks. Everyone is trying to optimize their ass-covering.

Elon Musk

And indeed the early years of Tesla Motors were far from smooth. Although the company (and Musk) were picking up awards for their designs, including the 2006 Global Green product design award and the 2007 Index Design award, both for the Tesla Roadstar, the company was burning through funds at an alarming rate. Musk was forced to cut the size of his team by 10% in 2007 to stave off financial disaster, and the following year *The Truth About Cars* website launched a "Tesla Death Watch", anticipating the end was nigh. *Valleywag*, the Silicon Valley gossip blog, had also earmarked Tesla its #1 tech company fail of 2007. Thankfully for Musk, they had both underestimated Musk's determination and the appeal of the Tesla product to investors.

Lesson 24: People will always try to rain on your parade. Keep your head down, keep working and ignore idle gossip. This is the only way to remain focus and not get bogged down by other people's negativity.

Elon said 'I will spend my last dollar on these companies. If we have to move into Justine's parents' basement, we'll do it.'

Antonio Gracias

Musk raised round after round of funding. He was confident, enthused constantly about Tesla and its potential, and investors believed what he had to say. He raised $45 million for the company in May 2007, $40 million in December 2008, and a further $50 million from Germany's Daimler AG (the makers of Mercedes-Benz) in May 2009. Musk had also contributed an estimated $70 million of his own money.

Now the company's fortunes began to turn for the better. Tesla delivered its first 147 cars by January 2009, showing that they were a credible prospect. Abu Dhabi's Aabar Investments bought 40% of Daimler AG's interest in Tesla and the company was advanced $465 million in loans from the United States Department of Energy part of the Advanced Technology Vehicles Manufacturing Loan Program. Mainstream car manufacturers Ford and Nissan also received funds from this programme, but Tesla was able to repay its loan well in advance of its competitors.

Lesson 25: Investment and growth are all about confidence. When one investor comes onboard and in doing so endorses your business, others will more than likely follow. The challenge is getting that first one to say "Yes"!

Tesla finally turned a profit for the first time in July 2009 on the back of sales of the Tesla Roadster.109 vehicles had shipped that month and as the company's fortunes now looked promising, Musk decided that the time was right for an initial public offering (IPO).

Tesla Motors launched its initial public offering on NASDAQ (the US-Canadian stock exchange) in June 2010. 13,300,000 shares were issued, each with a value of $17. IPO raised $226 million for the company, and it proved the catalyst for the company's epic growth: by the end of 2014 the share price had reached $240 per share and the total value of the company was nearly $29 billion. Tesla was the top performing company on the Nasdaq 100 index in 2013 and sold more than 33,000 cars worldwide in 2014.

Lesson 26: Right from the start you should know what your exit strategy for your company will be, and what the necessary conditions are for that exit. When the time is right, don't be afraid to let go. This is, after all, what you have been working for all along.

Although Tesla's long term goal is to produce cars for the mainstream consumer car market, in the meantime they are having fun creating some top end products that excite the automotive media. It is a shrewd business model because it creates aspiration, an appetite for Tesla's future products as and when they do become affordable for ordinary, middle class customers. The latest Tesla car the Model X SUV, was launched in September 2015 with a basic model costing around $80,000. If you want the top-of-the-range Signature Series, the prices rise to at least $132,000. The vehicle is exceptionally energy efficient, as you would expect from Tesla Motors, but there are also a number of other interesting features: the car continually scans the road with camera, radar and sonar systems so that it can automatically break before an accident and steer away from side collisions; the wing doors allow access in narrow spaces but also have sensors so that they won't crunch up into the roof of a garage; and the car can do 0 to 60 mph in 3.2 seconds. The Signature Series has a top speed of 275 mph (443 kmph).

Lesson 27: Creating aspiration creates demand for your brand. It is far easier to start at the top, selling and building a reputation for quality, than to begin at the bottom end of the market and to try to claw your way up.

Tesla's innovations are not just in the car market, however: Musk wants to bring affordable electrical energy into all walks of life. This is especially true regarding batteries. A Tesla batter is made up of thousands of lithium-ion 18650 commodity cells, typically used in laptops and other small consumer electrical devices. Made by Panasonic (itself an investor in Tesla), the cells are small, lightweight and cheap, costing around $200 per kWh, significantly less than any batter alternatives currently available on the market.

Lesson 28: Be aware of all the essential components in the product you sell. Their quality, reliability and cost will have a significant impact on your end product too.

Taking these batteries a step further, Tesla announced the Powerwall home and battery packs in April 2015. The standard version is a 7 kilowatt-hour wall-mounted unit, although industrial users can also opt for far larger batteries in units of 100 kWh. These will at first be made by Panasonic, then from 2016 onwards by Reno as this will enable Tesla to cut costs by around 30%. The move into household energy storage is hugely important because it means that for the first time consumers with solar panels on their houses can actually store the energy they produce in a cost effective manner. *Bloomberg* reported that Tesla consequently made $800 million of battery sales in their first week, smashing even Musk's expectations. Once it is operational, Musk's planned "Gigafactory" in Nevada will enable Tesla to more than double the world's total annual production of lithium-ion batteries. He is taking on the energy market in a spectacular manner.

Lesson 29: There is money to be made reworking your existing products in new and imaginative ways. Think outside the box for ways you can enter new markets.

Musk's interest in energy is not just in storage and use, but also in production. SolarCity, one of the USA's largest solar power companies, designs, finances, and installs solar power systems. Although it was founded in 2006 by Lyndon and Peter Rive, the idea for the company came from their cousin, Elon Musk, who is SolarCity's Chairman and provided its start-up capital.

SolarCity works in a number of complementary areas. It has a number of commercial solar installations in California, including on sites belonging to eBay, British Motors, Walmart and Intel; it offers energy efficiency evaluations and upgrades to home owners; there is a five-year plan to build more than $1 billion in solar photovoltaic projects (predominantly rooftop solar panels) for military housing estates in the US; it produced electric car charging points; and also installs snap together solar panels. SolarCity plans to build a major new manufacturing facility in Buffalo, New York in order to manufacture high-efficiency solar modules. When it is completed, this will be the largest such plant in the US and will enable SolarCity to compete aggressively against manufacturers in China.

Lesson 30: No market or business exists in isolation. Be constantly on the look out for ways to collaborate and build relationships that will stand you in good stead in the future.

Supporting SolarCity - which now has a market capitalisation in excess of $6 billion - is a good move for Musk as it sits well with his investment in Tesla. Not only can SolarCity produce the quality car chargers Tesla needs, but the household batteries produced by Tesla can also be used to store electricity produced by homes with SolarCity's photovoltaic cells. It is a win-win situation.

Musk's venture into public transportation, Hyperloop, is as yet just an idea on the drawing board, but if his track record is anything to go by, even the most far fetched idea might just come to fruition.

At its most basic, the Hyperloop is a theoretical high-speed transport system where pressurised capsules ride on a cushion of air through reduced pressure tubes, driven by linear induction motors and air compressors. Musk proposed the system to run parallel to Interstate 5 between Los Angeles and San Francisco in California, a journey of 354-mile (570 km). Musk believes that his system could cut the journey time to only 35 minutes, requiring an average speed of about 598 mph (962 km/h). Not only will this be significantly faster than any other available option, including air travel, but it would also substantially reduce congestion and traffic pollution on California's roads.

Lesson 31: Apply your expertise to real world problems if you really want to have a positive impact on the world in which you live.

Musk first proposed his idea for a "fifth mode of transport" in Santa Monica, California in 2011. He was addressing attendees at a web and tech event and spoke of his dream of a transport option that was immune to bad weather, could not crash, had an average speed twice that of a typical jet, required little power, and could store energy for 24-hour operations. Musk envisaged his Hyperloop as being a "cross between a Concorde and a railgun and an air hockey table".

The physical challenges that the Hyperloop project faces are the impact of air resistance and friction when anything moves at high speed. Maglev - the use of magnetically levitating trains in evacuated tubes - in theory at least eliminates these problems, but is an exceptionally expensive type of technology and it is difficult to maintain the necessary vacuum over any kind of distance.

To see if he could make it happen, Musk put together a team of engineers from Tesla and SpaceX. They worked on the conceptual foundation and modelling of Hyperloop and produced a white paper, inviting comment from the wider tech-minded community. Unusually, the design was open source: Musk wanted anyone to be able to understand it and to contribute ideas that might improve the design. He then announced his plan to build a prototype to test the concept in practice.

You want to be extra rigorous about making the best possible thing you can. Find everything that's wrong with it and fix it. Seek negative feedback, particularly from friends.

Elon Musk

Lesson 32: Commercial secrecy, though understandable, is an outdated model. You will make progress far faster if you can access the 'hive mind' of the wider community and harness their ideas.

154

Although initially it was reported that the Hyperloop test track would be in Texas, Musk then concluded it would be more convenient to situate it in California's Quay Valley, next door to SpaceX's Hawthorne facility. Here there will be a 1 mile (1.6 km) test track where they can trial pod designs submitted as entries in a Hyperloop design competition.

Musk came up with the Hyperloop concept, but to take the project to the next level he is happy for others to contribute and to do the running. He has allowed JumpStarter Inc. to create Hyperloop Transportation Technologies (HTT), a research company which is using a crowd funding and collaboration approach to develop the transportation system. More than 100 engineers, all of whom have taken stock options instead of upfront payment, are working together on designs. They expect to have completed their first feasibility study by the end of 2015, but admit that they are at least 10 years away from opening a commercially viable Hyperloop. HTT hopes that its IPO will raise $100 million to fund the project's development. They already have permission to build a 5-mile (8.0 km) test track alongside Interstate 5, and have also proposed a Hyperloop route between Los Angeles and Las Vegas.

Lesson 33: You don't have to be possessive about your ideas. If you really want something to succeed, be prepared to let others have a go at it if you don't have the skills or resources available to you at the time.

Initial calculations suggest that Musk's own version of the Hyperloop would be technically and commercially viable. Musk has suggested a price tag of $6 billion, though critics do think this is optimistically low, and in the alpha design he outlines a scenario where the Hyperloop covers its capital costs within 20 years. A one-way passenger ticket would be a very affordable $20. The challenges are likely to be scaremongering - every critic is terrified of spiralling costs - and the difficulty of moving support (financial and political) away from the state's current mega-project, California High-Speed Rail. The existing project inevitably has many vested interests and so focusing on an alternative route (such as Los Angeles to Texas) that does not bring the two projects into head to head conflict might be the best route forward.

Lesson 34: Vested interests can block even the best ideas. Look ahead and find ways to circumvent them so that your projects don't get mired in the mud.

Awards and Recognition

Musk's recognition is international in scope and touches on multiple disciplines. He is lauded as an inventor and innovator by universities and learned society's, is the darling of the business world, and a popular and respected figure by journalists too. There is space here to discuss only a small selection of his awards.

Lesson 35: In today's multi disciplinary world, it is not enough to be an expert in just one area. A true renaissance man will earn the appreciation of his peers in every field.

In *Background and Education* we looked at Musk's university career, and though he abandoned his own doctorate at Stanford University after only two days, other institutions have moved to recognise his contributions to technology regardless. In the UK, Surrey University (one of the world's foremost centres for the development of satellite technology) has awarded Musk an honorary doctorate (DUniv) in Aerospace Engineering, and he also has an honorary doctorate of Engineering and Technology from Yale University. His third honorary doctorate, this time in design, comes from the ArtCenter College of Design in Pasadena, California.

Recognising his contributions in the field of space technology, Musk was asked to serve on the United States National Academy of Sciences Aeronautics and Space Engineering Board. He received the 2007/08 American Institute of Aeronautics and Astronautics George Low award for his design of the Falcon 1, and also National Space Society's Von Braun Trophy and the Fédération Aéronautique Internationale's Gold Space Medal, both for this same outstanding achievement. The Kitty Hawk Foundation have recognised Musk as a Living Legend of Aviation, and in 2011 he received the Heinlein Prize for Advances in Space Commercialization, worth $250,000.

Lesson 36: Academic awards can enhance your credibility in the commercial world too. The two worlds, though they sometimes can appear to be poles apart, are in fact compatible and have mutual benefits.

As a businessman, Musk's line up of accolades is no less impressive. *R&D Magazine, Inc Magazine* and *Fortune* have all named him as their entrepreneur of the year (in 2007, 2007 and 2014 respectively). *Esquire* magazine listed Musk as one of the 75 most influential people of the 21st century, and in 2011 he also appeared in *Forbes'* "America's 20

Most Powerful CEOs 40 And Under". If that weren't enough to confirm his superstar status, in January 2015 an episode of *The Simpsons* entitled "The Musk Who Fell to Earth" was broadcast, poking fun at some of his inventions. Musk made a guest appearance.

Lesson 37: Even when selling high ticket items like space crafts and electronic cars, there is no harm in appealing to the general public through popular culture.

Politics and Beliefs

Often it is easy to spot the political leanings of a major businessman, especially in the US, but that is not the case with Musk: he has described himself as "half-Democrat, half-Republican... I'm somewhere in the middle, socially liberal and fiscally conservative." He has contributed to election campaigns for both of the mainstream political parties in the US.

Lesson 38: Politics, and indeed one's own political position, is not black and white. You can, and should, shift your allegiance as required by your commercial needs.

The donations are linked to Musk's lobbying efforts: he understandably lobbies hard on issues of importance to his companies. A report from the Sunlight Foundation found that SpaceX alone has spent $4 million lobbying both sides of Congress, and Musk himself has made $725,000 in campaign donations. His own campaign to win political support is "systematic and sophisticated". It is also consistent. SpaceX has its own in-house lobbyists and also works with the Washington-based lobbying group Patton Boggs LLP and other similar groups.

Lesson 39: When lobbying and making donations, focus on the causes that make most business sense. Consider these efforts as part of your core business development costs, and take them seriously.

Although Musk's own companies have been the recipients of government subsidies in the past, Musk has subsequently spoken out against this. He believes that a carbon tax, levied on those companies that are not environmentally friendly, is a far better policy than costly subsidies. His view is controversial, however: collectively SpaceX, Tesla Motors and SolarCity have benefited from an estimated $4.9 billion in government subsidies, and in their early days even these companies may not have been successful without it.

Lesson 40: If the criticism of hypocrisy is levelled at you, have a good reason for your change of heart.

One thing that is in no doubt at all is Musk's patriotism. Despite being born in South Africa and becoming a US national only as an adult, Musk is unashamedly pro-American. He has described his host country as "[inarguably] the greatest country that has ever existed on Earth" and "the greatest force for good of any country that's ever been". Whether or not you agree with him, you have to admire his enthusiasm, and the approach has certainly ensured he's a favourite amongst US politicians and investors alike.

Lesson 41: Playing to the gallery will earn you plenty of Brownie points amongst the elite. Look after your supporters, and they will look after you.

The conservative elements in the US tend to ignore Musk's religious beliefs (or rather lack thereof).

He is a rationalist, basing his personal views on his understanding of the laws of physics. He thinks that it is unlikely that religion and science could coexist. He does believe, however, that there is a significant chance that there simple life on other planets, perhaps something akin to mould growing in a petri dish. Musk has "hope that there is other intelligent life in the known universe" and thinks that statistically it is "probably more likely than not".

What concerns Musk is not extraterrestrial life but the threat posed to humanity by artificial intelligence, which he has described as "the most serious threat to the survival of the human race". He is very concerned about the lack of regulatory oversight, either an a national or international level, and when addressing the the MIT AeroAstro Centennial Symposium, he went on to say "There have been movies about this, you know, like Terminator – there are some scary outcomes. And we should try to make sure the outcomes are good, not bad."

I wouldn't say I have a lack of fear. In fact, I'd like my fear emotion to be less because it's very distracting and fries my nervous system.

Elon Musk

Lesson 42: If there is something out there that worries you or that you fear, be honest about it. Don't hide in the dark and hope that it goes away. Instead, think about what you can do to overcome the threat and tackle it head on.

Personal Life

I remember thinking it was a lot of drama, and that if I was going to put up with it, we might as well be married. I told him he should just propose to me.

Justine Musk

Musk met his first wife, Justine, whilst they were both students at Queen's University in Ontario, Canada. She was an aspiring writer, and he wooed her with ice cream and bunches of roses. She travelled to Japan to teach, but returned to the US to join Musk in Silicon Valley, and the couple married in January 2000. The board of x.com (later Pay-Pal) urged the bride and groom to sign a postnuptial agreement protecting his newly acquired wealth, and the sense of economic inequality within the relationship, combined with Musk's alpha male tendencies, caused notable strain.

Lesson 43: The characteristics that make you successful in business are not necessarily characteristics which will serve you well in other aspects of your life.

Nothing could have prepared the Musks for the trauma to come, however. Their first son, Nevada Alexander Musk, was born in 2002. The same week that Musk sold PayPal, catapulting his wealth to in excess of $100 million, the 10-week old baby was put down for a nap and stopped breathing. Although he was resuscitated by paramedics, Nevada had been deprived of oxygen for too long and was brain dead. Three days later his life support machines were turned off. The cause of death was sudden infant death syndrome (SIDS).

Lesson 44: No amount of money makes you immune from personal tragedy. What is important is how you respond when that tragedy strikes.

Musk bottled up his emotions, refusing to talk with his wife about their loss. At first Justine grieved openly, but Musk decried this behaviour as "emotionally manipulative" and so she was forced to hide her pain. In spite of being caught in a spiral of depression, she returned to the IVF clinic and gave birth first to twins and then to triplets, five small boys in all. Griffin and Xavier were born in 2004, and Damian, Saxon and Kai followed in 2006.

On the face of it, the Musks had a perfect family set-up and social life. They lived in a 6,000-square-foot house in the Bel Air Hills, partied with Bono, Paris Hilton and Leonardo DiCaprio, and travelled everywhere by private jet. What was missing, sadly, was intimacy and mutual respect. Musk was obsessed with his work and paid little attention to his wife. She had sacrificed her successful literary career to raise their children and support him, but he was dismissive. An intelligent, capable woman in her own right, Justine had been reduced to no more than a trophy wife, and she understandably resented that fact.

Lesson 45: A successful marriage depends on mutual respect and balance. If it is important to you, you need to work as hard at your relationship as you do at your career.

Faced with a collapsing marriage, and a wife who craved equality in their partnership, Musk agreed to begin marriage counselling. He lasted just three sessions, then impatiently issued Justine with an ultimatum: either we fix this marriage today or I will divorce you tomorrow. No relationship can be rebuilt in a day. Musk filed for divorce the next morning.

Their divorce, in spring 2008, was messy. Although by signing the post-nup Justine had in theory signed away all her rights as a married person, including to communal property, but there was some debate as to whether or not Musk had fully disclosed his finances at the time of signing, which was a marital fiduciary duty. Resolution was a matter for the courts.

Lesson 46: If you are going to mix marriage and money, make sure the paperwork is sorted out before you start. If you don't, only the lawyers will win.

I would like to allocate more time to dating, though. I need to find a girlfriend. That's why I need to carve out just a little more time. I think maybe even another five to 10 — how much time does a woman want a week? Maybe 10 hours? That's kind of the minimum? I don't know.

Elon Musk

Just six weeks after Musk filed for divorce, he announced his engagement to British actress Talulah Riley. Though the relationship between his ex-wife and new fiancee could have been acrimonious, Justine took the unusual step of reaching out to her replacement (who she has never met) in an email:

"I would rather live out the French-movie version of things, in which the two women become friends and various philosophies are pondered, than the American version, in which one is "good" and one is "bad" and there's a huge catfight sequence and someone gets thrown off a balcony."

Riley responded, "Let's do as the French do."

Lesson 47: In every walk of life, civility makes things far, far easier for everyone involved.

I remember him saying, 'Being with me was choosing the hard path.' I didn't quite understand at the time, but I do now. It's quite hard, quite the crazy ride.

Talulah Riley

A graduate of Cheltenham Ladies College, Riley probably first caught Musk's eye when she appeared as Mary Bennet in the 2005 film of *Pride and Prejudice*. She also had roles in *St. Trinian's*, *The Boat that Rocked*, and *Dr. Who*. The couple married in Dornoch Cathedral in 2010, and their marriage lasted two years. The *Telegraph* reported that Riley received a $4.2 million divorce settlement, but the couple were oddly reconciled, albeit temporarily, in 2014. The current status of their relationship is open to debate: legally Musk and Riley are still married, but the *Associated Press* announced another split on 31 December 2014, this time with an alimony payout of $16 million in cash and assets.

Lesson 48: The prying and speculating of the press puts every high profile relationship under pressure. Be clear about what you are and are not prepared to share with the media and the public, and defend your right to privacy to that those around you are protected.

In spite of these payouts to his ex-wives, Musk still has ample fortune to spend. He distributes some of this philanthropically through the Musk Foundation. Reflecting his commercial interests, the Musk Foundation provides solar powered energy systems to communities which have been hit by natural disasters. Recent donations have included a 25 kW solar power system for the South Bay Community Alliance's (SBCA) hurricane response centre in Alabama, and a $250,000 contribution towards a solar power project in a tsunami-affected area of Japan. Philanthropy and charity are not the same thing, and Musk understands this implicitly. It is perfectly acceptable to use the former to raise your profile and awareness of your products and services. Doing good for others can do you and your business good too.

In addition to this, Musk has made donations to individual projects which interest him. He donated $1 million towards the construction of the Tesla Science Center at Tesla's former Wardenclyffe Laboratory on Long Island, New York, as well as pledging to build a Tesla Supercharger in the museum's car park, and he gave $10 million to the Future of Life Institute to fund their global research programme. The purpose of this was to ensure artificial intelligence (something which concerns Musk greatly, see *Politics and Beliefs*) remains a net benefit to humanity.

Lesson 49: Support only the things which really interest you. If you make money, every cat and dog home will come begging, but you don't have to fund them all. Use your money wisely.

The board of the X Prize Foundation, which designs competitions intended to encourage technological development that could benefit mankind, reads like a who's who of the tech and business worlds, so it should come as no surprise that Musk sits on the boar alongside Larry Page, Arianna Huffington, Ratan Tata and others. Musk's interest in the non-profit organisation was likely piqued by the Ansari XPRIZE, which is a $10 million prize for the first privately financed team that could build and fly a three-passenger vehicle 100 km into space twice within two weeks. This particular prize was won by Mojave Aerospace Ventures, whose spacecraft SpaceShipOne successfully completed the challenge in 2004. Its successor award is the Google Lunar XPRIZE, launched in 2007, which will give $20 million to the first team to land a rover on the moon. The rover must travel more than 500m and transmit back high definition images and video. Bonus prizes of $5 million each are available for teams whose rover can travel long distances (considered to be more than 5km) or can survive the lunar night.

Lesson 50: As an entrepreneur, you have a responsibility to inspire the next generation of innovators. Doing so may well be the greatest legacy you leave.

Conclusion

I think it is possible for ordinary people to choose to be extraordinary.

Elon Musk

It would be hard, and probably unfair, to argue that Elon Musk is not a genius. Though his academic credentials are not remarkable - he did abandon his PhD incomplete after all - his breadth and depth of understanding of science and technology, combined with his willingness to keep on learning new things, means that he is uniquely well placed to try and solve some of the many challenges faced today in our world. Unlike an elected politician, Musk is not answerable to an electorate. He doesn't have to make populist choices, and he can take on projects where the results will not be seen until quite some time along the line. He is also not like other businessmen. His companies do have shareholders, of course, but he is also prepared to put his own money into a project, to test it out and get things up and running to the point when the idea is proven and other investors want to jump on his band wagon. He sees his role in life not just being about making money, though he does have a competitive, acquisitive side too, but also about addressing the major issues that humanity faces, challenges that seem to huge and insurmountable at the start that others are afraid to even try.

I came to the conclusion that we should aspire to increase the scope and scale of human consciousness in order to better understand what questions to ask. Really, the only thing that makes sense is to strive for greater collective enlightenment.

Elon Musk

Perhaps Musk's greatest and most admirable asset is that he can look at the big picture and take the long view. He is not in a rush, and he does not have to prove himself to others. His achievement to date, in business and in innovation, already put him on a level far beyond what most other entrepreneurs and/or inventors can ever hope to achieve, so what Musk does now is entirely up to him. If a challenge interests him, and if an idea inspires him, he can pursue it and see where it leads. This gives Musk a great deal of freedom to try things out, and the freedom to think and to dream is something that all of his disciples can emulate. We may be restrained by physical and financial barriers, but that does not mean that we can't open our minds and look at the challenges we face in new and imaginative ways. When our thoughts are unencumbered, we will come up with the best solutions.

164

[Physics is] a good framework for thinking. ... Boil things down to their fundamental truths and reason up from there.

Elon Musk

Musk's life and work so far also teaches us that you don't have to be a specialist in one narrow field: a true renaissance man like Leonardo Da Vinci, Musk is able to think creatively, and to excel, in multiple disciplines. Yes, he has undoubtedly mastered the basics of mathematics and physics, engineering and computer programming, not to mention public speaking, leadership and self promotion, but he is not (yet) a Nobel prize winning scientist, and his oratory skills fall short of those of, for example, Winston Churchill or Adolf Hitler. What Musk does have is a breadth of interest and knowledge, enough to understand the complexities of arguments and the nuances of details presented to him. He is perpetually curious, even to the point of obsession, wanting to know more and more. He has learned to surround himself with the greatest thinkers and doers in each industry he wants to work in. He inspires and leads them, but depends very much on their collective input and expertise to make his projects happen. Musk's mastery of the dual arts of leadership and delegation is what enables him to rise above his competitors, to see further, and to achieve far more.

It would be perfectly possible to replicate Musk's educational and professional career moves step by step without achieving the same outcome. He is, like any successful entrepreneur, the beneficiary of a particular, fortunate set of circumstances. Had he made the same decisions,   the same bids, at a different time in his career, the outcomes would likely have been very different: we have already seen how close SpaceX and Tesla Motors came to falling flat on their faces. The final lesson in this book which we should learn from Musk, then, is that what determines success is not your qualifications, where you were born, or how much money you have. Instead, it is how you choose to see the world, your openness to ideas, and how you respond to opportunities and challenges when you are faced with them. No one in this world, not even Elon Musk, goes through life with a completely easy ride. For all of us there are forks in the road, and vital decisions to be made. We must approach these times with confidence and conviction if we are to achieve our goals.

50 Life and Business Lessons from Mark Zuckerberg

Introduction

At the age of just 31, American Mark Zuckerberg is worth an estimated $46 billion. He has not inherited his wealth, but rather has made it from scratch in only 12 years, and with the creation of a single product: Facebook.

Unless you have buried your head in the sand for the past decade, ignoring not only the internet but also newspapers, television, cinema, and water cooler discussions, you cannot have missed the social media phenomenon which is Facebook. It has an estimated 1.5 billion users, in almost every corner of the globe, and is the driving force behind Free Basics, an app which provides free internet services in the developing world.

Zuckerberg himself has not only made exorbitant wealth, leaving relatively little controversy in his wake, but also positioned himself at the forefront of enterprise and innovation. He has been voted as *Time* magazine's man of the year, and is the poster child for the tech world. Along with Bill Gates and Warren Buffet, men many years his senior, he was one of the key signatories to The Giving Pledge, and as a result he is leading the way for philanthropists. His subsequent promise to donate 99% of his Facebook shares to charity, during his lifetime, shows his level of commitment to this ideal.

The early chapters of this book are laid out roughly in chronological order: first of all we discuss Zuckerberg's childhood and education; then his early forays into social media and programming; the birth and growth of Facebook; and his launch of Internet.org. In the second part of the book, we look more widely at his estimated wealth; awards and accolades; philanthropic efforts; political involvement; and, last but not least; his personal life.

Throughout the book you will find lessons we have drawn from Zuckerberg's life and work, which you can apply in your own life. Though not all of these lessons will be personally applicable, you can take inspiration from them, and put into practice those which are most relevant to you. You will find a summary of the overarching themes of those lessons — five unforgettable lessons from Mark Zuckerberg — in the book's conclusion.

Childhood and Education

Right from the word go, Mark Zuckerberg was a child prodigy, a fascinating and precocious child with seemingly infinite capacity to learn and to innovate. Born on 14 May, 1984 in White Plains, New York, the son of two professional parents, dentist Edward Zuckerberg and psychiatrist Karen Kempner, Zuckerberg and his three sisters were raised in New York state, and then in New Hampshire.

Lesson 1: A commitment to education, from an early age, stands you in good stead in later life. It need not be a formal, academic education, but you should instil in your children, and in yourself, a love of learning as early as possible.

All the members of the Zuckerberg family were academically gifted, and professionally high achievers. Zuckerberg was no exception. At Phillips Exeter Academy, a coeducational independent school for boarding and day students, Zuckerberg followed in the footsteps of numerous notable alumni, including Dan Brown, author of The Da Vinci Code; Lloyd Shapley, winner of the 2012 Nobel Prize in economics; and Adam D'Angelo, computer scientist and co-founder of the billion-dollar Q&A website, Quora. He won academic prizes in maths, astronomy, physics, and classical studies, was captain of the fencing team, and by the time he applied to Harvard University, he could read and write French, Hebrew, Latin, and ancient Greek, in addition to his native English.

Lesson 2: Don't ever be embarrassed about being smart, or about having a diverse range of interests. Bulling the geek is something for the school yard only; in the adult world, you do need to be modest, but not falsely so.

Zuckerberg's interest in computer programming began whilst he was still at middle school. He learned Atari BASIC programming from his father, then took private classes with software developer David Newman. Still in high school, Zuckerberg enrolled in a graduate class at the liberal arts college, Mercy College, in New York, and he built a number of programmes, including computer games illustrated by his friends; ZuckNet, a primitive version of AOL's Instant Messenger (released the following year), which enabled all the computers in his house to communicate with those in his father's dental practice; and the Synapse Media Player, which used machine learning to analyse and predict users' listening preferences. Zuckerberg's Synapse Media Player was featured in both *Slashdot* and *PC Magazine*, where it received a rating of 3/5 from reviewers.

I got my first computer in the 6th grade or so. As soon as I got it, I was interested in finding out how it worked and how the programs worked and then figuring out how to write programs at just deeper and deeper levels within the system.

Mark Zuckerberg

Lesson 3: It is never too soon to discover your passion and start developing your ideas. Encourage those around you, whatever their age, and do not dissuade yourself from trying something new because you think you are too young, or too old.

Zuckerberg enrolled at Harvard University, signing up for classes in computer science and psychology. He belonged to the Alpha Epsilon Pi (AEΠ or AEPi) fraternity, which is based upon Jewish principles (Zuckerberg was raised Jewish; see *Chapter 8: Personal Life*), and notable members have included Nobel Prize winners, Olympic sportsmen, attorney generals, film makers, entrepreneurs, and even the inventor of Tinder. It was a network which would stand Zuckerberg in good stead as he pursued his own commercial ambitions. Zuckerberg also belonged to Kirkland House, an undergraduate house popular with Harvard's athletes.

Lesson 4: The network of people around you has a significant impact on the likelihood that your projects will succeed. If you can connect yourself with intelligent, driven individuals, you will be more motivated to succeed.

Although Zuckerberg is undoubtedly academically able, and passionate about his subjects, he did not complete his degree at Harvard. He decided instead to take a semester off from studying to concentrate on developing Facebook (see *Chapter 2: Facebook*), then dropped out of the university entirely to devote his full attention to the company's growth.

All of my friends who have younger siblings who are going to college or high school - my number one piece of advice is: You should learn how to program.

Mark Zuckerberg

Lesson 5: A formal education at a university will not suit everyone. Be open to new ways of learning, gaining skills and qualifications.

Facebook

As we saw in Chapter 1: Childhood and Education, Zuckerberg was accomplished at computer programming from an early age, and saw it as much as a means of entertainment as something which had commercial value. The programming skills he learned in his teenage years, honed at Harvard, and encouraged and inspired by the fellow students he met there, set him on the path to developing what is the financially most successful, and widely used, social media platform in the world: Facebook.

Early Experiments

As a sophomore student, Zuckerberg created CourseMatch, a simple program which enabled users to select courses (informed by the previous choices of other users), and to form study groups. It was his first attempt at social networking and, though not terribly exciting, it laid the ground work for Zuckerberg's next project, Facemash.

Lesson 6: Spend time experimenting with your ideas so that you hone your skills. Your first project probably won't be a success, and it may well be that you have to test out a dozen or more ideas until you find something which is technically workable and commercially viable.

A computerised variant of the *Hot or Not?* game, Zuckerberg built Facemash with three friends, Andrew McCollum, Chris Hughes, and Dustin Moskovitz. He took images from the online face books (student profiles) of nine Harvard Houses (halls of residence), and laid them side by side, two photos at a time. Users could then vote as to who was hot, and who was not. Zuckerberg launched the site on on October 28, 2003, and wrote in his personal blog:

> *I'm a little intoxicated, not gonna lie. So what if it's not even 10 pm and it's a Tuesday night? What? The* <u>*Kirkland dormitory*</u> *face book is open on my desktop and some of these people have pretty horrendous face book pics. I almost want to put some of these faces next to pictures of some farm animals and have people vote on which is more attractive.*
>
> *— 2:49 pm*

Yea, it's on. I'm not exactly sure how the farm animals are going to fit into this whole thing (you can't really ever be sure with farm animals...), but I like the idea of comparing two people together.

— 11:10 am

Let the hacking begin.

— 2:57 pm

Lesson 7: You need to be excited about what you create. If and idea doesn't thrill you, it won't thrill anyone else either, so there is little point in pursuing it.

The hacking was a reference to the fact that Zuckerberg had no ownership of the face books' content: the images the books contained were intended for reference purposes only, to help students identify one another. He had to hack the Harvard server in order to extract the images for his own site.

The Hacker Way is an approach to building that involves continuous improvement and iteration. Hackers believe that something can always be better, and that nothing is ever complete.

Mark Zuckerberg

Facemash was an immediate hit. Zuckerberg forwarded the site to several Harvard University servers one weekend, and by Monday it had to be shut down because its popularity had overwhelmed one of the network switches. When it was discovered what he had done, Zuckerberg faced charges of violating copyright, breach of security, and violating individual privacy, and faced expulsion from the university for his actions, but these charges against him were later dropped.

Lesson 8: Be aware of security and privacy laws. Ignorance is no defence in court, and you might well find yourself in hot water if you breach such regulations. Zuckerberg got away with it by luck; you are unlikely to be so fortunate.

Not one to let the site go entirely, however, he reformatted it for his art history final, uploading 500 Augustan images, and allowed classmates to share their notes in the comments section alongside each image. According to Zuckerberg's art history professor, the project had the best grades of any final he had ever given. This was Zuckerberg's first social hack.

The facemash.com URL was auctioned off to an unknown buyer for $30,201 in October 2010.

Lesson 9: Be prepared to rework your ideas. If something isn't working out quite the way that you planned, have a Plan B up your sleeve so that your early efforts aren't wasted.

The Birth of Facebook

I literally coded Facebook in my dorm room and launched it from my dorm room. I rented a server for $85 a month, and I funded it by putting an ad on the side, and we've funded ever since by putting ads on the side.

Mark Zuckerberg

His experience with Facemash taught Zuckerberg several important things. Interviewed in *The Harvard Crimson*, a widely read magazine on the university campus, he said:

> *It is clear that the technology needed to create a centralized website is readily available ... the benefits are many...Everyone's been talking a lot about a universal face book within Harvard. I think it's kind of silly that it would take the University a couple of years to get around to it as I can do it better than they can, and I can do it in a week.*

He was aware of a need in the marketplace, that he had the skills to fulfil it, and that as he could fulfil that need faster than anyone else, he would have the first mover advantage. Zuckerberg wanted to create a website which would allow members of the university not only to see each other's images and profiles, but also to connect with one another. The idea for Facebook was born.

Lesson 10: The very best ideas are simple. You don't need a great deal of infrastructure or money to develop them, just time and effort.

Zuckerberg started coding Facebook in January 2004. Unsure exactly how to promote his new site, he asked his friends for his advice. His roommate, Dustin Moskovitz, remembers Facebook's entrance into the world like this:

> When Mark finished the site, he told a couple of friends ... then one of them suggested putting it on the Kirkland House online mailing list, which was ... three hundred people.... By the end of the night, we were ... actively watching the registration process. Within twenty-four hours, we had somewhere between twelve hundred and fifteen hundred registrants.

Lesson 11: Poll your friends and other contacts about your ideas. Make use of your collective brain power, and test out your ideas in real-life market research.

The Facebook, as it was then known, was an instant hit, but it too was not without its problems. Three of Zuckerberg's fellow students at Harvard, Cameron Winklevoss, his brother Tyler Winklevoss, and Divya Narendra, all accused Zuckerberg of agreeing to help them built a social network called Harvard Connection, and then running off with their idea. They took their complaint to *The Harvard Crimson*, to get a voice amongst the university community at large, who began to investigate the matter.

Lesson 12: Be very careful who you talk to, and who you work with, during the early stage of your projects. Keep a paper trail (email is fine) so that it is clear who the copyright belongs to, and thus who might be entitled to benefit from it in the future.

Zuckerberg was not about to sit by blindly whilst the investigation was taking place: he wanted to know what was going on so that he would be in a stronger position to respond. Using The Facebook, he was able to identify users who also worked at *The Harvard Crimson*. He cross-referenced their names with the list of failed logins to The Facebook, and then used those same passwords to try and access the users' Harvard email accounts. He successfully accessed two accounts, and was thus able to read their communications as the investigation progressed. Three of the users subsequently brought a lawsuit against Zuckerberg for this abuse of trust and breach of privacy, but the case was settled.

When The Facebook was launched, it was only available to members of Harvard University. You had to have a Harvard email address to sign up. This, whether deliberate or not, was a shrewd move, as a social network can only work if it has sufficient penetration within a group of people. People will only join if their friends have already joined, or if they expect to find people they know, and this is far easier to achieve if the pool of people is small. In the first month after The Facebook was launched, half of Harvard's undergraduate population had signed up. The appetite for the site was proven, and its model was working.

Lesson 13: Launch your products in a market you understand. It will increase your chances of success, and you can always use that as a platform from which to expand into less familiar markets at a later date.

The Facebook's Founders

To date, The Facebook had been more or less a one-man band. It was Zuckerberg's baby. But he wasn't arrogant: he knew that in order for the project to grow and realise its full potential, he had to bring other people onboard. He recruited four colleagues from amongst his social circle at Harvard to help him develop and promote The Facebook further.

Each of Zuckerberg's new recruits had their own area of expertise and responsibility. Eduardo Saverin, a Brazilian student who was president of the Harvard Investment Association, had already proven his business skills by making a $300,000 profit from strategic investments in the Brazilian oil industry. He became The Facebook's chief financial officer and business manager. It was Saverin's money, along with Zuckerberg's, which sustained the company during its first few months, and both men took equity stakes in the company.

Zuckerberg's room mate, Dustin Moskovitz, who had been there, watching, the night Zuckerberg launched The Facebook, came onboard as a programmer. He was the company's first chief technology officer and then vice president of engineering, and in March 2011 *Forbes* magazine would declare him to be the youngest self-made billionaire in history. He was just 28 years old.

Andrew McCollum did the graphic design work. He worked at the company for its first three years, then returned to Harvard University to complete his undergraduate degree, and then to do a Masters.

The final member of this founding team was Chris Hughes. A pretty, blonde boy, he had met Zuckerberg during his freshman year in 2002, and beta tested many of Zuckerberg's early designs, as well as making product suggestions. Hughes became The Facebook's spokesman, and it was his idea to open the site to schools, paving its way for global expansion. He travelled with The Facebook team to Palo Alto in the summer of 2004, but unlike his colleagues, decided to return to Harvard to complete his degree. He would rejoin them in California after his graduation in 2006.

Lesson 14: Even if you are the person with the original idea, you don't have to develop it alone, and should avoid even trying to do so. Identify your own weaknesses or shortcomings, and recruit a team around you who compensates for those gaps in your own capacity.

The Growth of Facebook

My goal was never to just create a company. A lot of people misinterpret that, as if I don't care about revenue or profit or any of those things. But what not being just a company means to me is not being just that - building something that actually makes a really big change in the world.

Mark Zuckerberg

The Facebook's expansion began in March 2004, when the site was opened up to students at the universities of Columbia, Stanford, and Yale. The utility of the network, combined with the sense of exclusivity — you had to be at one of these elite universities to join — made it instantly popular.

Lesson 15: Exclusivity is a powerful marketing tool as you can create demand for a product before it is even available. Then, once people can finally buy into your idea, or sign up for your product, they will be far more likely to do so.

In the summer of 2004, Zuckerberg and his colleagues travelled to Palo Alto, in the centre of Silicon Valley. They incorporated The Facebook as a company, and Sean Parker, co-founder of the file sharing site Napster, became the company's first president. He had already been advising Zuckerberg informally for some time, and he convinced Zuckerberg and his colleagues (bar Hughes, see above) to stay. Venture capitalist Peter Thiel, who had made his money as the co-founder of PayPal alongside Elon Musk, made a $500,000 angel investment in exchange for a 10.2% equity stake in The Facebook.

Other seed round investments were made by Reid Hoffman, CEO of LinkedIn; entrepreneur Mark Pincus, who had sold his first start-up, Freeloader, Inc., for $38 million and would later found online games company Zynga; and Maurice Werdegar of Western Technology Investment.

Lesson 16: Even digital businesses need to have a physical home. Find somewhere where you will have a lot of support, professional and technical as well as financial, and which is accessible to potential investors and clients.

2005 was to be the year that The Facebook really took off. The company now had its base in Palo Alto, where tech entrepreneurs and investors were two a penny, yet all excited about Zuckerberg's idea. He dropped the "The" from The Facebook's name, and henceforth the company was simply Facebook. The company opened out to 21 universities in the United Kingdom (Oxford and Cambridge first amongst them, in keeping with the idea that this was a network for elite university students and alumni); they launched a version for high schools, which was by invitation only; and additional networks were created for the employees of Apple, Microsoft, and other major tech companies. By the end of the year Facebook was available to more than 2,000 colleges and universities, and 25,000 high schools, in the United States and Canada, the United Kingdom and Ireland, Australia and New Zealand, and Mexico. The company raised $12.7 million in venture capital from Accel Partners, valuing Facebook at $98 million.

Lesson 17: A company cannot grow without money, either from income that it has generated, or from investors. The advantage of seeking funding from venture capitalists is that they bring their expertise and connections to the table, as well as cash, and have a vested interest in seeing your company succeed.

In summer 2006, Facebook opened up to anyone around the world, so long as they were aged 13 and older, and had a valid email address. Zuckerberg closed Facebook's Series B funding round with investments from Greylock Partners and Meritech Capital, as well as additional funds from Thiel and Accel Partners. The valuation of Facebook stood at $500 million, not bad for 18 months work.

I mean, we've built a lot of products that we think are good, and will help people share photos and share videos and write messages to each other. But it's really all about how people are spreading Facebook around the world in all these different countries. And that's what's so amazing about the scale that it's at today.

Sales Negotiations and Profitability

Facebook had grown very quickly, and it seemed inevitable that Zuckerberg and his co-founders would want to realise their investment, selling out at least part of their stakes as soon as possible. Facebook's main competitor, MySpace, was sold to News Corp in 2005, and market analysts thought Zuckerberg would avail himself of a similar exit strategy. In quick succession, however, Zuckerberg turned down a $750 million offer from an unknown bidder, and a $1 billion offer from Yahoo! Microsoft suggested it would make a $300–500 million investment in exchange for a 5% stake, and Google followed suit. But Zuckerberg wasn't interested. He wanted to keep Facebook independent, stating:

> We're not really looking to sell the company... We're not looking to IPO anytime soon. It's just not the core focus of the company.

His view may well have been shaped by the fact that Thiel had already created an internal valuation of $8 billion for Facebook, based on its predicted revenues. Microsoft was allowed to invest $240 million for a 1.6% stake, implying a valuation of $15 billion, and Hong Kong billionaire Li Ka-shing invested a further $60 million.

Lesson 18: Every company must have an exit strategy — its the way you and your investors recoup your investment — but you do not have to disclose it to others, and it is often beneficial to hold that plan close to your chest.

The interesting thing is that all of these investments were speculative: Facebook had a huge network of users, but they paid no subscription fees, and the site generated almost no revenue. Zuckerberg was quite open about his failure to monetise the site, saying:

> I don't think social networks can be monetized in the same way that search did ... In three years from now we have to figure out what the optimum model is. But that is not our primary focus today.

For Facebook's board members, monetisation was a priority, however. The board recruited Sheryl Sandberg, Vice President of Global Online Sales and Operations at Google, as Facebook's chief operating officer in 2008. Zuckerberg had known Sandberg for just a few months, having met her at a Christmas drinks party and then again at the World Economic Forum in Davos, but he was convinced she was the perfect fit for the role. He wasn't wrong.

Lesson 19: A company has to make a profit: that is its purpose. If you don't intend it to generate a profit, you should look at other models, such as a not-for-profit (or charity).

Sandberg was the first woman in a senior role at Facebook. As far as she was concerned, the company was "primarily interested in building a really cool site; profits, they assumed, would follow." Sandberg decided a more proactive approach was required. She brainstormed ideas with Facebook employees, and concluded that advertising revenues would be the main source of monetisation. The board agreed with her findings, and Sandberg changed the company's advertising model. As a result, Facebook had positive cash flow for the very first time in September 2009.

Advertising works most effectively when it's in line with what people are already trying to do. And people are trying to communicate in a certain way on Facebook - they share information with their friends, they learn about what their friends are doing - so there's really a whole new opportunity for a new type of advertising model within that.

Mark Zuckerberg

Lesson 20: If you are unsure about how to develop your income streams, or even what those streams should be, ask for expert advice.

Acquisitions

Once Facebook became profitable, it was in a position to start investing in other companies, and to make wholesale acquisitions when it was useful to do so. These acquisitions were usually of competing products, or services which could be added to Facebook's portfolio to make their own offering more attractive.

Lesson 21: You do not need to build every aspect of your company from scratch. It is perfectly possible — and often advisable — to buy in expertise or capacity.

Examples of early acquisitions include FriendFeed, a real-time news feed aggregator which brought together users' feeds from multiple social media platforms, blogs, etc. and was the brainchild of Bret Taylor (co-creator of Google Maps) and Paul Buchheit (the lead developer of Gmail, who also prototyped Google AdSense); Octazen Solutions, a Malaysian start-up whose software could be used to import contacts from multiple sources; photo sharing system Divvyshot; and the team behind Storylane, a start-up which allowed users to share their interests with a given community.

Such acquisitions made Facebook increasingly attractive to investors as they enriched the platform's portfolio and technical capacity. After the company had its IPO in February 2012 (see *IPO*, below) Facebook had a much larger pool of cash to draw from, and the board decided to make two further, phenomenal acquisitions: Instagram, and WhatsApp Inc.

Lesson 22: Only buy into other companies which enhance your core offering, or prevent your competitors increasing their share in the marketplace.

First released in October 2010, Instagram is a social network focused on photo and video sharing. It's square, Polaroid-style images were distinctive (though in later versions of the app alternative aspect ratios were also popular), and users also liked the fact that they could add filters to their images. The free app had 100 million users in its first 18 months, and in April 2012, Facebook acquired Instagram for $1 billion in cash and stock. It was a shrewd investment: Instagram trebled its number of users over the next two-year period, a rate of growth which even Facebook itself could not match.

Lesson 23: If you see a company which has significant growth potential, and is cash generative, think seriously about adding it to your portfolio. It will probably be a sound decision.

Although Facebook paid a gargantuan sum for Instagram, it would shell out even more money for messaging service WhatsApp. Created by two former employees of Yahoo!, who had ironically enough been turned down for jobs at Facebook, WhatsApp launched in November 2009. By spring 2014, it had 500 million users a month, and today that figure is estimated at around 1 billion users. Facebook acquired WhatsApp in February 2014 for $19 billion, of which $4 billion was paid in cash, $12 billion was in Facebook shares, and the remaining $3 billion was in restricted stock options for WhatsApp's founders.

Lesson 24: Communications are key to everyday life, and any idea which can piggyback on that in an intuitive, but unobtrusive, way is worth exploring.

Immediately after the acquisition of WhatsApp, Zuckerberg gave the keynote address at the Mobile World Congress in Barcelona. He explained that the acquisition of Whats-App was a key component of his Internet.org vision (see *Chapter 3:* internet.org), later explaining in an interview with TechCrunch that:

> *The idea… is to develop a group of basic internet services that would be free of charge to use – 'a 911 for the internet.' These could be a social networking service like Facebook, a messaging service, maybe search and other things like weather. Providing a bundle of these free of charge to users will work like a gateway drug of sorts – users who may be able to afford data services and phones these days just don't see the point of why they would pay for those data services. This would give them some context for why they are important, and that will lead them to paying for more services like this – or so the hope goes.*

Lesson 25: Even if you think that something you have done, or plan to do, is a good idea, you need to be able to explain it in a cohesive, convincing way to other people.

Developments in WhatsApp subsequent to the app's acquisition by Facebook include the ability to handle voice calls, and the dropping of its annual $1 subscription charge. Both of these changes increased its appeal to customers, with *Forbes* magazine predicting that WhatsApp and Skype would have lost conventional communications companies a combined total of $386 billion between 2012 and 2018. Facebook and its subsidiaries, once again, are changing the way in which we communicate, and in which money is made.

Initial Public Offering (IPO)

Despite Zuckererg's own initial resistance to the idea of an IPO (see *Sales Negotiations and Profitability*, above), it was inevitable that Facebook would one day have a public share offering: no one company could afford to buy Facebook in its entirety, and yet the investors had some how to realise their investment.

Zuckerberg's leadership, and conviction about the potential of Facebook, was essential because it enabled him to grow the company to well beyond the size estimated, and valuation offered, by Yahoo!, Microsoft, and Google. His confidence, and his face in his product, paid off, and by ensuring that he assembled around himself a world-class team, he was able to gain the largest valuation to date for a newly public company. Facebook's IPO raised $16 billion, making it the third largest in U.S. history.

So how did it happen? What steps did Zuckerberg take?

By resisting both buyouts and taking the company public for a protracted period, Zuckerberg was able to grow Facebook (increasing its ultimate valuation), and create an appetite in the marketplace for its shares: numerous investors wanted a piece of the action, but couldn't buy in, and this made the company even more tantalising. He told *PC Magazine* in 2010, "we are definitely in no rush."

Lesson 26: Bide your time. If you understand what people want, you can whet their appetite, and allow it to build over time, until you are ready to deliver and they will pay the best possible price.

On 1 February, 2012, Zuckerberg filed Facebook's S1 document with the US Securities and Exchange Commission in Washington DC. Key points of the document were an outline of the company's current position (845 million active monthly users; 2.7 billion daily likes and comments; and an increasing but decelerating increase in the number of users and income); a statement that Zuckerberg would retain 22% of Facebook's shares, but 57% of the voting shares; and an indication that Facebook expected to raise $5 billion from the IPO. It would therefore be one of the largest IPOs in history.

Zuckerberg personally led the roadshow for the Facebook IPO, and he did it in his own inimitable way. He turned up at the first investors' meeting wearing a hoodie, not a suit, which caused consternation in more conservative business circles, and generated plenty of column inches. Perhaps that was the idea of it. Once investor described the move (which may or may not have been deliberate) as "mark of immaturity," but it could also be seen as Zuckerberg reminding would-be investors that the ball was in his court, and he would run the roadshow and the IPO as he saw fit: he didn't need the money, and therefore had power.

Lesson 27: You need to strike a careful balance between being yourself, and doing what investors and customers expect. Investors tend to be naturally conservative, and easily put off by eccentricities.

Valuations of Facebook fluctuated significantly during this period, though overall they increased. The low initial estimate was $28 to $35 per share, but this was quickly revised up to $34 to $38 per share. This top estimate gave a total valuation for the company of $104 billion, and yet there was still strong demand from would-be investors, especially from retail investors. The previous strong performance of Google and LinkedIn have investors confidence, and no one wanted to risk missing out.

Lesson 28: You can make predictions about how your company will fare based on the performance of other similar companies, though this is by no means a fail-safe strategy.

Two days before the IPO, Zuckerberg announced that due to high demand, 25% more shares would be released. The stock would debut with 421 million shares. Some analysts did express concern, thinking that the estimates overvalued Facebook, especially given concerns about the company's advertising model: just days before the IPO, General Motors announced publicly it was going to cancel its $10 million advertising campaign on Facebook due to underperformance.

The Facebook IPO was fascinating to watch as it was a cultural event as much as a business one: *Reuters* declared it to be "a cultural phenomenon", and Zuckerberg, ever the showman, ran a series of events in the run up to the IPO. The night before it was due to take place, he led an all-night hackathon; CBS coined the word Zuckonomics to describe the way in which the IPO was playing out; and Zuckerberg rang a bell in the Facebook campus's Hackers Square to announce, in a time-honoured fashion, that the company was going public.

Lesson 29: Even fairly standard financial transactions can appear exciting if marketed in the right way.

Trading in Facebook shares was due to begin at 11 am on 18 May, 2012, but it was delayed by half an hour due to technical issues at NASDAQ. This didn't bode well, as there were to be technical glitches throughout the day, and buyers couldn't always see whether or not their trades had been successful. The opening share price had been set at $38, and shot up as high as $45, but Facebook couldn't maintain this price. When the price fell below $38, the underwriters had to wade in to keep the price steady, and the day's trading closed with a disappointing share price of just $38.23. The stock did set a new record for the trading volume of an IPO (460 million shares), and it raised $16 billion. The IPO confirmed Zuckerberg's own stake as being worth $19 billion, so all in all, it wasn't a bad day for him.

Lesson 30: You can't control everything, and there will be multiple factors outside of your control which affect how your business fares. Be prepared to be pleasantly surprised on some occasions, and sorely disappointed on others.

In the fortnight following the IPO, Facebook's share price declined. Trading curbs were used to slow the decline, but Facebook closed its first full week of trading down at $31.91, and after two weeks, the share price was just $27.72. It would be four weeks before the company made a modest gain, and when the *Wall Street Journal* described the IPO as a fiasco, they weren't the only ones holding that opinion. More than 40 legal suits against Facebook's lead underwriters, Morgan Stanley, JP Morgan, and Goldman Sachs, followed, with Morgan Stanley being forced to settle allegations of improperly influencing research analysts for $5 million. The reputation of both Morgan Stanley (the primary underwriter) and NASDAQ was damaged due to the botching of the IPO.

Those investors who did keep their Facebook shares (and nerve), rather than dumping them in panic and fury shortly after the IPO, made a shrewd decision. Today the share price stands at $111, and it has been growing consistently since it hit an all-time low of $18.06 in August 2012. The current forecast, drawn from 54 polled investment analysts, is that Facebook will outperform the market in the coming year, and they have a median 12-month target of $135, with some predicting the share price could go as high as $170 by the end of that period. It seems that the IPO wasn't such a fiasco after all.

Lesson 31: You need to be in business for the long haul. Any company can increase or decrease dramatically in value in the short term, but on the whole a well managed company with a steady stream of quality products will grow and make money over time.

Legal Disputes The extraordinary success of Facebook, and the wealth which the company has generated for Zuckerberg, have meant, perhaps inevitably, that there are plenty of people who are extremely jealous of what he has received. Some of them believe that they are entitled to a slice of the Facebook pie for the early involvement or ideas; others are just chancing their luck. Whatever the background, such individuals are canny enough to realise that whether their claim is valid or not, simply making allegations will quite likely catapult them into the limelight, giving them their 30 seconds of fame.

For the Winklevoss brothers, that period of fame has lasted even longer, though it hasn't exactly shown them in a good light.

When I was in college I did a lot of stupid things and I don't want to make an excuse for that. Some of the things that people accuse me of are true, some of them aren't. There are pranks, IMs.

Mark Zuckerberg

From the week of Facebook's launch, until June 2008, Zuckerberg was at loggerheads with twins twins Cameron and Tyler Winklevoss, and their classmate Divya Narendra, all three of whom had studied alongside him at Harvard. The plaintiffs alleged that they had hired Zuckerberg in 2003 to help them build a campus dating site called Harvard Connection, but that he had stalled their project and ultimately stolen their idea, turning it in to Facebook. Zuckerberg filed countersuit, accusing the plaintiffs of unfair business practices, and the case was settled out of court.

Lesson 32: Be prepared for people you have worked with in the past to turn against you when you start to taste success. Their jealousy can be your downfall, so protect yourself accordingly.

But the story doesn't end there. The settlement was based on stock, and by extension, Facebook's valuation. The plaintiffs argued that Zuckerberg had fraudulently misrepresented the value of Facebook stock, and took him back to court. It was a public relations nightmare, and one which Zuckerberg surely thought he had seen the back of.

Thankfully for Zuckerberg, Judge James Ware of Federal District Court in San Jose sided with Zuckerberg, enforcing the earlier decision. The judge noted that the plaintiffs were upset that Facebook's valuation was not the $15 billion that recent media reports had suggested, but that Facebook's own valuation was fair. He also suggested that the Winklevoss twins' father, Howard Winklevoss, was the main force behind the dispute. The Winklevosses and Narendra took their handout and slunk away, and Facebook issued the following statement:

We are happy that Judge Ware enforced the agreement settling our dispute with the ConnectU founders [ConnectU is the company founded by the Winklevoss twins]. *ConnectU's founders were represented by six lawyers and a professor at Wharton Business School when they signed the settlement agreement. The ConnectU founders understood the deal they made, and we are gratified that the court rejected their false allegations of fraud. Their challenge was simply a case of "buyer's remorse," as described by the Boston court earlier this month.*

We were disappointed that we had to litigate the settlement, as we believed we were caught in the middle of a fee dispute between ConnectU's founders and its former counsel. Nevertheless, we can now consider this chapter closed and wish the Winklevoss brothers the best of luck in their future endeavors.

Lesson 33: When you win, be gracious, and humble. People will have far more respect for you as a result.

The sincerity of that final clause may be questionable, because as you might imagine, there is no love lost between Zuckerberg and the Winklevoss twins. Their original idea might in some way have contributed to Zuckerberg's formulation of Facebook, but even if the Harvard Connection had been successful, and Facebook never even born, it was so limited in its scope and application that it could never have realised even a fraction of the growth that Facebook has seen. Unadulterated greed and jealousy are the driving forces behind their law suits, nothing more.

The Winklevoss twins were not the only people to claim Zuckerberg had acted in a less than honorable fashion, however. His co-founder of Facebook, Eduardo Saverin, had a claim to make too, and in his case it was rather more valid.

As well as putting his own money into the project, Saverin was Facebook's first chief financial officer and business manager (see *Facebook and its Founders*, above). In 2012, *Business Insider* magazine obtained a private email sent by Zuckerberg suggesting that he had knowingly cut Saverin out of Facebook in 2005, and diluted his stake in the company. Saverin's exit was central to the plot of the 2010 film, *The Social Network*, but even the film's writers could not have anticipated this particular turn of events.

The email, copied below, made Zuckerberg's intentions, and the impact on Saverin, clear.

[Redacted],
This email should probably be attorney-client privileged, not quite how to do that though.
Anyhow, Sean and I have agreed that a price of one-half cent per share is the way to

go for now. We think we can maybe almost justify and if not, we'll just deal with it later.

We also agreed that if the company bonusing us the amount we need for the shares, plus tax, is a good solution to the problem of us all being completely broke.

As far as Eduardo goes, I think it's safe to ask for his permission to make grants. Especially if we do it in conjunction with raising money. It's probably even OK to say how many shares we're adding to the pool. It's probably less OK to tell him who's getting the shares, just because he might have adverse reaction initially. But I think we may even be able to make him understand that.

Is there a way to do this without making it painfully apparent to him that he's being diluted to 10%?

OK, that's all for now. I'll send you the list of grants I need made in another email in a second. Sean can send you grants for his people when he stops coughing up his lungs.

Hope you guys both feel better,

Mark

His lawyer's response made it explicitly clear to Zuckerberg that as Saverin would be the only only shareholder diluted by the grants issuances, he would have a legitimate claim to Facebook breaching fiduciary duty, and recommended that to avoid this happening, Zuckerberg should get Saverin's consent for the issuances in writing. Zuckerberg did not heed his advice, and Saverin successfully sued Facebook for approximately 5% of the company. At the IPO, that stake was work around $5 billion.

Lesson 34: Treat those you work with fairly. Not only is it the right thing, morally speaking, to do, but if you breach their trust and abuse them, it might well come back to haunt you in the future.

A number of smaller lawsuits have also been brought against Facebook, by users and their representatives. A brief summary of two of the more interesting cases is below.

Lane v Facebook was a class action challenging Facebook's privacy settings. When Facebook launched Beacon (which broadcast users' purchases from Facebook's affiliate sites), the default privacy settings required users to opt out, rather than to opt in. Many users were unaware of this fact, and as their purchases were then broadcast to their social and professional networks via their Facebook newsfeed, they felt that their privacy had been breached. The lawyers representing the plaintiffs claimed that Facebook had broken Electronic Communications Privacy Act, Video Privacy Protection Act, and

California Consumer Legal Remedies Act, and also violated the violated the California Computer Crime Law and the Computer Fraud and Abuse Act. Facebook denied wrongdoing but did establish a cash settlement fund of $9.5 million. This was used to open and run a privacy foundation designed to educate users. Facebook terminated the Beacon program, paid the lawyers fees, and made small compensation payments ($1,000 to $15,000) to the class representatives.

Lesson 35: Legal cases can be expensive, and even if they don't upset your firm financially, they do no good for your reputation in the public eye.

In recent years, Facebook has collaborated with academics to conduct a number of experiments on its users. These include "A 61-Million-Person Experiment in Social Influence And Political Mobilization," which Facebook ran during the 2010 Presidential election in the US; and "Emotional Contagion Through Social Networks", a controversial study in 2014 which manipulated the balance of positive and negative messages which 700,000 users saw. The study was criticised for its ethics, causing the privacy watchdog group Electronic Privacy Information Center (EPIC) to file a formal complaint with the Federal Trade. They alleged that Facebook had conducted the study without the knowledge or consent of their users, and secretly conducted a psychological experiment on their emotions, breaching their privacy. The outcome of this case is as yet undecided, but the law professor James Grimmelmann has stated that he believes the action is "illegal, immoral, and mood-altering".

Lesson 36: The ethics of research is a mine field. Take advice on what you are doing, and if you think that you might be straying into grey waters, take a step back, and think carefully what the repercussions might be.

Internet.org

There is a huge need and a huge opportunity to get everyone in the world connected, to give everyone a voice and to help transform society for the future. The scale of the technology and infrastructure that must be built is unprecedented, and we believe this is the most important problem we can focus on.

Mark Zuckerberg

With billions of dollars in personal wealth, not to mention command of the Facebook platform, Zuckerberg has to decide what his legacy will be. He's only in his early 30s, and will unlikely be inclined, or able, to replicate the commercial success of Facebook, but that doesn't mean he is unable to make a world-altering changes in other fields. We will talk about his charitable giving in *Chapter 6: Philanthropy*, but potentially far wider reaching is his Internet.org initiative.

Internet.org is a partnership between Facebook and Ericsson, MediaTek, Nokia, Opera Software, Qualcomm, and Samsung. It was launched in August 2013, and Zuckerberg issued a 10-page white paper, and gave a detailed video interview for TechCrunch, elaborating on the idea.

Lesson 37: If you achieve a position of dominance in any given market, you can leverage that position to bring onboard partners to help you achieve more than you would be capable of doing alone.

Put simply, Zuckerberg believes that "connectivity is a human right," and that basic web servers should be available worldwide for free. The first Internet.org summit was held in October 2014 in India, where Zuckerberg met with Indian Prime Minister Narendra Modi to discuss the project.

Internet.org provides free internet services through an app called Free Basics. Although on the face of it it is an admirable initiative, with much to recommend it, it has its detractors, and their concerns do have some basis.

Lesson 38: No idea is without flaws. Be prepared to take criticism, and to adapt your idea accordingly.

Firstly, critics argue that Internet.org violates net neutrality. Facebook is, in essence, an unregulated gatekeeper to the Free Basics platform, deciding which services will and will not be provided on it. Facebook's rivals might well be discriminated against.

To date, more than a dozen countries are offering Free Basics, delivering it through approved mobile network providers. The service was launched in India in October 2015, but Zuckerberg was, perhaps unfairly, accused of targeting India's poor with Facebook proxies. The Telecom Regulatory Authority of India (TRAI) banned the service in the country just a year after its launch on the grounds that Free Basics' commercials were misleading, and they had masked the identity of its supporters in a manner nicknamed "astroturfing".

Lesson 39: You need to tread carefully with regulatory bodies, carefully researching their remit, and building relationships with their decision makers. Doing so will increase your chances of survival in what can otherwise be hostile waters.

To date, the Internet.org project has brought an estimated 19 million new internet users online. Kids are able to do their homework and enhance their education, entrepreneurs are able to establish, expand and market their businesses, and millions more people are able to learn about keeping healthy, their rights, and in general about the world around them. Any app can be offered on the platform so long as it meets Free Basics' guidelines, granting developers access to vast new markets in the developing world.

Lesson 40: When you do good, you can also earn benefits for yourself.

Wealth

In December 2015, Business Inside magazine estimated Zuckerberg's personal wealth (including his shareholding in Facebook) at $46 billion. He made nearly $12 billion of that wealth in 2015 alone. As his salary from Facebook is just $1 a year, this increase was driven almost entirely by Facebook's rising share price, though he has made personal investments in companies such as Mastery Connect ($5 million), Alt School ($100 million), Vicarious ($52 million), and Panorama Education ($4 million), as well. Since 2010, Time magazine has declared him as one of the 100 wealthiest and most influential people in the world, and his income stream looks as though it will only increase in the coming years.

Awards and Accolades

Unusually for a virtuoso billionaire, Zuckerberg hasn't actively courted awards and accolades. He has been satisfied to be allowed to run his company the way he wants to, and to generate vast sums of money from doing so.

But awards have come his way: his achievements are so remarkable that they cannot be ignored. In In 2010, he was named the Person of the Year by *Time* magazine, and *The Jerusalem Post* followed up with a similar accolade the following year, declaring him as one of the 'Most Influential Jews'. In 2016, Zuckerberg was nominated as CEO of the Year at the 9th Annual Crunchies Award, TechCrunch's recognition of the leaders in the tech field, and won the award in spite of stiff competition from Tim Cook (Apple), Jack Dorsey (Twitter/Square), Susan Wojcicki (YouTube), and Elon Musk (Tesla).

Lesson 41: You will only be considered truly successful if you are recognised outside of your specific sector, and gain general acclaim.

For a self-proclaimed geek like Zuckerberg, however, one of his proudest moments is likely to be his cameo appearance on *The Simpsons*. In the "Loan-A-Lisa" episode, Lisa takes Nelson to a start-up event to meet successful founders, in the hope that they will inspire him to stay on in education rather than dropping out to run his business. Unfortunately for Lisa, the founders they meet are Zuckerberg, Bill Gates, and Richard Branson, none of whom completed their degrees. The episode aired in October 2010, two days after the release of *The Social Network*, and it was watched by an estimated 8.63 million households in the US. Critics agreed it was generally entertaining, though by no means the most hilarious, or insightful, of *The Simpsons*' episodes.

Lesson 42: Be prepared to laugh at yourself. Popular culture creates heroes and villains, and if you are game for a laugh, you are more likely to be considered as one of the former.

Philanthropy

A squirrel dying in front of your house may be more relevant to your interests right now than people dying in Africa.

Mark Zuckerberg

Having come from a very ordinary background, and achieved great things as a result of his own education and the educational background of his parents, Zuckerberg was never going to be the spoilt rich kid. He has worked for his money, and understands acutely how much power it gives him. His early donations included an undisclosed sum to Diaspora, an open-source personal web server; and $100 million to the public schools system in Newark. Modest, Zuckerberg wanted to make the latter donation anonymous, but New Jersey's Governor, Chris Christie, and Newark's Mayor, Cory Booker, convinced him to go public.

Lesson 43: Although you shouldn't boast about your generosity, there is no need to hide it either. By giving in a responsible way, you can inspire others to do likewise.

In 2010, Zuckerberg decided to sign The Giving Pledge, a commitment to give at least 50% of his wealth to charity, and to give it during his lifetime. Other signatories of the pledge include Bill Gates and Warren Buffet. The reason for spending before you die are numerous, and include the ability to decide which projects you support, to leverage your own professional network and skills to maximise the positive outcomes of the donations, and the reduction in administration costs if you don't have to use a succession of trust vehicles and lawyers to make decisions for you.

Lesson 44: If you make money, you have a responsibility to give back to the community which has helped you succeed, and to do so in an as effective manner as possible.

Since signing the pledge, Zuckerberg has donated 18 million Facebook shares (with a value totalling $990 million) to the Silicon Valley Community Foundation, the largest community foundation in the US, which makes grants to domestic and international charities working in community building, economic security, education, immigration, and widening opportunities; and he also have $25 million to help combat the spread of the ebola virus in 2014.

Chan Zuckerberg Initiative

The question I ask myself like almost every day is, 'Am I doing the most important thing I could be doing?'

Mark Zuckerberg

Zuckerberg's daughter, Max, was born on 1 December, 2015, and a week later Zuckerberg and his wife, Priscilla Chan (see *Chapter 8: Personal Life*) marked the occasion by publishing an open letter to their child. In the letter, they pledged to donate 99% of their Facebook shares (valued at the time at around $45 billion) to a new foundation, the Chan Zuckerberg Initiative. The foundation works in health and education, and the money will be spent over the course of Chan and Zuckerberg's lifetimes.

Lesson 45: Consider the fact that changes in your personal and professional life can significantly alter your outlook on life. Be flexible, and if need be, change the course of your actions accordingly.

Technically the Chan Zuckerberg Initiative is neither a private foundation nor a charity: it is a limited liability company. This means that it is able to generate a profit, to lobby government bodies, and to make political donations. This model has drawn some criticism, as the donations Zuckerberg makes to the initiative will be tax deductible. In the words of Michael Miello at *The Daily Beast*, "If purity is the essence here, there seems no reason that the tax system should support it. Zuckerberg can afford to dabble in politics and society without massive subsidies from the rest of the country."

The published mission of the Chan Zuckerberg Initiative is to "advance human potential and promote equality in areas such as health, education, scientific research and energy". Zuckerberg and Chan intend to take the long view, targeting their resources at the biggest challenges they expect the next generation to face. The timeframe for their work is clear, as in the open letter they wrote:

Consider disease. Today we spend about 50 times more as a society treating people who are sick than we invest in research so you won't get sick in the first place...

Medicine has only been a real science for less than 100 years, and we've already seen complete cures for some diseases and good progress for others. As technology accelerates, we have a real shot at preventing, curing or managing all or most of the rest in the next 100 years.

Lesson 46: Put your money and your influence behind issues you really care about. Be passionate about your giving, and you will be more likely to have a quantifiable, sustainable, and beneficial impact.

Today, the Chan Zuckerberg Initiative is just a few months old, so we cannot yet see its impact on the causes which Chan and Zuckerberg so clearly feel strongly about. In a year's time, hopefully we will see the budding of something great, and in a decade or so, real, positive changes will be visible.

Political Involvement

Politically, Zuckerberg is a pragmatist. He does not appear to have any particularly strong ideological leanings, and as he has never specified his own political views, there are those who would place him in both the conservative and liberal camps. It is likely, and indeed a shrewd business move, that he supports those politicians and parties best able to represent the commercial interests of Facebook, and the philanthropic interests of the Chan Zuckerberg Initiative, at the current moment in time.

Lesson 47: There is no shame in being a pragmatist. As a company director, you are legally obliged to do your best for the company and its shareholders, and this might well involve lobbying, or campaigning for, different political groups.

That is not to say that Zuckerberg doesn't get involved in politics, however. In February 2013, he hosted his first fundraising event, for New Jersey Governor Chris Christie. Zuckerberg knew Christie from the time of his $100 million donation to Newark's public schools (see *Chapter 6: Philanthropy*), and he would later that year run a similar fundraiser for Cory Booker. On both of these occasions, Zuckerberg's own interest was pushing for education reform, and he believed that these two men would help him do it.

In April 2013, Zuckerberg also launched a new lobbying group, FWD.us, which had three core aims: immigration reform; improving state education; and enabling more technological breakthroughs of benefit to the general public. FWD.us was backed by a number of Silicon Valley entrepreneurs, and its first President was Zuckerberg's friend, Joe Green. The lobbying group is not aligned to a particular political party — it favours the bipartisan approach —and though there is some positive evidence of its impact on policy (TechCrunch reported that FWD.us drove 33,500 calls to Congress in summer 2013, and a total of 125,000 actions including social media shares), that is less than the founders might have liked. Other criticisms of FWD.us is that it has a poorly defined long-term agenda, and doesn't articulate its vision well.

Lesson 48: Be open about the issues which are important to you, and use your platform to advocate change.

In terms of other, politically charged issues which he cares about, Zuckerberg has openly supported gay and trans-gender rights, riding with Facebook's carnival float at the annual San Francisco Lesbian, Gay, Bisexual, and Transgender Pride Celebration in 2013. In the aftermath of the Paris terror attacks in December 2015, he spoke out in support of the Muslim community, explaining that he wanted "to add my voice in support of Muslims in our community and around the world" and reminding others that "as a Jew, my parents taught me that we must stand up against attacks on all communities." Zuckerberg has also voiced his support for the Black Lives Matter campaign, explaining in a memo to staff that "*Black Lives Matter* doesn't mean other lives don't — it's simply asking that the black community also achieves the justice they deserve." The memo was a response to his discovery that some Facebook employees crossed out Black Lives Matter graffiti, overwriting it with All Lives Matter. He was angry about this fact, on the grounds that the very act of crossing something out is a "means silencing speech, or that one person's speech is more important than another's."

Personal Life

Zuckerberg is still only 31 years old, and so the timeline of his personal life is correspondingly short. We discussed his early years in *Chapter 1: Childhood and Education*, and so this chapter can only really consider his personal relationships and religion.

Nothing much is known about Zuckerberg's teenage dating exploits, though that might well be because his forays into relationships were few and far between. He met Priscilla Chan at a frat party in his sophomore year at Harvard, where she was also studying, and the couple started dating in 2003, a year before the birth of Facebook.

Chan was born in Braintree, Massachusetts, and grew up just outside Boston. The oldest of three sisters, here parents were two ethnically Chinese refugees, who arrived in the US from the Vietnamese refugee boats. In her childhood she spoke Cantonese at home.

Though quiet and usually in the background, Chan is at least as smart as Zuckerberg, which is no doubt what attracts him to her. She was her class' Valedictorian in high school, and she graduated from Harvard University with a BA in biology, and a minor in Spanish. On graduating, she taught science for a year, then when on to medical school at the University of California. She graduated in 2012, married Zuckerberg the same year, and works as a paediatrician. It is likely that it is Chan who pushed for the focus on health at the Chan Zuckerberg Initiative.

Lesson 49: Find a partner, in life as well as in business, who is your equal, intellectually speaking, and shares your values. This will create the richest kind of relationship.

Maxima Chan Zuckerberg (Chén Míngyǔ, to give her her Chinese name) on 1 December 2015, and her parents presented her to the world with their announcement of the Chan Zuckerberg Initiative (see *Chapter 6: Philanthropy*). The baby, known as Max, was long-awaited: Chan had suffered from three previous miscarriages, and so it was inevitably with trepidation that the couple announced her pregnancy, and with relief when the baby arrived safely.

Zuckerberg blogged to his 33 million followers about Chan's miscarriages. Although there were those who felt this was over sharing, plenty more were positive about his honesty. He wrote:

We hope that sharing our experience will give more people the same hope we felt and will help more people feel comfortable sharing their stories...

Most people don't discuss miscarriages because you worry your problems will distance you or reflect upon you - as if you're defective or did something to cause this. So you struggle on your own.

For anyone, but a man in particular, to speak out about the pain and loneliness of losing a child (and, in this tragic case, three children), took many by surprise, but has hopefully opened up a forum for others to discuss what they have been through, and to find support online. It also moves Zuckerberg from his pedestal as a godlike figure in the tech world, and reveals to both his fans and his detractors, that he too is a mortal, capable of misfortune and suffering like any other man.

Lesson 50: Personal loss can happen to any of us, however much money we have. Be sensitive to those around you in their time of need, offer support, and be prepared to ask for help from others when you need it

Conclusion

Not all of us can be like Mark Zuckerberg, sadly. Intellectually, he is far ahead of most of his Harvard University peers, let alone the general public, and his breadth of interests and knowledge — from art history to Latin — is unquestionably unusual too. There are only a certain number of Facebooks which can be founded in any one generation, one man at a time for can be *Time* magazine's Person of the Year, and with $46 billion currently behind him (and more with every passing day), Zuckerberg indisputably has an advantage on the average man on the street.

But that is not to say that his personal attributes, his values and interests, and the career path he has chosen cannot be a source of inspiration to us all. There are plenty of lessons we can learn from him, and apply in our own lives, which will put us in a stronger position intellectually, personally, financially, and in business.

If we were to summarise the content of this book into five unforgettable lessons from Mark Zuckerberg, those lessons would have to be as follows:

1. If you have an idea, develop it. And if it doesn't work out, have another idea, and develop that one too. Eventually you will come up with an idea that you are satisfied with and which is commercially viable.

2. When you have found that idea, focus on it. Zuckerberg has focused on Facebook every single day for the past 12 years. It's taken a great deal of blood, sweat and tears, not to mention brain power, to get this far.

3. Remember that human communication and interaction are the most powerful and emotional channels we have. If you can tap into our desire and need to engage with one another, in a way which is effective but unobtrusive, you have the basis for a successful company.

4. Give back to the society you live and work in. No one succeeds on their own, and whether you are at the top of your game, or still climbing the ladder, you have a responsibility to contribute your time, money, energy and ideas to making the world you live in a better place.

5. Even if you live and sleep work, you still need someone in your life to support you when things are tough. Don't overlook your personal life if you want to be truly rich.

Think carefully about what you can do, in each aspect of our life, to apply Zuckerberg's lesson. Your ultimate goal is not just to make money, but to be fulfilled, and to play a positive role in the world. Zuckerberg is a role model for us all.

50 Life and Business Lessons from Oprah Winfrey

Introduction

If there is a queen of chat shows in the USA, it is Oprah Winfrey. This self-made billionaire is far more than a talking head, however: she has leveraged her public profile to make a $3 billion fortune. She is the richest African American, and greatest black philanthropist, in history. Oprah has honorary doctorates from both Duke and Harvard Universities, and in 2013 President Barack Obama awarded her the Presidential Medal of Freedom. Her rise from childhood poverty in rural Mississippi, and her teenage years as a single mother in inner city Milwaukee, having become pregnant aged just 14, is nothing short of a miracle. Even in fairytales, heroines don't triumph over adversity like this.

Be thankful for what you have; you'll end up having more. If you concentrate on what you don't have, you will never, ever have enough.

Oprah Winfrey

So what is it that has enabled Oprah Winfrey to succeed when countless others have fallen by the wayside? What are her personal attributes, how does she position herself, and what is it that drives her to go on? Having come from nowhere, with no obvious advantages in life, the lessons she can teach us are invaluable. If someone as disadvantaged in life as Oprah Winfrey can go on to achieve the things she has, such possibilities are open to any one of us. She is the ultimate role model, an inspiration whether you are black or white, female or male, rich or poor.

Oprah Winfrey has been in the public limelight for more than 40 years, and her life was not uneventful before that. In this book we will examine the key periods of her life, the events which made her the women she is today, and endeavour to extract from them key lessons which you can apply in your own life and business. Some of these lessons will be complex, and require time to think about. Other will be simple, and you can begin to action them straight away. We have highlighted these bite-sized lessons throughout the book so that if you are short of time, you can spot them quickly, returning to read each chapter in more detail at a later date.

Chapter 1 examines Oprah's childhood and education, the period which probably most shaped her as a person, and which undoubtedly was the most difficult in her life. It describes what happened to Oprah, and what she did about it, before she began her career in television.

Chapter 2 looks at Oprah's television career, from co-anchoring local news channels, to being the face of the most successful talk show in the history of American broadcasting: *The Oprah Winfrey Show*. Oprah's personality, her insight into guests and viewers alike, and her desire to use her television platform for good, all shine through. This is followed by *Chapter 3: Other Media Projects*, a discussion of her publishing, film, radio, and online initiatives, many of which were spin-offs from her television show, but which have not always been commercial successes. Oprah's business empire - the company structures which own and create her numerous products - is explored in *Chapter 4*.

After this, the book then shifts away from Oprah's career to examine in detail her awards and honours (*Chapter 5*) her philanthropic efforts, in the US and overseas (*Chapter 6*); and her thought leadership and influence over the American public (*Chapter 7*). This chapter considers in particular Oprah's ability to change public ideas on contemporary issues such as homosexuality, her ability to influence the outcome of political elections, and the impact that her endorsements have on the sale consumer items.

Oprah's private life, including her early relationships and long-term partnership with Stedman Graham, is discussed in *Chapter 8*. The book finishes with a conclusion, summarising the most important lessons which Oprah can, and would want to, teach us.

Childhood and Education

Few people's formative years are bleaker than those of Oprah Winfrey. She was born on January 29, 1954 in Kosciusko, Mississippi to Vernita Lee, an unmarried teenage housemaid, who had conceived her daughter on a one-night stand with a coal miner turned barber scarcely older than she was. The child was named Orpah on her birth certificate, a biblical name suggested by her aunt, which was taken from the Book of Ruth. None of her relatives knew how to spell the name when they wrote it down, and in any case, anyone who saw it from then on always mispronounced it as Oprah. This inadvertent moniker stuck.

Oprah grew up in desperate poverty. Her mother left to look for work shortly after she was born, and Oprah was cared for by her grandmother, Hattie Mae Lee. The family's situation was such that Oprah wore dresses made from potato sacks, which even in the impoverished society where she lived marked her out as different. She was inevitably bullied for her appearance by her peers.

Lesson 1: Economic poverty, however desperate, can be overcome. Just because you start with nothing does not mean that you are fated to always be poor.

Young Oprah was smart, however, and by the age of three, her grandmother had already taught her to read. She had a good memory and a strong voice, so the congregation at the local church nicknamed her "the Preacher".

Lesson 2: Early years education is vital to success later in life. Whatever your financial position, invest in the education of your children from the very start.

Oprah's mother came back into her life when Oprah was six, uprooting her from her grandmother's home and moving her to Milwaukee. Vernita Lee worked interminable hours for minimal pay, and had little time for her daughter. She gave birth to a second daughter, Patricia, and sent Oprah away once again, this time to be cared for by her biological father, Vernon Winfrey. During her absence, two more children were born: another daughter, who was put up for adoption for financial reasons; and a son.

Not even having reached puberty, Oprah was molested by a relatives, notably a cousin and an uncle, and also by a family friend. When she attempted to raise the abuse with her immediate family, years later, they refused to accept what she said, and it was not until 1986, on one of her own programmes about sexual abuse, that Oprah felt able to talk about what had happened to her publicly. In any case, the emotional and psychological damage of these years was permanent: Oprah told an interviewer on the BBC News that the reason she had chosen not to be a mother because she herself had not been mothered well.

Lesson 3: The repercussions of physical and emotional abuse will last a lifetime. Although you might be able to function, and even to thrive, that does not remove the underlying scars.

Aged just 13, Oprah ran away from home. She became pregnant at 14, but her son was born prematurely, and died not long after he was born. Oprah was, regardless, just a child herself, with no capacity to care for a baby. Having returned to live with her mother, Oprah attended Lincoln High School, and then the more affluent Nicolet High School, but she was acutely aware of her poverty, and felt it was constantly rubbed in her face by her peers. Oprah fell into a bad crowd, and stole money to keep up appearances.

The struggle of my life created empathy - I could relate to pain, being abandoned, having people not love me.

Oprah Winfrey

Again, Vernita Lee sent Oprah to live with her father, but this time the arrangement was much more of a success. Vernon Winfrey valued education, and made it a priority for Oprah. He sent her to East Nashville Hill School, where she quickly found her feet. She joined the high school speech team, and won a prestigious oratory competition, the prize for which was a full scholarship to study communication at Tennessee State University. Education gave Oprah the springboard she needed to leave Milwaukee, her poverty, and many of her troubles, behind.

Where there is no struggle, there is no strength.

Oprah Winfrey

Lesson 4: Education is the single most important means of creating ambition, and the means by which those ambitions can be realised.

Television Career

Whilst she was still a student, Oprah began putting her communication skills to work. She presented the news part time at WVOL, a Nashville-based radio station which broadcast predominantly to Tennessee's African-American community. On graduating, the moved to WLAC-TV (a CBS-affiliated TV station), also in Nashville, and became their first black female news anchor. Oprah was also the youngest news anchor hired by the channel.

Lesson 5: Youth need not be a drawback to achievement. If you have energy, and are good at what you do, opportunities will avail themselves.

The late 1970s saw Oprah move through a succession of jobs in local television news, first to anchor the six o'clock news at WJZ-TV in Baltimore, and then to co-host the channel's local talk show, *People Are Talking*, and *Dialing for Dollars*. Oprah's warmth and enthusiasm engaged listeners and viewers alike, and having a young, dynamic black woman on screen was something fresh, which appealed to channel executives.

Oprah's big break, her leap from local broadcasting to a national stage, occurred in 1983 when she was headhunted by WLS-TV in Chicago. She took over their morning talk show, *AM Chicago*, and in a matter of months transformed it from a low-performing programme, to the highest rated talk show in Chicago. All eyes were on Oprah to see what she would do next.

Lesson 6: You can't sit at home and expect opportunities to pop up there. You need to be prepared to move, sometimes long distances, in order to take the next step.

One of those watching closely was film critic Roger Ebert. He convinced Oprah to sign a syndication contract with King World, and her morning talk show was renamed *The Oprah Winfrey Show*. Fans now turned on the box for an hour every morning, entranced by her intelligence and sassiness, and when national broadcasting of the show began in September 1986, it quickly became the number-one daytime talk show in America. Writing at the time in TIME magazine, journalist Richard Zoglin was to the point:

> Few people would have bet on Oprah Winfrey's swift rise to host of the most popular talk show on TV. In a field dominated by white males, she is a black female of

ample bulk. [...] What she lacks in journalistic toughness, she makes up for in plain-spoken curiosity, robust humor and, above all empathy. Guests with sad stories to tell are apt to rouse a tear in Oprah's eye [...] They, in turn, often find themselves revealing things they would not imagine telling anyone, much less a national TV audience. It is the talk show as a group therapy session.

The Oprah Winfrey Show was broadcast nationally from 1986 until 2011, making it one of the longest running daytime talk shows in history. Initially tabled as a tabloid talk show, Oprah went on to make the programme a platform for her educational and philanthropic initiatives too.

With viewer figures estimated to have reached 20 million a day at the peak of the show's popularity, everyone who was everyone wanted to make an appearance, and Oprah had no shortage of celebrity guests. CBS Anchor and Oprah's best friend, Gayle King, made a record 141 appearances on the show, and singer Celine Dion clocked up 28. Oprah interviewed Tom Cruise, Elizabeth Taylor, and even Michael Jackson. That interview, filmed at the singer's home, Neverland, and broadcast live, was watched by 90 million people, making it the most-watched television interview in history.

Lesson 7: People are interested in celebrities, and want to hear what they have to say. Surrounding yourself with celebrities is a good way to increase your own popularity.

But Oprah wasn't only interested in the lives of the rich and famous: she was fascinated by the lives of ordinary people too, and wanted to bring their experiences to light, prompting discussion amongst her audiences. She interviewed the parents of murdered children, those with life-threatening and incurable diseases, and the victims of abuse. It was in one such interview, with a woman named Trudie Chase in the show's 1989-90 season, that Oprah broke down on hearing about her guest's violent sexual abuse, and then recounted her own experiences of childhood molestation (see *Chapter 1: Childhood and Education*). Oprah invited 200 men who had been victims of childhood abuse to appear on an episode during the show's final season, along with director and producer Tyler Perry, himself an abuse survivor, in the hope that it would encourage other victims to realise they did not have to suffer in silence and in shame, but could be open about what the had endured, and bring the perpetrators to justice.

Real integrity is doing the right thing, knowing that nobody's going to know whether you did it or not.

Lesson 8: The stories of ordinary people can be just as enthralling as those of the famous. Don't ever discount someone, or their experiences, because you think they are too mundane.

Oprah knew early on that her show was about more than just entertainment. By discussing prominent issues of current affairs, such as gun crime, racism, mental illness, or abuse, she could change public attitudes. She also realised the show could be a tool for educating middle America, and because of this, she created *Oprah's Book Club*.

Originally a segment of *The Oprah Winfrey Show*, each month Oprah would select a book (usually a novel) to discuss on air. Four of the books she featured generated multi-million sales, and they invariably shot straight to the top of the best-sellers lists, even if they had been originally published years before. Eckhard Tolle's *A New Earth* sold 3,370,000 copies after being included on Oprah's reading list in 2008. Oprah combined her book discussions with author interviews and other related features, including a visit to the Auschwitz concentration camp with Elie Wiesel, an author, Holocaust survivor, and Nobel Laureate.

Lesson 9: Entertainment and education can go hand in hand, and when new information is delivered in an engaging format, people are more keen to learn.

In her book, *Reading with Oprah: The Book Club That Changed America*, writer and publisher Kathleen Rooney described Oprah as being, "a serious American intellectual who pioneered the use of electronic media, specifically television and the Internet, to take reading—a decidedly non-technological and highly individual act—and highlight its social elements and uses in such a way to motivate millions of erstwhile non-readers to pick up books." *Business Week* was similarly impressed with the leverage Oprah had on the publishing industry, claiming, "No one comes close to Oprah's clout: Publishers estimate that her power to sell a book is anywhere from 20 to 100 times that of any other media personality."

Books were my pass to personal freedom. I learned to read at age three, and soon discovered there was a whole world to conquer that went beyond our farm in Mississippi.

Oprah Winfrey

Lesson 10: Learning should be a life-long process. Whatever your age, and whatever your situation, you are never too old or too busy to learn something new.

Oprah also used *The Oprah Winfrey Show* to reach out to audiences, encouraging them to improve their health and well-being, and to increase their aspirations. Having come herself from such impoverished, desperate beginnings, she knew the importance of role models, and that she herself could set an example to others. We'll discuss her leadership and influence more in *Chapter 7*, but here we can specifically consider her talk show's self-help elements.

Lesson 11: People in positions of power, and influence, have a moral responsibility to educate the people who look up to them, and to set a positive example.

Although Oprah's own opinions held great weight with her television audiences, she understood that for important matters such as health, finance, and marital issues, it gave the show credibility if she brought on experts in their respective fields. Iyanla Vanzant, life coach and spiritual teacher, began appearing on the show in the late 1990s, advising mostly on relationship issues, and in 2000, *Ebony* magazine rated her as one of the "100 most influential Black Americans". Dr. Phil McGraw ("Dr Phil"), a psychologist from Oklahoma, used his academic background to give advice on relationships, bad habits, bad attitudes, and weight loss, and his spin-off show, *Dr. Phil*, began in 2002. Last year, *Forbes* magazine ranked him the 15th highest earning celebrity in the world. It is a similar success story for financial expert Suze Orman, who spoke on the show about credit card debt, budgeting, etc.

The greatest discovery of all time is that a person can change his future by merely changing his attitude.

Oprah Winfrey

Lesson 12: Your professional relationships should be mutually beneficial. If someone else's efforts add to your own credibility, you should give them a leg-up in return.

The Oprah Winfrey Show ran until 2011. The 25th season was Oprah's last, but my was it impressive: Oprah flew all 300 audience members to Australia, with John Travolta as the pilot; she interviewed President Barack Obama and First Lady Michelle Obama; and the final episode included appearances from Arethra Franklin, Tom Cruise, Stevie Wonder, Will Smith, and Beyonce. Hundreds of graduates who had received the Oprah Winfrey Scholarship at Morehouse College were in the audience, and the show received its highest ratings figures in 17 years. Oprah's own feelings about this end of an era were frank, and generally celebratory. She said to her viewers:

> I've been asked many times during this farewell season, 'Is ending the show bittersweet?' Well, I say all sweet. No bitter. And here is why: Many of us have been together for 25 years. We have hooted and hollered together, had our aha! moments, we ugly-cried together and we did our gratitude journals. So I thank you all for your support and your trust in me. I thank you for sharing this yellow brick road of blessings. I thank you for tuning in every day along with your mothers and your sisters and your daughters, your partners, gay and otherwise, your friends and all the husbands who got coaxed into watching *Oprah*. And I thank you for being as much of a sweet inspiration for me as I've tried to be for you. I won't say goodbye. I'll just say...until we meet again. To God be the glory.

During the show's lifetime, it received 47 Daytime Emmy Awards, eight GLAAD Media Awards, five Image Awards, and a TV Guide Award. In 2013, TV Guide also ranked *The Oprah Winfrey Show* as the 19th greatest show of all time.

Lesson 13: Even the greatest projects have a natural shelf life. One of the hardest things in business is to anticipate when that end is nigh, and to draw things to a close gracefully.

Other Media Projects

By the mid 1980s, Oprah Winfrey was already a household name, and this meant that she had her pick of other media projects. She was savvy in those she chose, however, always selecting opportunities which furthered her career, or related to issues she cared about.

Films Oprah made her big screen debut in *The Color Purple* in 1985. Directed by Steven Spielberg, this period drama was an adaptation of the novel of the same name. The film's themes of poverty, racism, and sexism in the southern United States must have resonated with Oprah. The film was a box office success, earning $142 million worldwide, and it was favourably received by critics: the online review site *Rotten Tomatoes* amalgamates critics' reviews to give the film an overall score of 88%, and describes it as "a sentimental tale that reveals great emotional truths in American history." Oprah appeared in the film as Sofia Johnson, the daughter-in-law of the film's female protagonist, who is herself a victim of sexual abuse, but refuses to be cowed by her attackers.

The themes of *The Color Purple* are also evident in some of Oprah's later films. She appeared as Sethe, a former slave living in Cincinati in the aftermath of the American civil war, in the 1998 horror-drama *Beloved*; and in 2005 she was the executive producer for *Their Eyes Were Watching God*, a television movie based on Zora Neale Hurston's novel, itself considered to be a seminal work of African-American fiction. Her preparations for her role in *Beloved* were particularly thorough and harrowing: she was tied up, blindfolded and left alone in the woods to have an idea of what it must have been like to be a slave.

Lesson 14: If you want something to be a success, you have to give it your all. This is much easier if it is something you truly believe in.

Harpo Productions (see *Chapter 4: Business Empire*) also developed and produced a number of films and documentaries for HBO, and Oprah made small appearances, often as a voice-over artist, in children's cartoons. She voiced Gussie the goose in *Charlotte's Web*, Judge Bumbledon in the *Bee Movie*, and also recorded the voice of Eudora in Disney's *The Princess and the Frog*.

Magazines Oprah published two magazines, *O at Home*, and *O, The Oprah Magazine*, which *Fortune* declared to be the most successful ever start-up in the publishing industry.

O, The Oprah Magazine, abbreviated as *O*, was first published in 2000, and is targeted primarily at middle-aged, female readers - the same sort of people who watched *The Oprah Winfrey Show*. Oprah appears on every cover, sometimes accompanied by other high-profile women such as Michelle Obama and Ellen DeGeneres, and topics covered in the magazine include fashion and beauty, health, finances, and books. It is intended to project Oprah's opinions and style, and her image and comments are present throughout.

The paid circulation of *O* peaked in 2004, at 2.7 million copies. Although most magazines experienced declining print sales in the late 2000s, *O* held strong in the marketplace. Today, the magazine's circulation hovers around 2.4 million copies, two-thirds of which are sold by subscription, and the rest through news stands. Nearly 2/3 of readers are Caucasian, and the balance African-American, Hispanic, and Asian. The digital issue of the magazine was launched in 2010, for iPad users, and the app gives readers access to videos and the ability to purchase books from Oprah's book list.

Lesson 15: If you are lucky enough to create a product which people want to buy in to, be prepared to spin it in different ways. Give your fans (your customers) a variety of products to choose from.

O at Home was a spin-off from *O, The Oprah Magazine*, was published by the Hearst Corporation, and after it was launched in 2004, it quickly grew to have a circulation of 1.4 million. *O at Home* was published quarterly, and focused on home furnishings, decorating tips, and good interior design on a budget. The magazine closed in 2008, as Hearst tried to cut costs in the face of falling advertising revenues, and its content themes were reincorporated into *O, The Oprah Magazine*.

Think like a queen. A queen is not afraid to fail. Failure is another steppingstone to greatness.

Oprah Winfrey

Lesson 16: There is no shame in failing: it is a natural part of learning and developing. If something does not work out, for whatever reason, try something else instead.

Books To date, Oprah has co-written five books, on a variety of topics.

In 1996, writing with Bill Adler, Oprah released *The Uncommon Wisdom of Oprah Winfrey: A Portrait in Her Own Words*. The moving story of her early life and rise to fame, in the book she explores themes of family, success, weight loss, relationships, as well as her own pains, passions, and ambitions. Her views and insight are provided in the form of quotes, which Adler then elaborates on.

Lesson 17: Play to your strengths, and let others play to theirs. It is perfectly acceptable to delegate responsibility to other people, especially if they can do something better than you can.

Capitalising on interest in the self-help field, which itself developed in no small part due to *The Oprah Winfrey Show*, Oprah co-wrote *Make The Connection: 10 Steps To A Better Body And A Better Life* with personal trainer, Bob Greene. This book was also published in 1996. In the book, Oprah is blunt about her own struggles with weight - she had tried, and failed at, every diet imaginable - but the book then shifts to looking at how Greene helped her to lose (and largely keep off) more than 70 lbs by eating more healthily and exercising regularly. The 10 steps referred to in the book's title are the core of Greene's weight loss programme, and include ways to increase your metabolism. Oprah's own story runs alongside these practical tips, providing encouragement through inspiration. Though the book is now 20 years old, it is still well-reviewed by dieters, many of whom return to Oprah and Greene's advice again and again.

Lesson 18: Partnering with an expert in a specific field is the best way to create a quality product, and thus increase the likelihood that your project will succeed.

Journey to Beloved was published two years later, in 1998. Written by Oprah and with photographs by Ken Regan, it is the story of how Oprah fell in love with Toni Morrison's Pulitzer Prize-winning novel, *Beloved*, and decided to make it into a film (see *Films*, above). The book is principally a production diary, with an essay to preface it, but even in this somewhat sterile format, we see Oprah's emotions and vulnerabilities. She is filled with doubts about her ability to play her character, Sethe. Even in the company of so many experienced film makers, she worries that she lacks the skill and strength to pull the project off. And Oprah clearly feels a great weight of responsibility to do justice to the book, its characters, themes, and the real people who have inspired it, writing:

> Tomorrow is the first day of dialogue. Am I ready? I think so. I bring the force and grace of history and pain with me, carrying the Ancestors in my heart, hoping, but

also knowing, they, too, carry me.... I ask God for grace, and the power of the spirits whose lives went unnoticed, demeaned and diminished by slavery. Calling on you. Calling on you. I try to prepare in terms of logic, reasoning, what would [Sethe] be thinking - chronologically - but I really believe I can call her up. Her and so many others. I'm counting on them.

Those who have read the book are often moved by Oprah's accounts to read the original novel, or to watch the film.

Lesson 19: People don't buy products, they buy emotions. When you are creating something, you therefore need to be aware of how it will make people feel.

The most recent of Oprah's books is *What I Know For Sure*, published in 2014. Originally the title of her column in *O, The Oprah Magazine* (see *Magazines*, above), this book is a cloth-bound collection of the best of her columns, many of which have been specially revised and updated. Candid and moving, uplifting and frequently funny, the essays provide insight into the way that Oprah thinks and feels. The essays are arranged by theme - joy, resilience, connection, gratitude, possibility, awe, clarity, and power - and are intended to help readers to define their ambitions, work towards realising them, and be fulfilled. Oprah combines her own experiences with messages for others, for example:

> My highest achievement: never shutting down my heart. Even in my darkest moments—through sexual abuse, a pregnancy at 14, lies and betrayals—I remained faithful, hopeful, and willing to see the best in people, regardless of whether they were showing me their worst. I continued to believe that no matter how hard the climb, there is always a way to let in a sliver of light to illuminate the path forward.

Lesson 20: Adding your own opinions and experiences to your products adds authenticity, and is an effective means of marketing.

Unlike some celebrities, who seem to have a new, ghost-written book out every other week, Oprah has held off on publishing a second memoir or autobiography for many years. Perhaps she was just too busy, or perhaps she felt that she had more to achieve before putting pen to paper. In any case, having retired from *The Oprah Winfrey Show*, she had more time, and thus began to write. Her forthcoming memoir, entitled *The Life You Want*, will look at Oprah's own life, and also give inspirational advice: much like this book, in fact! *The Life You Want* is scheduled for publication by Flatiron Books in 2017, and critics are already chomping at the bit to read it. Writing in the *New York Times* in December 2015, Alexandra Alter has already predicted that Oprah's memoir will be the best-selling book of the year.

Lesson 21: Building suspense is a very effective marketing tool. Work out what your customers want, and dangle it just out of reach, and they will want it even more.

Radio *Oprah Radio* (originally called *Oprah and Friends*) was a talk-show radio channel which ran from 2006 to 2014. Oprah's first three year contract with the station's owners, XM Satellite Radio, was said to be worth $55 million.

Broadcast from Oprah's own studio in Chicago, the channel featured not only Oprah, but also key figures who frequently appeared on *The Oprah Winfrey Show*, such as personal trainer Bob Greene, interior designer Nate Berkus, cardiothoracic surgeon and alternative medicine support Dr. Mehmet Cengiz Öz ("Dr. Oz"), and spiritual teacher Marianne Williamson. Oprah was contractually to be on the air 30 minutes a week, 39 weeks a year, and she often presented her segment along with CBS anchor Gayle King.

Lesson 22: Every business has key personnel. Understand who they are, work out what you need from them, and how you can keep them engaged.

The topics discussed on *Oprah Radio* were very similar to those on *The Oprah Winfrey Show*: current affairs, self-improvement, health, nutrition, fitness, relationships, and tips for your home all featured. The channel was broadcast by a number of companies in succession, but ceased broadcasting on 31 December, 2014. Listeners were not informed of the channel's shutdown in advance.

Do the one thing you think you cannot do. Fail at it. Try again. Do better the second time. The only people who never tumble are those who never mount the high wire. This is your moment. Own it.

Oprah Winfrey

Lesson 23: Even the most successful entrepreneurs sometimes make flawed decisions. The important thing is not that you failed, but that you get back up and try something else.

Online Presence In order to coordinate all her activities, and to create a hub where fans to access everything in one place, Oprah created **oprah.com**. According to Quantcast, the website currently receives 4.8 million unique visitors every month (down from 6 million in 2008), 70% of whom are in the US. The vast majority of visitors to the site are women in the 35-65 age bracket, and by far the largest ethnic group of users is African-American.

oprah.com is a mine of information, and thankfully well organised enough that you can usually find what you are looking for. The latest stories from *O, The Oprah Magazine*, are on the home page, along with advertisements for courses, events, and branded products available from the *O Store*, Oprah's online shop. The home page also includes some video content, and an invitation for readers to share their own experiences on a variety of topics, so that they feel engaged. The topics - everything from *Dads: Is your ex blocking you from your child?* to *Are you a Caribbean woman who feels shunned?* and *Are you an ex-con who can't seem to catch a break?* - are all slightly sensationalist, encouraging readers to read and comment on what others have said, even if they have nothing to contribute themselves.

Lesson 24: Engaging your customers and building a sense of rapport with them increases their sense of loyalty to your brand.

The bulk of the website's content is divided into several dozen different categories, all of which are accessible from the side bar menu. These include common topics such as *Fashion & Beauty*, *Food*, *Health & Wellness*, and *Inspiration*, but also special sections for all of Oprah's courses, and television shows produced by the Oprah Winfrey Network (OWN, see *Chapter 4: Business Empire*). The website has a dedicated discussion area (*Community Conversations*), an area for competitions and promotions (*Sweepstakes*), and also a book store tied in with Oprah's Book Club (see *Chapter 2: Television Career*).

The *Books* section is one of the most interesting parts of oprah.com: it is at once a valuable information source which promotes Oprah's educational objectives, and also a lucrative money spinner. Numerous book lists are provided under the *Reading Room*, and all of them can be purchased online, generating oprah.com a referral fee from the vendors. A second income stream is generated through advertising: pay-per-click adverts, typically for products and services unrelated to the book, appear beneath each book review.

Lesson 25: Your business' website has two purposes: to inform customers, and to make money. Both of these purposes go hand in hand, and you should not overlook one in favour of the other.

Business Empire

What I know is, is that if you do work that you love, and the work fulfils you, the rest will come.

Oprah Winfrey

Oprah is acutely aware that she herself is a multi-billion dollar brand: people want to hear what she says and thinks, and she can capitalise on this, through endorsements and advertising, to make mega bucks. A single tweet from Oprah's Twitter account, for example, is thought to have boosted Weight Watchers' earnings by $150 million.

Lesson 26: Your brand, and that of your company, are intimately linked. You should therefore think about your personal and professional platforms as one and the same.

Although she is personally shrewd, she has also been very well advised throughout her career, enabling her to make the best business decisions. The fact that *Forbes* magazine currently estimates her net wealth at $3.1 billion, is testament to this fact. Unlike many of her wealthy peers, she has not inherited a cent, but made it entirely herself.

Lesson 27: The easiest way to become a millionaire is to inherit it. If you aren't lucky enough to be in that position, however, you can still reach the same levels of wealth, it is just much harder work.

In *Chapter 2: Television Career* and *Chapter 3: Other Media Projects*, we have talked about the products Oprah has created, for film and television, publishing and radio, and online. In this chapter, then, we will look at the commercial vehicles which have enabled her to build her business empire, to promote herself on so many different platforms, and to capitalise, professional and financially, on all of them.

It is easy to think of Oprah as a talk show host, a celebrity, but she is a businesswoman first and foremost. Indeed, Nicole Aschoff, writing in The Guardian, went as far as to describe her as, "one of the world's best neoliberal capitalist thinkers." Oprah embodies the American Dream, although, as Aschoff is at pains to point out, for most people:

> [the American Dream] is a fiction. If all or most forms of social and cultural capital were equally valuable and accessible, we should see the effects of this in increased

222

upward mobility and wealth created anew by new people in each generation rather than passed down and expanded from one generation to the next. The data do not demonstrate this upward mobility.

In any case, we still aspire to be like Oprah. Reality, however brutal, does not blunt our dreams, and a role model like Oprah - someone who has made it against all the odds - just makes us work harder to try and realise them.

The biggest adventure you can take is to live the life of your dreams.

Oprah Winfrey

Lesson 28: The American Dream is, for most people, just a dream, something which they aspire towards, but will never reach. For a lucky few, however, that dream can become a reality.

Oprah's business empire is managed, and expanded, by two companies, Harpo Productions, and the Oprah Winfrey Network (OWN).

Harpo Productions Founded in Chicago in 1986, Harpo Productions (the sole subsidiary of Harpo, Inc.) employs more than 12,000 people and handles the bulk of Oprah's business empire. The name, Harpo, is Oprah spelt backwards, but was also the name of Oprah's on-screen husband in *The Color Purple* (see *Films*, in *Chapter 3: Other Media Projects*).

Lesson 29: Choose a business name which is catchy, and ideally which means something to you.

Each of Oprah's business areas forms a subsidiary of Harpo Productions, though not all of those subsidiaries are still operational.

Harpo Print, in partnership with Hearst Magazines, publishes *O, The Oprah Magazine* (see *Magazines* in *Chapter 3: Other Media Projects*) and also the now-defunct *O Home*.

Harpo Films, founded in 1993, was once the largest division of Harpo Productions, and it developed and produced motion pictures and long-form television programmes. Harpo Films had an overlap of interests with Harpo Studios, the home of *The Oprah Winfrey Show* in Chicago, and where many of her other film and television projects, including *Beloved*, were filmed. Harpo Films closed in 2013, but with most of its staff moving to Harpo Studio and OWN (see below).

Harpo Studies now controls much of Oprah's television output, plus that of the protégés whose careers she has helped to launch. In addition to producing *The Oprah Winfrey Show* (1986-2011), Harpo Studios also produces *Dr. Phil* (2002-present), *Rachael Ray* (2006-present), *The Dr. Oz Show* (2009-present), and many more. Oprah's own shows, notably *Oprah Prime*, *Oprah: Where Are They Now?*, *Oprah's Master Class*, and *Oprah's Life Class*, are all products belonging to Harpo Studios.

Harpo Radio was the holding company for *Oprah Radio* (see *Radio* in *Chapter 3: Other Media Projects*), which ran from 2006 to 2014.

Harpo Productions also owns oprah.com (see *Online* in *Chapter 3: Other Media Projects*).

Lesson 30: Take expert advice and think carefully about how to structure your own business enterprises. It is sometimes necessary to spread risk, and liability, between multiple legal entities.

The Oprah Winfrey Network (OWN) The Oprah Winfrey Network (OWN) is an offshoot of Harpo Productions (see above), though it too is an umbrella for multiple different projects. Founded in 2011, the company has two stakeholders, Harpo Productions and Discovery Communications, both of which own 50%.

OWN is a television channel, available to 82 million households in the US, and its content is also syndicated to TLC UK (UK), Discovery Home & Health (Australia), DStv (South Africa), and local channels in Bulgaria, Poland, Romania, and Russia. Its viewing ratings - averaging 581,000 in the first quarter of 2015 - are reasonable when compared to OWN's competitors, but a fraction of the 7 million viewers Oprah herself could expect to attract during a particularly juicy episode of *The Oprah Winfrey Show*. The network's viewing figures are generally boosted by one-off occasions when a celebrity comes on a show and what they say makes breaking news: disgraced Tour de France winner Lance Armstrong's public confession that he had used performance enhancing drugs attracted 4.3 million viewers; and Oprah's interview with Bobbi Kristina Brown, broadcast a month to the day after her mother Whitney Houston's death by drowning, broke even that record.

Lesson 31: Exclusivity is a very powerful marketing tool: it makes people want what you have. Work to find something which no one else can give your customers, and they will then flock to you.

OWN broadcasts a mixture of talk shows and films, both original series and re-runs of popular shows. Much of the content is broadcast as marathons - back to back episodes of the same programme - and the majority of shows broadcast are products of Harpo Studios (see above). All of Oprah's own shows are broadcast on the channel, as are those of Nate Berkus, Rachael Ray, and Dr. Phil. Tyler Perry, one of the highest paid performers in the US, signed a contract with OWN in 2012 to produce 90 episodes of original content, and to broadcast all his new material through the channel. His series, which include *The Haves and the Have Nots*, and *Love Thy Neighbor*, have been great commercial successes, and so the partnership was renewed. Perry's viewer figures actually now exceed those of Oprah herself.

Lesson 32: Successful products don't have to be original. You can rework, and redistribute, existing products in multiple ways, and still make money doing so.

Awards and Honours

Oprah's awards and honours are almost too numerous to count: if there is a prize in existence, she has probably already won it, or at least been nominated.

In *Chapter 2: Television Career*, we discussed some of the awards won by *The Oprah Winfrey Show* which, of course, was made possible by Oprah herself. As an individual presenter, she also received the People's Choice Award on four separate occasions across three decades (1988, 1997, 1998, and 2004), she was twice nominated for Academy Awards for her film roles (1986 and 2015), she was given a Lifetime Achievement Award by the Emmy Awards (1998), and in 2005 she was inducted into the National Association for the Advancement of Colored People (NAACP) Hall of Fame in recognition of her work in television and film.

Lesson 33: Gaining recognition within your industry is an effective way to raise your business' profile, as other people will publicise your achievements on your behalf.

Oprah's awards stretch beyond the worlds of film and television, however: she was honoured with the Jefferson Award for Public Service in 1998, and the Peabody Award, also for meritorious public service, in 1995. Oprah received the Bob Hope Humanitarian Award in 2002, and the Kennedy Center Honors in 2010.

There is one award, however, which Oprah is more proud of than all the others, and rightly so. On November 22, 2013, Oprah was invited to the White House, where President Barack Obama presented her with the Presidential Medal of Freedom, the highest civilian award of the United States. The award recognises those who have made "an especially meritorious contribution to the security or national interests of the United States, world peace, cultural or other significant public or private endeavors," and as a recipient, Oprah follows in the footsteps of the Apollo 13 crew, Mother Teresa, and scientist Stephen Hawking.

Lesson 34: If you excel in your field, whatever it is, and campaign tirelessly for issues you believe in, you and your efforts will ultimately come to wider attention.

Philanthropy

Acutely aware of where she has come from, and the potential which her personal wealth has to change lives, Oprah is an active philanthropist. In fact, *Businessweek* records that she became the first black person to rank among the 50 most generous Americans, and by 2012 she had already given away $400 million to educational causes alone. She has donated more than 400 scholarships to Morehouse College in Atlanta, Georgia, and in 2013 made a one-off donation of $12 million to the Smithsonian's National Museum of African American History and Culture.

Lesson 35: No one achieves wealth, or greatness, on their own. If you make money, you have a moral obligation to give something back to the communities which have enabled you to excel.

Oprah create Oprah's Angel Network in 1998 to support charitable projects and provide grants to NGOs. She personally covered all administrative costs of the network, and so every cent of the $80 million it raised went to the front line of charities' work. This included a donation of $11 million ($10 million of which was a personal donation from Oprah) for relief efforts in the wake of Hurricanes Katrina and Rita, which devastated predominantly poor, black communities in Texas, Mississippi, Louisiana, and Alabama.

Lesson 36: Sometimes the most effective gift you can give is not your money, but your time, platform, and endorsement. Leverage your position to encourage others to support causes you believe in.

The philanthropic project which Oprah is most proud of, however, is the Oprah Winfrey Leadership Academy for Girls, close to Johannesburg in South Africa. The root of the idea formed in 2000 when Oprah was a guest of Nelson Mandela at his home in Western Cape. The pair discussed poverty at some length, and agreed that education was the best way of giving poor South African youths - and girls in particular - a chance to improve their lives.

Oprah initially pledged $10 million for a school, and began developing a state-of-the-art campus. Her financial commitment increased to $40 million as the scope of the project grew. She began recruiting students in 2006, stipulating that only the brightest but most disadvantaged girls would be accepted. The surroundings she created for her students were lavish, even by western standards, which drew controversy from multiple quarters, but Oprah was adamant that, "If you are surrounded by beautiful things and wonderful teachers who inspire you, that beauty brings out the beauty in you."

Today the school has nearly 300 students, and is a huge success. In a country where only 14% of black girls graduate from high school, these girls buck the trend: every one of the 72 students in the first graduating class won a place at university. Graduates frequently go onto study for degrees in the US, and Oprah not only pays their tuition fees but also for their living costs, equipping them with everything they need. They call her "Mom-Oprah", and she feels very strongly that these girls are her heirs. What they achieve in life will be her proudest legacy.

When I look into the future, it's so bright it burns my eyes.

Oprah Winfrey

Lesson 37: Support initiatives you feel passionately about. Not only will they be more likely to succeed, but you will have a far greater feeling of accomplishment when they do.

Leadership and Influence

In 2001, TIME magazine called Oprah "arguably the world's most powerful woman". Life listed her as the most influential black person of her generation, and called her "America's most powerful woman." *Forbes* named her as the world's most powerful celebrity in five different years (2005, 2007, 2008, 2010, and 2013), and even President Barack Obama said that she, "may be the most influential woman in the country". Whoever you speak to, at home or abroad, there is no doubt that Oprah is, and has been for three decades, one of the most influential people on the planet.

Lesson 38: People in conventional positions of power - politicians, military figures, and religious leaders - no longer exert as much influence as they did in the past. Ordinary people can spearhead significant change.

To describe Oprah's influence on middle America, *The Wall Street Journal* coined the word "Oprahfication". The term has been used in particular to refer to speaking out about personal issues, and to bringing ones private life into a public sphere. Although it was originally used to talk about public confession as a form of therapy, particularly for issues such as sexual abuse, weight problems, and a tumultuous love life, it went on to have applications in the world of politics too, encouraging politicians to speak emotionally about their problems and issues of importance to them. As *Newsweek* stated, "Every time a politician lets his lip quiver or a cable anchor 'emotes' on TV, they nod to the cult of confession that Oprah helped create."

Lesson 39: A message, delivered with conviction and emotion, will always be more effective than one based solely on rational argument.

Oprah has consistently used her position to deliberately influence public opinion, on moral and spiritual issues, as well as consumer choices. By providing a safe forum on her talk show, and encouraging guests to speak out, she was able to put previously taboo issues, such as homosexuality, on the discussion table in ordinary homes.

Although her critics have accused Oprah of blurring the lines between "normal" and "deviant" behaviour, the general view is that Oprah just made people understand that differences in sexual preference exist naturally within any given population, and talking about them is nothing to be ashamed of. As early as 1988, Oprah invited audience members to stand up and announce their sexuality on air, in observance of National Coming Out Day. She visited a West Virginian town and publicly confronted residents paranoid about the presence of a local man with HIV, chastising them for their lack of Christian love. She also invited, and actively promoted, gay celebrities on her show, and when Ellen DeGeneres announced to the world she was a lesbian, it was to Oprah.

Lesson 40: Public attitudes are constantly in flux; there are very few issues about which opinions are completely black and white. Given time and the right figurehead, public opinions can be led in a particular direction.

Oprah has guided her fans spiritually too, both through her own teachings, and through the teachings of those she has given a platform to on her show. *Christianity Today* described her in an article, 'The Church of O', as, "a post-modern priestess—an icon of church-free spirituality." In the comic cartoon series *Futurama*, an episode set a thousand years from now has "Oprahism" as the mainstream religion.

It isn't until you come to a spiritual understanding of who you are - not necessarily a religious feeling, but deep down, the spirit within - that you can begin to take control.

Oprah Winfrey

Although Oprah herself is a Christian, she has actively promoted spirituality in all its forms. The American spiritual teacher Gary Zukav, who promotes the alignment of personality with soul to create "authentic power" and transform humanity, was invited to appear on *The Oprah Winfrey Show* on 35 separate occasions, and less than a month after the 9/11 terror attacks, she controversially aired a show called Islam 101, describing Islam as, "the most misunderstood of the three major religions". Rudy Giuliani, then mayor of New York, asked her to host the Prayer for America service at the Yankee Stadium in New York, which she did, and in 2002, George W. Bush asked her to join a US delegation to Afghanistan. Concerned that it would portray the War on Terror in a positive light, however, Oprah declined the invitation, and the trip was cancelled. Without its figurehead, the foremost opinion leader in the country, it was not worthwhile.

What God intended for you goes far beyond anything you can imagine.

Oprah Winfrey

Lesson 41: Contrary to what is often said, religion is not a personal business. People care deeply about what others believe, and will frequently manipulate belief for political ends.

Oprah's backing in elections is, unsurprisingly, fiercely sought-after. Interestingly, she kept her political views (at least in a party political sense) to herself until 2008 when, for the first time, she openly came out and supported a presidential candidate: Barack Obama. Oprah held a fundraise for Obama at her Santa Barbara estate, joined him on the campaign trail in Iowa, New Hampshire, and South Carolina, and economists at the University of Maryland calculated that her endorsement was responsible for between 420,000 and 1,600,000 votes for Obama in the Democratic primary alone. Rod Blagojevich, Governor of Illinois, described Oprah as, "the most instrumental person in electing Barack Obama president."

Lesson 42: Democratic politics is, to a great extent, a popularity contest. He who receives the most publicity, and gets the most influential endorsements, is most likely to take home the prize.

"The Oprah Effect" has as great an impact on consumer purchases as it does on public opinion. When Oprah introduced Oprah's Book Club (see *Chapter 2: Television Career*) in 1996, even previously obscure novels would rocket to the top of the best sellers list. According to *The New York Times*, a book recommendation by Oprah could easily generate 1 million additional sales.

The opposite is true also: if Oprah doesn't like something, and says so publicly, sales fall. During a 1996 programme about mad cow disease, Oprah was horrified by what she heard, and said she was, "stopped cold from eating another burger." Cattle prices tumbled, allegedly costing beef producers $11 million. Texas cattlemen attempted to sue Oprah for for "false defamation of perishable food" and "business disparagement", but after a two-month trial, Oprah was found not liable for damages. It was during this court case that Oprah first met Dr. Phil, and she subsequently invited him to appear on *The Oprah Winfrey Show*.

Lesson 43: Be aware of the potential impact of what you say on others. Use your platform for public good, and be prepared to defend your endorsements.

Personal Life

Oprah has spent the entirety of her adult life as a public figure, speaking openly about her personal life: the whole concept of Oprahfication (see *Chapter 7: Leadership and Influence*) is, after all, about making your private life and emotions public as a means of therapy. Oprah practises what she preaches.

Relationships Oprah's romantic life, particularly in her early years, was chequered. A self-confessed promiscuous teen, she became pregnant at the age of 14, but her son died in infancy. After that, as she began to focus on education and pull her life together, she had a number of more meaningful relationships, including with a childhood sweetheart, Anthony Otey, who she met whilst still at school.

Lesson 44: Delinquent teenage years do not necessarily portend delinquent adulthood. If someone makes mistakes, especially whilst they are young, be prepared to give them a second chance.

In 1971, shortly after starting university, Oprah met William "Bubba" Taylor, her first great love. Oprah got Taylor his first job, and was absolutely besotted by him, begging him to stay with her, but when she moved to Baltimore in 1976, he refused to follow her there. It is with some nostalgia, and lingering fondness, that Oprah says, "We really did care for each other [...] We shared a deep love. A love I will never forget."

In the late 1970s, Oprah had a succession of love affairs. She dated musician and radio host John Tesh, but according to her biographer, the couple split due to the pressure of having a mixed-race relationship. She also dated reporter Lloyd Kramer, and a married man who had no intention of leaving his wife. She has talked at length about that relationship and the desperation it made her feel, saying, "I'd had a relationship with a man for four years. I wasn't living with him. I'd never lived with anyone—and I thought I was worthless without him. The more he rejected me, the more I wanted him. I felt depleted, powerless. At the end I was down on the floor on my knees grovelling and pleading with him." When the relationship broke down, Oprah contemplated suicide, even going as far as to write a suicide note. Though she did not follow through with the idea, the emotional turmoil led to significant weight gain. Again, Oprah has spoken frankly about this issue:

> The reason I gained so much weight in the first place and the reason I had such a sorry history of abusive relationships with men was I just needed approval so much.

I needed everyone to like me, because I didn't like myself much. So I'd end up with these cruel self-absorbed guys who'd tell me how selfish I was, and I'd say 'Oh thank you, you're so right' and be grateful to them. Because I had no sense that I deserved anything else. Which is also why I gained so much weight later on. It was the perfect way of cushioning myself against the world's disapproval.

Lesson 45: Do not underestimate the emotional impact of a relationship breakdown. Whether it has happened to you, or to someone you work with, be sensitive, supportive, and allow time to start to heal the trauma.

In the early 1980s, Oprah dated Randolph Cook, film critic Roger Ebert (who encouraged her to syndicate her show, see *Chapter 2: Television Career*), and possibly also filmmaker Reginald Chevalier. She got together with Stedman Graham in 1986, and although they were engaged to be married in 1992, Oprah and Stedman never actually tied the knot. They are still happily together, unmarried, and without children. They prefer to have a "spiritual union".

Lesson 46: It is fine to buck convention, in your private and professional lives. Find out what works for you and those around you, and make fulfilling those needs your priority.

Graham (born 1951) is a successful businessman and speaker, though his fame and wealth have come as result of his relationship with Oprah. He is the author of a dozen self-help books, and also has a column for *The Huffington Post*. Prior to meeting Oprah, he had a long-term relationship WBBM-TV anchor Robin Robinson.

Lots of people want to ride with you in the limo, but what you want is someone who will take the bus with you when the limo breaks down.

Oprah Winfrey

Lesson 47: Relationships don't have to be exciting all the time. Perhaps the most important thing is that you can depend on each other when things are tough. You can then enjoy the good times together even more.

Oprah's closest friend is the former news anchor Gayle King, who Oprah first met in her early twenties. Over the years, some people have suggested that Oprah and King's relationship was partly sexual in nature, but this is something which both women refute.

Writing in the August 2006 issue of *O, the Oprah Magazine*, Oprah said "I understand why people think we're gay. There isn't a definition in our culture for this kind of bond between women. So I get why people have to label it—how can you be this close without it being sexual? [...] I've told nearly everything there is to tell. All my stuff is out there. People think I'd be so ashamed of being gay that I wouldn't admit it? Oh, please." As well has having a close friendship, Oprah and King have also work together extensively. King was a frequent guest on *The Oprah Winfrey Show*, and she is now an editor for *O, the Oprah Magazine*.

Lesson 48: Your friends have helped to make you the person you are today. Celebrate your friendship and support one another.

Oprah considers the writer Maya Angelou to be both a friend and a mentor, referring to the older woman as "mother-sister-friend." When Angelou turned 70 in 1998, Oprah arranged a week-long cruise for Angelou and 150 of her guests, and a decade later, to mark Angelou's 80th birthday, Oprah hosted a similarly lavish affair at the Mar-a-Lago Club in Palm Beach, Florida.

Homes Winfrey has invested some of her wealth in property, and she alternates between her different homes. Her main base, at least since having stopped filming *The Oprah Winfrey Show*, is The Promised Land, a 42-acre estate in California. She also owns homes in the US states of Colordao, Florida, Hawaii, Illinois, and New Jersey, and on the Caribbean island of Antigua.

I still have my feet on the ground, I just wear better shoes.

Oprah Winfrey

Lesson 49: Investing in property, especially across different regions, makes economic sense and the ability to call somewhere "home" gives you a sense of stability and reassurance.

Conclusion

I don't think of myself as a poor deprived ghetto girl who made good. I think of myself as somebody who, from an early age, knew I was responsible for myself, <u>and I had to make good.</u>

Oprah Winfrey

Regardless of how Oprah feels about herself, she is, for more than a generation of Americans - and African American women in particular - the ultimate pin-up girl, a woman who has made it in spite of seeming to have all of life's odds stacked against her. Her story is one of hope, and Oprah embodies, perhaps more than anyone else in the country, the American Dream.

What is indisputable, however, is that she has made it for herself. She didn't inherit her wealth, marry it, or receive any other notable handouts of money. She has earned every cent through legitimate business interests: there is not even a hint of scandal, or of wrongdoing in her past, and that in itself is remarkable.

Although Oprah's life is long and complex, there are some lessons which come through stronger than any others, and though the chances of any one of us following in her footsteps exactly are slight, by implementing them in our own lives, we can certainly improve our lot.

First of all, education is the single most effective way of lifting people out of poverty. If you cannot access education, you cannot hope to advance. It was learning to read which brought young Oprah to the attention of congregation members at her church; and a good high school and a college scholarship in Nashville which enabled her to turn her life around. Oprah understands, from personal experience, just what a different a good education can make to aspiration and lifetime achievement, and this is why she invests so much of her time, money and effort, in her educational initiatives.

Secondly, no one else is going to do it for you. If you are fortunate, there will be other people around you who encourage you, support you, teach you, and give you lucky breaks. But it is up to you to position yourself in such a way that you are able to take full advantage of them, to remain focused, and to work hard consistently.

Thirdly, and perhaps most importantly, as a person you must have credibility. If you are the face of your brand, your customers will no differentiate between what you do and what your company does. If you are providing advice, it must be of the highest quality, and this might require you to get input from experts. If you are creating a product, it must be something which others want to buy, and which they believe in. You cannot do one thing, and say something else. You must be open about your shortcomings, and the things which you have got wrong. Be prepared to accept criticism, and to learn from it. Show others that you are still human, and they will respect you all the more for it.

Lesson 50: You, and you alone, are the driving force behind your achievements. Whether or not you succeed depends on a variety of factors, but without determination, and taking responsibility for your decisions, you won't every get anywhere.

The Life and Business Lessons of Richard Branson

Screw It, Let's Do It!

"Screw it, let's do it!" This is Richard Branson's motto, and it has become so closely associated with him that it even inspired the title of his 2011 book, *Screw Business as Usual*. Richard Branson is known for his direct approach to everything he does. He is a mischievous chap with a cheeky grin; he gets to the point without bothering with airs and graces, treading frequently and knowingly on the toes of the establishment; and when there is something that he wants, personally or commercially, he dives straight into the deep end and grabs it with both of his hands. Every now and then, this ballsy approach pays off spectacularly well.

In 1979, Branson first saw Necker, an extraordinarily beautiful Caribbean island in the British Virgin Islands. The asking price was $6 million, and when Branson scraped together absolutely every penny he had, it came to a total of $100,000. Rather than fearing what might happen, or thinking it couldn't be done, he put all his cash on the table, and was immediately laughed out of the room by the sellers. A year later, the estate agents came back to him, grovelling. They were no longer laughing at the young man with a seemingly ridiculous dream. No one else had put in a bid for Necker, and the seller's wanted Branson's money after all. Branson bought his $6 million island for just $100,000 in cash. Today, 35 years on, it is worth somewhere in the region $200 million. It is the party island of choice for the world's celebrities, from Kate Winslet to Prince Harry, and it is quite possibly the best investment Branson ever made. It was an impulse buy and one with no commercial basis, but Branson followed his gut, invested in something he wanted and would enjoy, and passion and good fortune combined to ultimately make it a runaway success. Branson now lives on Necker for much of the year, and he wouldn't part with it for the world.

This book offers an introduction to Branson, his businesses and the lessons that they teach us. It is not a text book nor a biography, but more of a cheat sheet for reading on the bus or in the bathroom, so that you can pick out the most significant points without having to carry around a bag of weighty tomes. You can read it all in one sitting, or look up specific case studies as and when you are looking for inspiration or direction. The key lessons outlined here are drawn from interviews Branson has given over his more than 40 years in business, from the numerous blogs and articles written by him and about him, and, most importantly, from the successes and failures of many of his commercial ventures. Though his theories and analysis are certainly important, and this book does indeed give them credence, the hardcore details of what worked and what didn't, combined with the reasons why, are the most useful sources you have as a businessman, whether you are following in Branson's footsteps as an entrepreneur, or contemplating his businesses from afar.

In this book you will find three main sections. In **Part 1**, you will learn about Branson's early life, his family background and his formal education, short-lived though it was. In short, this part of the book is about how he became the man he is. In this chapter we also discuss his earliest business ventures, including *The Student* and Virgin Records, the pitfalls he ran headlong into, and how he picked himself up, turned his life around, and was motivated to learn from his mistakes and succeed.

Part 2 is about Branson's many successes. There are case studies of three of his most important companies, Virgin Trains, Virgin Media and Virgin Atlantic, and these case studies look at the different models the companies have, and how they make their money. This chapter is also about how Branson diversifies his commercial options, spreading his risk to maximums return and hedge his bets against failure, and how in recent years he has used his money and public profile to pursue humanitarian agendas he believes are particularly important.

Branson would argue that part of success is knowing how to fail, and being prepared to get back up and try again when it has all gone wrong. For this reason, **Part 3** is about how Branson handles failure and criticism. We look in detail at three Virgin companies that went wrong - Virgin Cola, Virgin Brides and Virgin Vie - why they went wrong, and how Branson was able to live to fight another day. There is a short examination of the criticism heaped on Branson by competitors and the press, and how he handles that too.

Without anymore to do, however, let's meet the man in question.

Getting Into Business

Sir Richard Charles Nicholas Branson is quite possibly the world's most famous businessman. From Australia to Zimbabwe, Atlanta to Zagreb and everywhere in between, the Englishman and his infamous publicity stunts get people talking. Even if you cannot name a single one of his more than 400 companies, you will recognise this laid-back celebrity, his goatee beard and the cheeky grin. Richard Branson is the master of self promotion, and the column inches he personally generates are one of the major contributing factors to the Virgin Group's success. He was knighted by Prince Charles at Buckingham Palace in March 2000 for his services to entrepreneurship, and in 2014 *The Sunday Times* voted him the most admired business person over the last five decades. Just how did he manage to get there?

Richard Branson was born on 18 July 1950, the eldest of three children. His father, Edward Branson, was a barrister, respected and comfortably wealthy but by no means a society figure, in spite of the fact that his own father, Richard's grandfather, was a titled high court judge. Richard's mother, Eve, had been a professional ballet dancer and air hostess prior to getting married. A stay at home mum, she supplemented the family's income with small, entrepreneurial projects, including producing craft items to sell. Branson and his two younger sisters were encouraged to help her with the things she made. The family was always close, and Branson right from the start Branson had a particularly strong relationship with his mother.

Branson and his sisters grew up in the south of England. They enjoyed an idyllic childhood, though discipline at home was strict: in his biography Branson describes how at the age of five his mother put him out of the car three miles from home and told him to walk the rest of the way. It was his punishment for causing a disturbance on the back seat. Branson sees this as a turning point in his childhood: for the first time he had to take responsibility for his actions, and he was forced to overcome his innate shyness and talk to strangers in order to be able to get home. It was a lesson that would stand him in good stead in later life.

Schooling was a trial for Branson, and in all honesty he probably didn't get a great deal out of the experience, at least not academically. He was privately educated, first at Scaitcliffe School, a prep school in Berkshire, and then at the independent Stowe School in Buckinghamshire. He suffered, then as now, from dyslexia, which was neither diagnosed nor supported, and so he performed poorly in both exams and coursework. Though a popular and lively student, he was often disruptive, and on his final day at school, aged 16, his headmaster, Robert Drayson, foretold that young Branson would either end up in prison or become a millionaire. Time would show Drayson understood his student well and was a particularly insightful man: Richard Branson has done both, though you can add a few extra noughts to the millions.

Fresh out of school and with no commercial experience or formal qualifications, 17 year old Branson founded *The Student* magazine, his first business venture and the first brick in the Virgin story. It was 1968 and Branson recognised early both the significant consumer power of young people and also that their interests different substantially from those of their parents. The publication was timely and it capitalised on fashions and moods in universities and colleges across the UK. The inaugural issue featured insightful interviews with prominent celebrities such as the actress Vanessa Redgrave and artist David Hockney; there was a short story by writer John Le Carre; and the magazine carried inspiring feature articles on topics such as white slavery and resistance to the Vietnam War. All the content was designed to encourage discussion amongst readers and their friends, publicising the title.

Right from this first step into business, Branson had his eye on the bottom line: interviewing celebrities and publishing magazines was fun, but financially it still had to wash its face. Making calls from phone boxes, young Branson recruited advertisers who paid for their products to appear in the magazine. Branson gave them the opportunity to promote their goods in front of a very specific group of consumers, and they recognised the value of this. These sums were small, but they were a start.

With *The Student* up and running, Branson realised that he could not only advertise other people's products, but that he had a ready made platform for selling his own products too and, what is more, he wouldn't have to pay anyone else to advertise them. He opened his own shop, Virgin Records and Tapes, with friend Nik Powell in Nottingham Hill in 1971 and sold vinyl records over the counter and by mail order. Branson advertised the bands, tracks and records in the magazine, and he substantially undercut the prices of high street competitors such as WH Smith. The name, Virgin, was suggested by one of Branson's first employees. Although it was seen as a bit risque, it referred principally to the fact that they were all new to business and had little idea of what to expect or do.

Branson and Powell didn't sell just any records: they chose the coolest artists of the day and specialised in so-called Krautrock (German electronic music, a particular favourite of BBC Radio 1 DJ John Peel), as well as progressive rock. Both of these styles were on the cusp of reaching the big time and appealed to Virgin's student market. Hanging out at the shop was half of the appeal for customers: you could meet with friends, sit on the bean bags and tuck into vegetarian snacks. The entire shopping experience was new, a departure from the everyday, and so even if it weren't for the competitive record prices, customers would still have come to Virgin in preference to other record stores because it was the place to see and be seen.

By the early 1970s, we can already see aspects of Branson's *modus operandi* emerging. The characteristics of these early two businesses, *The Student* and Virgin Records and Tapes, didn't guarantee their overnight success or, in fact, long-term survival, but they would be key factors in Branson's later commercial endeavours. The features can be summarised as follows:

1. **The Virgin name**

The Virgin brand has been at the heart of Branson's businesses from these very early days. It is a name that certainly catches people's attention and that they remember. It wins by virtue of its associations with sex but is not, in itself, something overtly sexual or offensive. If anything, it falls in the great British tradition of innuendo, making people smile. By promoting his diverse range of products under the single Virgin umbrella, Branson capitalises on brand familiarity and respect. If people recognise the name Virgin, be it in the context of mobile phones, airlines, cosmetics or records, they immediately associate the product with Branson, and expect it to be affordable, fun and well done.

2. **Creating brands with overlapping interests**

Branson understood right from the start that a company needn't exist in isolation and, indeed, it can be mutually beneficial if two companies work together. *The Student* gave Branson's record store a boost and, later, he used the market knowledge he gained through both of these businesses to build up Virgin Records. The same pattern is evident throughout his career: why sell just air tickets when you can use your knowledge and customer base also to sell holidays and even space travel?

3. **Selling fashionable products**

Branson always aims to be ahead of the curve. He does his market research, and acts on his hunches about what the next big thing will be. This enables him to have the first mover advantage over his competitors and means that customers always see Virgin as being at the cutting edge of innovation. Branson identified brands and musical styles and marketed them to the public just as they were becoming popular, riding on the back of their growth. Likewise, he made sure that Virgin planes were the first to be equipped with in-flight Wi-Fi, anticipating customer demand, and founded Virgin Galactic right back in 2004, long before space tourism was a reality.

4. **Prioritising customer experience**

Customer service and customer experience set Virgin apart from other companies. With Virgin Records and Tapes, we see Branson's desire (and ability) to create an environment that customers loved: it was not just a shop but a place to meet, eat and share ideas. No one else had thought to sell records in this way, and that put Virgin at a distinct advantage. Customers have always come first for Branson: as he puts it, "good customer service will win every time". He still calls a random selection of customers personally to ask for their feedback, and makes his personal phone number and email address available so that people can always come to him with ideas and criticism.

Branson's rise to power was not smooth, however, and one particular event in his early career could well have stopped the Virgin empire in its tracks. By the end of 1971, Virgin Records and Tapes also had a shop in Oxford Street. Branson was caught selling vinyl records that had been declared as export stock: no tax had been paid when he bought them. Although this had enabled him to keep prices low and increase his sales margins, it was a criminal offence and one that HM Revenue & Customs and the Metropolitan Police took very seriously indeed. Branson spent a night in jail, he had to pay all of the unpaid taxes, and was heavily fined.

Most small businesses would have folded at this stage: there was no way to pay the fine and the back taxes, either from savings or from future profits. It was Branson's mother, Eve, who stepped into save the day. She remortgaged their family home to help pay the settlement, and Branson could continue trading. He was heavily indebted to her for her generosity.

Branson learned three important lessons from this event:

1. ***Your family are your greatest supporters and an asset to your business***. Don't take advantage of them, but be aware that they are there to help when you need them. 40 years on Branson is still close to his mother (his father, sadly, died in 2011), and

his children, Holly and Sam Branson, are equally important public brand ambassadors for Virgin, though they have their own, independent careers.

2. ***Keep on the right side of the law***. Bending the rules can help you get rich quick, but in the longer term it will come back to bite you. Knowing the rules and regulations and complying with them has meant that Virgin and Branson himself are respected around the world and that he has largely avoided the damaging tax scandals that have hit the public reputations of companies such as Google, Starbucks and Vodafone.

3. ***Cash flow (or, specifically, lack thereof) kills small companies***. If Branson's mother hadn't stepped into the breach, Virgin would have died a premature death. Branson understands from personal experience that "In business, protecting against the downside is critical." You have to plan for the rainy day and make sure that there is money in the pot to cover all eventualities, even if you don't expect them to occur. Think of it like an insurance policy.

Thanks to his good fortune and his mother's generosity, Branson recovered from this set-back and used Virgin Records and Tapes as the springboard for his next project, that business that would catapult him from being a school drop-out and criminal into the big time. He launched Virgin Records in 1972 with existing business partner, Nik Powell, and two other men, Simon Draper and Tom Newman. Branson's life would change forever.

Branson's time spent in the record shop interacting with his customers meant that he had done his market research thoroughly and had a fair idea about what his future customers would actually want to buy. Interviews he had conducted for *The Student* gave him a ready-made network of musicians, DJs and agents he could work with, and this again gave him a fighting chance in the company's early days.

Luck was on Virgin Records' side: they picked their first artist well and made sure he signed to their label. The artist in question was multi-instrumentalist Mike Oldfield, and they sealed the deal by offering him a free session in their recording studio, The Manor Studio, which was inside Branson's Oxfordshire home. The progressive rock album that Oldfield recorded and Virgin released was *Tubular Bells*. It has sold more than 15 million copies worldwide (including nearly 3 million in the UK), stayed in the charts for 279 weeks, and was played during the opening ceremony of the 2012 London Olympics. Several more chart successes followed, including the electronic album *Phaedra*, and *The Faust Tapes*.

Branson had two priorities: getting the right artists, and selling records at the right price. He famously sold the *Faust* album for 49p, which was usually the price of a vinyl single. To students with limited budgets, the choice was obvious: why would you buy one track on vinyl when you could have a whole album from Virgin Records on tape?

Virgin Records was gaining traction but principally recorded and distributed music by new or little-known artists. That would all change in 1977 when Branson signed the Sex Pistols. The band had previously recorded on both the EMI and A&M labels, but their erratic behaviour and frequent scandals made them unreliable and they were dropped, considered by management to be too much of a liability. Branson saw his opportunity, and Virgin Records stepped into the vacuum. This decision catapulted the record company into the mainstream. Some of the most important progressive rock artists of the late 1970s and early '80s now clamoured to join Virgin Records, including Culture Club and Human League, whose single *Don't You Want Me* went straight to #1 in the UK singles charts in 1981.

Yet again realising the potential of cross-pollinating his businesses, Branson purchased the gay nightclub Heaven, a super club beneath London's Charing Cross Station. Not afraid of courting controversy (gay clubs were still relatively unusual at the time) he promoted his artists and DJs through the club, widening the appeal of his records and also using the column-inches generated about Heaven to raise the profile of Virgin Records.

For the first time Branson was making money, and lots of it. He bought the Kensington Roof Gardens in 1981 and in quick succession founded Virgin Vision (later Virgin Communications), Virgin Games, Virgin Atlantic Airways, Virgin Holidays and BSB (British Satellite Broadcasting, a joint venture with Anglia, Granada and Pearson). He was no longer thinking just about the London or UK markets but was building a global brand with a strong footprint in the USA as well as in Europe.

It is beyond the scope of this book, unfortunately, to look at all these companies in detail, but the early days of Virgin Atlantic (founded in 1984) are particularly worthy of note.

Virgin Atlantic actually had its routes in another airline, formed the year before as British Atlantic Airways (BAA) to operate flights between the UK, US and the Falkland Islands, where the war had just finished. Branson met one of BAA's founders, American Randolph Fields, at a friend's drinks party in London, and after lengthy negotiations,

Branson came onboard as a business partner. The airline was renamed Virgin Atlantic, and shortly afterwards, Branson bought out Fields for a lump sum of £1 million and a further payment from the airline's first dividend.

Branson wasn't actually looking for an airline: he was looking for an opportunity, and when one came along, he seized it with both hands. In the 1980s, British Airways (Virgin Atlantic's main competitor) was the only British airline operating long-haul routes. British Airway's customer service, then as now, was known to be poor, and so Branson quickly realised he could attract customers not by slicing fares but by offering more comfortable planes and superior service during the booking process and onboard. Virgin Atlantic at first was restricted to only operating flights out of Gatwick (for bureaucratic reasons) but in 1991 was granted permission to fly from Heathrow too, much to British Airway's chagrin.

Virgin Atlantic got off to a fairly strong start because Branson identified a genuine customer demand and made sure his new airline filled it. It was not plain sailing (or should that be plane sailing?!), however, and the company experienced financial difficulties throughout the early 1990s. In spite of his deep fondness for Virgin Records, Branson sold the brand to EMI in 1992 for approximately £560 million and used the proceeds to shore up the airline's financial situation. This was a hard decision for Branson - he cried when the deal was done - but he knew the importance of prioritising financial stability and long-term returns above and beyond personal attachment to an individual product or brand. The gamble paid off and Branson and Virgin Atlantic both lived to fight another day, but they were not yet out of the woods.

Throughout the 1990s British Airways ran a serious publicity campaign against Virgin Atlantic, nicknamed the "dirty tricks" campaign. British Airways objected to Branson's publicity stunts and attacked him as viciously as they attacked the airline in a bid to put the company out of business. The plan backfired, however: Branson sued British Airways for libel and won. British Airways had to pay a legal bill of £3 million, personal damages of £500,000 to Branson, and a further £110,000 to Virgin Atlantic. If anything, the failed British Airways campaign actually improved Virgin's standing in the public eye as people enthusiastically backed David against Goliath and were elated when David won.

Today Virgin Atlantic has an annual turnover of £2.87 billion, employs around 10,000 people and carries 5.5 million passengers on its international flights each year. It is one of the largest and best-known brands in Branson's Virgin Group, and a major trend-setter in the global airline market.

Managing 400 Companies

The Virgin Group is a global success story. The group employs 50,000 people world-wide, and in 2012 had worldwide revenues in excess of $24 billion. According to the Forbes 2014 Rich List, Richard Branson personally is worth nearly $5 billion, making him the seventh richest person in the UK. How has he made this money, and how does he manage such success? In this section of the book we are going to look at three Virgin case studies, three successful businesses that Branson has grown and operated in quite different ways, and then some of the more unusual but personally rewarding projects he has launched using the money and profile he has generated through his more conventional commercial platforms.

Virgin Media was a flagship brand for the Virgin Group. Founded in 2006, and with headquarters in New York (executive office) and Hook in the UK (operational headquarters), Virgin Media offered digital television, broadband Internet, fixed-line and mobile telephone services. The company's revenue in 2012 was £4.1 billion, and total assets were in excess of £10.5 billion. Virgin Media was one of the Virgin Group's most successful companies, but Branson sold it to Liberty Global for $23.3 billion (£15 billion) in 2013. This makes it a particularly interesting case study.

Two earlier companies, NTL and Telewest, merged in March 2006 and four months later bought Virgin Mobile UK, founded by Branson in 1999 as the world's first Mobile Virtual Network Operator (MVNO). The offer price of £962.4 million was a package of cash and shares, so Branson acquired a 10.1% stake in the new company, which was rebranded as Virgin Media early in 2007. It was the first "quadruple play" network in the UK (a reference to the four services it provided), and Branson licensed the Virgin name to the new company for a 30-year period, recognising the Virgin name's importance to Virgin Media's long-term success.

Virgin Media was an innovative company in many ways, not least by offering quadruple play. Virgin Media owned and operated its own fibre-optic cable network, the only nationwide cable network in the UK; it launched Virgin Central, one of the first on-demand TV services; and in both 2009 and 2010 the company came top of the class in Ofcom's broadband speed tests, showing investment in infrastructure was paying off. The company experimented with various different ways of streaming content, including via VDSL2 and using telegraph poles, and when in 2010 Ofcom ordered BT to open up its own fibre-optic network to other service providers, Virgin Media was the first to capitalise on the opportunity. Most recently, in 2012, Virgin Media won an exclusive contract to provide wifi on the London Underground network until 2017.

Why then, if Virgin Media had first-rate products and was making money, did Branson sell out to Liberty Global? It comes down to a question of ownership and leverage. As we mentioned above, Branson only ever had a 10.1% stake in Virgin Media. In 2007 Branson had hedged 37% of this stake for a $224 million loan with the bank Credit Suisse, and when the repayment became due, Branson decided not to buy back the 12.8 million mortgaged shares. Instead, he reinvested the money in other Virgin Group projects, including the Virgin Green Fund (an investor in the renewable energy and energy efficiency sectors). The decision to sell Virgin Media in 2013 was therefore not Branson's alone: he was only the company's third largest shareholder, and the shareholders collectively approved the sale. Branson's personal feelings, if indeed he did oppose the deal, were overshadowed by the views of the majority.

Branson made money from Virgin Media, and has used the profits he made to diversify his portfolio, which is, in any case, an admirable strategy: he stayed with Virgin Media throughout its most rapid period of growth, and then sold out before competitors caught up and ate into Virgin Media's profits. It is also likely that just as he did when he sold Virgin Mobile, Branson also accepted shares in Liberty Global as part of the deal for Virgin Media: a deal which combined cash and shares was certainly agreed at the time of the sale, though subsequent to this Branson may have sold his own shares for cash. We cannot be sure on this either way as the parent company is a Delaware-registered organisation that due to local legislation does not have to disclose controlling shareholders in its annual reports.

We discussed the formation of Virgin Atlantic in Part 1 of this book, but we are going to return to it briefly here and examine it from different angles: how it makes money, and how the different parts of the business interrelate.

When consumers think of Branson and airlines, they think of Virgin Atlantic. In fact, the Virgin Group operates a number of airlines, all of which are separate legal entities. In addition to Virgin Atlantic, these include Virgin America, Virgin Australia and Virgin Samoa, as well as the now defunct Virgin Nigeria and Virgin Express (today part of Brussels Airlines, Belgium's national carrier). The strength of this model is that if any one airline fails, it does not automatically endanger the survival of other routes: Virgin Nigeria, for example, could simply be cut off; its losses did not have a detrimental impact on other parts of the company.

Virgin Atlantic has its headquarters in Crawley, England, and it shares the offices with Virgin Holidays. Both Virgin Atlantic and Virgin Holidays are controlled by the same holding company, Virgin Atlantic Ltd., which is in turn owned by the Virgin Group (51%) and Delta Air Lines (49%). The physical and legal proximity of Virgin Atlantic and Virgin Holidays is important because it enables them to have a symbiotic relationship: just as Branson used *The Student* to sell records in his record shop, and his music industry network to sign artists to the Virgin Records label, so too can he up-sell and cross-sell products from the airline to the holiday firm and vice versa. He has, in essence, created a one stop shop for consumers planning their vacations, and so he can make an enviable profit on every part of the holiday package.

In 2009, Virgin Atlantic made £68.4 million in pre-tax profits in spite of the recession and rising oil prices. This was compared to British Airways' losses of £401 million in the same period. How did Branson achieve this, defeating the odds? Firstly, Virgin Atlantic carried 5.8 million passengers in 2009, a large proportion of them in premium classes, increasing their profit margins on sales. Planning ahead, they had also pre-purchased fuel and so when oil prices soared to $147, they didn't have to pay the sky high prices. This alone meant that Virgin Atlantic's fuel bill that year was only £1 billion, a third of that paid by British Airways.

Since 2009, Virgin Atlantic hasn't been so lucky, and in the financial year 2012 to 2013, the airline suffered record losses in the region of £135 million. Virgin Atlantic announced it would axe its long-haul flights to Sydney and would also end its Little Red operations, which had been created to provide domestic flights in the UK after BMI was bought out and its landing slots at Heathrow became available. Cutting costs and increasing profits on long-haul flights became the two greatest priorities, and some critics wondered if Branson would be able to turn around Virgin Atlantic's fortunes at all.

Though some may say Branson is little more than a publicity artist, in fact he is a shrewd businessman and looks ahead. He managed to half Virgin Atlantic's losses in 2013 and expects to return to profit by 2015. He has put Craig Keeger, who he talent spotted whilst Keeger was working for American Airlines, at the helm, showing careful investment in experienced personnel as well as a willingness to look at fresh ideas. In Branson's own words, "The art of delegation is absolutely key."

Virgin Atlantic's turn-over and load factor (the percentage by which an aircraft is filled), have in fact already increased. The relationship with Delta Airlines, who bought into Virgin Atlantic in 2013 (taking over the minority share previously owned by Singapore Airlines), has also widened the appeal of the airline in the US market by opening up 84 new destinations in the States. New uniforms designed by Vivienne Westwood have generated press coverage and made the airline seem far more glamorous than its competitors, and the arrival of 16 brand new Boeing 787-9 Dreamliners means Virgin Atlantic's long-haul routes will be even more comfortable than before.

Not one of these changes is dramatic, and individually they count for relatively little. What Branson is good at, however, is looking at the bigger picture, and then working back to identify the many little steps required to make an impact overall. The parts of Virgin Atlantic that are not viable in the long-term will be cut off; those with commercial potential will be strengthened with the funds released from elsewhere, and in this way, Virgin Atlantic will remain a fixture in our skies for many years to come.

One of the major brands that the Virgin Group operates in the UK market is Virgin Trains, a company that Branson founded back in 1997. Virgin Group is the majority stakeholder (51%) in a partnership with Stagecoach (49%). The company currently operates train services on the West Coast Main Line between London Euston, Manchester, Liverpool, Edinburgh and Glasgow, and has recently had its franchise for that route extended until 2017, after which time Virgin will have to reapply for the license. Virgin Trains also operated Virgin Cross Country services from Birmingham New Street from 1997 to 2007, but they ultimately lost that franchise to competitors Arriva.

Branson's aim with Virgin Trains was to substantially increased the speed of journeys and the quality of service received by customers after the notoriously inefficient British Rail was privatised. He invested heavy in upgrading lines and purchasing new rolling stock, enabling trains to run at 125 mph on some routes. Branson had hoped to get his trains to run at 140 mph, but cutbacks at Railtrack after project costs escalated from £2.5 billion to £10 billion sadly thwarted that ambition.

Operating railway services in the UK is highly capital intensive and risky, as you have to invest in infrastructure but with no guarantee your franchise will be renewed. Branson was hit in exactly this way when he lost the Cross Country franchise to Arriva. The costs are, however, in part off-set by tax payer subsidies, and though these keep Virgin Trains afloat, some critics (including Aditya Chakrabortty of *The Guardian*) have gone to great pains to attack dependence on subsidies.

Chakrabortty believes that Branson's modus operandi is thus: identify industries with little competition; benefit from taxpayer subsidies; and then to cash out, profiting from the tax payer's hard-earned cash. There is some truth in what he says.

One of Branson's strengths is certainly in identifying industries with little competition: this is, in part, what being a good entrepreneur is about. When Branson has gone head to head with fierce, multi-national competitors (see Virgin Cola, *Handling Failure and Criticism*), he has got his fingers burned, so a business which gives him a monopoly, albeit in a certain, narrow area, is undoubtedly attractive. Being awarded the franchise in the first place does, of course, require going head to head with competitors, and you may well lose it in the next round of selection, but Chakrabortty seems to have over-looked that fact.

It is true that Virgin Trains has received large taxpayer-funded subsidies since its inception. Chakrabortty estimates that, in today's money, Virgin Trains received £2.79 billion of direct subsidies between 1997 and 2012. Other subsidies are indirect. Railtrack has reduced its fees to Virgin from £3 billion a year to £1.5 billion. Line upgrades and the fleet of Pendolino trains Virgin Trains uses were subsidised by the British Government, and yet it is Virgin which receives the income stream from ticket sales. According to Manuel Cortes, leader of the TSSA rail union, ticket prices on the West Coast Main Line have risen 245% since the line was privatised and taken over by Virgin Trains.

Even with these subsidies and increases in fares, Virgin Trains has not always made a profit: in 2006 the company made a £13 million pre-tax loss, and total losses from 2011 to 2014 are thought to be in the region of £250 million. Dividends have been paid out by Virgin Trains to its investors (Branson said he had shared £499 million in dividends with Stagecoach in 2013), but such dividends can only be paid in years when the company makes a profit, and based on its track record (excuse the pun), Virgin Trains loses money as often as it makes it. Branson does sometimes profit from the tax payer subsidies, but on those occasions when rail fares and government subsidies do not equal the train operator's running costs, Virgin Trains is in effect subsidising the rail service. It is swings and roundabouts.

The profits Branson has made from his various successful commercial enterprises, and the public platform his success and wealth have given him, have put him in an enviable position from which he can launch a variety of personal projects. These include vanity projects, humanitarian projects, and projects that, though not commercially viable in the short-term, may generate a profit in the future. Branson likes to think big. He sums it up as follows: "I sometimes think in life you've got to dream big by setting yourself seemingly impossible challenges... If you don't dream, nothing happens. And we like to dream big."

Everyone needs a hobby, and if you have got a fortune at your disposal, you can afford to have an expensive hobby. In Branson's case, that hobby is hot air ballooning. Branson laid out a series of challenges for himself: they were all balloon journeys no one had accomplished before. He broke the distance record for a hot air balloon when he crossed the Atlantic Ocean in 1987, reaching speeds of up to 142 mph. Four years later, he crossed the Pacific, and this time set a new speed record of 245 mph. The biggest challenge remained, however: Branson wanted to be the first person to circumnavigate the globe by balloon. He attempted this twice, in 1995 and 1998, but was ultimately beaten to the record by the crew of the Breitling Orbiter 3 later that same year. Branson took his defeat gracefully, and instead turned his attentions to a number of other record breaking feats, including the fastest crossing of the English Channel in an amphibious vehicle (1 hour, 40 minutes and 6 seconds in March 2004). That record still stands today.

Branson's celebrity has made him a popular choice for TV casting agents, who have often asked him to play himself in hit shows. He has willingly obliged, and looks completely relaxed in the limelight. He's made guest appearances in *Friends*, *Baywatch*, *Birds of a Feather* and *Only Fools and Horses*, and his cartoon self appeared in *The Simpson's* episode "Monty Can't Buy Me Love".

Although Branson has a great deal of fun playing himself on TV, in films and on stage, he does actually take his public role very seriously, and consequently he deploys his wealth, time and contact base to the benefit of a number of significant humanitarian projects.

One of the most interesting of these is The Elders, a dedicated group of leaders that work together to solve global conflicts. The idea for the group came out of a series of discussions Branson had with Nelson Mandela and the musician Peter Gabriel in the early 1990s, and it was announced formally in 2007 in a speech given by Nelson Mandela on the occasion of his 89th birthday. Former UN Secretary General and Nobel Peace Prize winner Kofi Annan chairs the group, and other high-profile members include Gro Harlem Brundtland (former Prime Minister of Norway), Martti Ahtisaari (former President of Finland, Nobel Peace Prize winner and the UN's Special Envoy to Kosovo) and Jimmy Carter. During his lifetime Nelson Mandela was an honorary Elder, as is

Desmond Tutu. Branson is not an Elder himself, but along with Gabriel he uses his money to fund their work and to raise the profile of issues they are working to resolve.

Branson also uses his money and influence to support the International Centre for Missing & Exploited Children (ICMEC); and the Branson School of Entrepreneurship, which aims to improve economic growth and stability in South Africa. He has backed the Global Zero campaign to eliminate nuclear weapons; and has spoken out on a wide range of issues, from calling Uganda to account for its anti-homosexuality legislation, to increasing public awareness about wildlife poaching and trafficking. Although he does maintain an interest in the running of the Virgin Group, he has delegated the day to day affairs and now concentrates his efforts primarily on his humanitarian projects.

The last category of Branson's projects are his dream projects, those that are not yet viable but at one stage might well be. Perhaps the most ambitious of these, and the one now reaching viability, is Virgin Galactic, Branson's commercial space flight company.

Branson founded Virgin Galactic in 2004 with the intention of developing a commercial space craft and offering suborbital flights to space tourists. He anticipated the first flight would happen in 2009, but a number of set-backs meant that Branson's dream has not yet become a reality. He does, however, remain optimistic.

The Virgin Group initially invested $100 million into Virgin Galactic, and this was followed by investments of $380 million from the sovereign wealth fund of Abu Dhabi, paid in two instalments, and $200 million from the New Mexico Government. NASA has invested a relatively small sum of $4.5 million for research flights. When you dream big, it seems, other people will dream big too.

So far, it is hard to establish when and how the investors expect to get their money back. It may well be, in fact, that the Emiratis in particular have got carried away with the hype and not actually done the maths. The latest figures (August 2013) state that 640 potential space tourists have signed up, each paying $200,000. This makes a total of $12.8 million, a fraction of what has been invested, and though investors argue that the price of space travel will come down, Virgin Galactic tickets have actually already increased in price, to $250,000. The fourth and most recent test flight of a Virgin Galactic space craft, VSS Enterprise, ended in disaster in October 2014 when it broke apart in mid air and crashed into the Mojave Desert, killing test pilot Michael Alsbury and seriously injuring his co-pilot, Peter Siebold.

It is not known when Virgin Galactic will sort out its space craft designs and make them safe enough to transport space tourists. What we do know, however, is that although Branson started out in the space tourism early, the decade of delays has meant that he has lost his head start. Three other companies, the Sierra Nevada Corporation, XCOR Aerospace, and SpaceX are now all developing their own reusable crewed suborbital and orbital spaceplanes. SpaceX has been awarded a a $2.6 billion contract by NASA, and as the company has scheduled a crewed flight for 2016, it is likely that they, not Virgin Galactic, will become the first private company to successfully launch men into space.

Branson will hopefully have more success with Virgin Green, the fund he has established to invest in renewable and efficient energy sources in Europe and the US. It is a venture capital firm, which will enable Branson to spread risk across a large number of projects, and also to cherry pick the very best ideas and teams. Some of the companies Virgin Green Fund is already investing in include Gevo Inc., and advanced biofuels company which converts renewable raw materials into hydrocarbons and isobutanol; Quench, an ultraviolet water filtration company; and Metrolight, a provider of electronic ballast solutions for high-intensity discharge lighting systems. Not all the investments will come to fruition, however: Solyndra, a Californian company which manufactures film solar cells, looked initially to be a good investment, but collapsed in 2011 because although the idea was strong, the company could compete with conventional solar panels made from crystalline silicon.

Yet again, Branson's success will be dictated to a large extent by his ability to identify commercial opportunities and to spread his risk across multiple companies. He is quite clear about his approach: "Business opportunities are like buses, there's always another one coming." Branson does not expect every project he touches to turn to gold, but he does expect that if he tries enough times, one of them will generate a substantial return, and that alone is enough to motivate him to keep on trying. In business, persistence and optimism pays off.

Failure and Criticism

Not everything that Richard Branson touches works out as he'd like it to, as he is the first to admit, and even those companies that ultimately turned a profit often struggled financially in their first few years. Branson's message to his disciples is clear: "In a company's first year, your goal should be simply to survive, and this will likely take everything you've got. No matter how tired or afraid you are, you have to figure out how to keep going." If you can get over this initial hurdle, you have at least a chance of long-term success.

There is, however, an argument that to be a good businessman you also have to know when to quit. It doesn't matter how good a business idea looks on paper, there are numerous reasons why it might not actually work in practice, and you have to be able to look critically at the product you are offering, what is going wrong, and if it is both feasible and cost-effective to rectify the problems. In this section of the book we are going to look at some of Branson's failures, why they occurred and how he responded to them. The case studies contain lessons for us all.

Branson has launched more than 400 brands worldwide since 1966. Many of these companies have been commercial success stories and stood the test of time; others have fallen by the wayside. Perhaps the most well publicised failure of a Virgin brand is Virgin Cola.

Branson founded Virgin Cola in 1994, believing that he could go head to head with the two biggest carbonated drinks brands in the world, Coca Cola and Pepsi, who he referred to as the "cola duopolists". The product launch was public relations gold dust: Branson drove a vintage Sherman tank through New York's Times Square, crushing Coca Cola bottles under the tracks before opening fire on Coca Cola's billboard. He erected a 40-foot Virgin Cola billboard above the Times Square Virgin Megastore; the drink's bottle was shaped to resemble Pamela Anderson's voluptuous curves and was popularly known as "the Pammy"; and Branson paid a fortune to the makers of the hit US TV show *Friends* to ensure the sitcom's characters were seen drinking Virgin Cola in the episodes. So far, everything was fine, but sadly the honeymoon period would not last.

Branson disagreed over the business development strategy with his partner, the Canadian drinks manufacturer Cott Corporation, who owned a 50% stake in Virgin Cola. Branson had to buy out their stake and go it alone in the US market, whilst in the UK he partnered with two relatively small drinks companies, Prince's and then, a short while later, Silver Spring, neither of whom had much clout in the marketplace.

The serious pitfall, however, was that Branson underestimated the strength of Coca Cola and Pepsi's market domination, particularly where brand recognition and distribution networks were concerned. Branson himself freely admits, "We often move into areas where the customer has traditionally received a poor deal, and where the competition is complacent," but Virgin Cola was a case in which this did not apply: customers were happy with the existing products on the market, and Coca Cola and Pepsi were far from complacent when dealing with new competitors snapping at their heels. Coca Cola's immediate response to Virgin Cola's appearance was doubling its advertising and promotion budget overnight, drowning out Virgin Cola's publicity.

By 1999, Virgin Cola had only captured 3% of the UK's cola market and had never made a penny in profit. This was largely due to Branson's difficulties distributing the product: most restaurant chains, cinemas and bars already had exclusive, long-term distribution contracts with either Coca Cola or Pepsi that they were unable or unwilling to break, even if Virgin Cola was more competitively priced. By the early 2000s, even the major supermarket chains had stopped stocking Virgin Cola: the only place you could consistently buy it was in 2 litre bottles in Asda, and it was seen as second-rate, low-price product. Asda too dropped Virgin Cola in August 2009, stating that they were no longer prepared to give it shelf space when competitors would sell far better.

The failure of Virgin Cola taught Branson an important lesson about the difficulties of taking on genuinely strong competitors: humility can be just as importance as confidence. He reflected on Virgin Cola: "That business taught me not to underestimate the power of the world's leading soft drink makers. I'll never again make the mistake of thinking that all large, dominant companies are sleepy!"

With Branson, however, even bleak situations often seem to have an unexpected silver lining. Virgin Cola is still sold profitably under license in Nigeria and the Philippines, two markets where the Virgin Group would not otherwise have a prominent presence, and, as Branson proclaims proudly, "We're still number one in Bangladesh!" This may not have been what he set out to achieve, but at least he is still able to think positively.

Another of Branson's failures, though less well known than Virgin Cola, was Virgin Brides, which Branson launched in 1996, generating publicity in his own inimitable style by shaving off his beard and donning a lacy white wedding dress and veil. When the company closed its last store in Manchester in 2007, Branson joked to reporters, "Why did Virgin Brides fail? Because we soon realised there weren't any!" Branson's critics suggested the unflattering originally promo shots of Branson in drag may well have been an own-goal too. The reality is more likely to be that, as with carbonated drinks, the wedding dress and accessory market was already highly saturated and as every bride is searching for individuality, a somewhat gimmicky change of stores simply didn't appeal to the target market.

The third of Branson's failures we are going to examine in this book, albeit briefly, is Virgin Vie, which was founded as The Virgin Cosmetics Company in 1997. The company was created by two individuals, Mark and Liz Warom, but they had financial backing from Branson and he allowed them to operate the firm under the Virgin umbrella. The company sales model was through parties, mail order and other retail outlets at first, but it was expected that Virgin Vie would open 100 of its own stores within the first five years.

Virgin Vie struggled to gain traction. It was rebranded as Virgin Cosmetics in 1999, apparently to make it more obvious what the product it sold was, but in fact the range included not only skin care products and make up, but also bath and body products, aromatherapy oils, jewellery, and home ware. It was a bit of a mishmash really. The company was headquartered in Tangmere, England, but there were few sales in the UK. Virgin Vie signed a partnership agreement with Luxasia pte Ltd. in 2001 in a bid to open up markets in Asia, and the following year had 7,000 distributors, mostly in China, South East Asia, and South Africa, but the company was overstretched and forced to close all stores in 2003, quite suddenly.

Virgin Vie limped on throughout the 2000s until there was a management buyout in 2009 by former marketing director Ros Simmons and her business partner, Ratan Daryani. Virgin had to pay £8.8 million to extract the Virgin name (which was surely the company's most valuable asset), and also write off an estimated £21 million in loans. The new company was even less successful than its Virgin forerunner, and Vie at Home (the company's new name) went into administration in 2011 owing more than £5 million to its suppliers and to HM Revenue & Customs.

Though little analysis has been done to date on the failure of Virgin Vie, I would suggest the principle reason it went bust was that Branson had, in reality, little or no involvement in the firm. It was not his idea, he had not researched the market, and though he put funding into the enterprise, neither he nor his core team were involved in the company on a day to day basis. Virgin Vie had the Virgin name above the door, but that alone was not enough to make it a success: the Virgin magic is about the ideas, the team and the drive behind Virgin products. The name on its own is not enough.

Branson lost money on Virgin Vie, undoubtedly, but he got out before the other investors. In short, it could have been an awful lot worse. One of Branson's strengths in business is his timing - knowing when to enter a market but also, as importantly, when to get out - and this sensitivity to shifting circumstances and markets is very clear in his swift exit from Virgin Vie.

How Branson handles failures and set-backs is a large part of why he is successful entrepreneur. His nickname, Dr Yes, is telling: he is perpetually optimistic and will jump at new opportunities, which pushes him forward into businesses and markets where others would be cautious to tread. His personal motto, "Screw it, just do it", is particularly telling about his approach. The flip side of the coin of unending optimism, however, is that every now and then Branson plunges head first into a new business venture without doing sufficient market research. Over all, his gambles pay off (see above for the example of the sale of Virgin Records to keep Virgin Atlantic afloat), but as every gambler knows, every now and then even the best gambler gets his fingers burned.

Fortunately for Branson, the Virgin brands that have failed have been relatively small. They have not been, in the greater scheme of things, capital intensive (unlike, for example, Virgin Atlantic or Virgin Trains), and their decline has not had a detrimental impact on the overall reputation of the Virgin Group.

Branson has also been able to see the funny side in failure and, more often than not, turn the joke to his advantage, even when it is on him. In 1985 Branson created the Atlantic Challenger, a boat that he used to try to break the Trans-Atlantic crossing record to win the coveted Blue Riband award. The Atlantic Challenger sunk 300 miles off the British coast, and Branson and his crew had to be rescued, embarrassingly, by a banana boat. This could have been a humiliating event, but having just launched Virgin Atlantic, Branson rode high on the publicity generated by the sinking and took out a double page advert in the newspapers. The advert showed the hull of the boat sticking out of the water, and above it there was a caption: "Next time, Richard, take the plane." The public loved it, Virgin Atlantic's brand recognition increased substantially, and people saw it as a younger, cooler and more irreverent company than its competitors, which appealed to the airline's target market.

In considering Branson's strengths and failings, and in a bid to understand the man and what drives him to succeed, it is relevant to look at how he handles criticism and scandal. Earlier in the book we discussed his run-in with the tax authorities in the 1960s and how he sued British Airways for libel when they attacked him and Virgin Atlantic. Although journalists and competitors do like to stick their oar in to Branson every so often, there is surprisingly little juicy gossip about him online: he is a happily married father of two; he sits on the Global Drug Commission and avoids involvement in the drugs industry (medical or recreational) so as not to lose his credibility as an impartial commissioner; and though he is open abut loving sex and uses innuendo and scantily clad female models to generate publicity for his products, there is not so much as a whiff of adultery, harassment or abuse anywhere in his past. Much to his critics' frustration, Branson is pretty much squeaky clean.

One issue that does rear its ugly head now and then is that is Branson's personal tax evasion, and the tabloid press is particularly fond of returning to it when there is a dearth of any actual news. The accusation levelled at Branson is that he moved to Necker, his private island in the British Virgin Islands, in 2006 to avoid paying income tax. Unlike US tax law, which demands US nationals and green card holders pay tax anywhere in the world, British nationals living overseas more than 180 days a year do not pay tax to the British Government. These so-called "non-doms" (non-domiciled Brits) are within the law, but critics question the morality of their actions.

In Branson's case, even the morality aspect is not clear cut: Branson has owned Necker since 1979 but lived and paid taxes in the UK for 40 years. His Virgin Group companies continue to pay full taxes in the UK (unlike the likes of Starbucks, Google and Vodafone, at whom the same criticisms are levied). Branson has retired, more or less, to Necker, which is undoubtedly and extraordinarily beautiful place, and his principle residence is indeed on the island: it is not that he has declared Necker as his residence but in reality continues to live elsewhere. What is more, Branson claims that his personal earnings now go to charity, and so even if he were to still be living in the UK, he would not be paying tax on them.

As is probably to be expected, Branson has paid no heed to these criticisms: there is not really any basis to them, and as they have little or no impact on his bottom line, he has sensibly decided to focus on his businesses and personal projects rather than give the tabloid accusations air. He showed his ongoing love for the UK by posing in a (rather hideous, but probably deliberately so) Union Jack suit on the beach at Necker, which in itself generated quite a few column inches.

Conclusions

Richard Branson is one of the best known entrepreneurs in the world: his face is synonymous with the Virgin brand, and were it not for his personal charisma and willingness to play up to the media, it is unlikely any of the Virgin Group's companies would have achieved the international profile that they have today. In spite of this incredible public persona, however, we know relatively little about the man behind the mask. How does Branson see himself?

In a 2012 interview with *Entrepreneur* magazine, Branson let slip that his childhood hero was Peter Pan, the JM Barry character who never gets old. At the age of 64, Branson certainly shows no signs of slowing down: in the past year he has published another best-selling book, *The Virgin Way: How to Listen, Learn, Laugh and Lead*; opened a new Virgin Hotel in Chicago; floated 15% of his stake in Virgin Money for £85 million; and made the groundbreaking (and column inch generating) decision to grant his personal staff as much annual holiday as they want, whenever they want to take it. When asked whether ageing is an advantage to entrepreneurs, Branson is divided in his opinions: he values experience and is inspired by the likes of the Rolling Stones, still playing together after 50 years, but believes senior business leaders do get stuck in a rut of working always with the same people. Branson stresses the importance of reaching out to the young, the energetic and the imaginative, including by volunteering as a mentor, in order to always keep your own mind bright and offering fresh.

Who else, then, has inspired Branson to succeed and to follow his current path? When asked this question, which does pop up repeatedly in interviews, Branson's first answer is always Nelson Mandela, "one of the most inspiring men I have ever met and had the honour to call my friend." Branson has read *Long Walk to Freedom* many times over, and it was his close personal relationship with Mandela that gave birth to The Elders in 2007. In spite of his dyslexia, Branson is an avid reader and the books he reads often have a profound effect on him. Al Gore's *An Inconvenient Truth* and James Lovelock's *The Revenge of Gaia* both developed his interest in humanitarian and ecological issues, and he reads historical titles too, mentioning *Stalingrad* by Harriet Beecher Stowe and *Mao: The Unknown Story* by Jung Chang as particular favourites. Not all Branson's reading matter is so serious, however: he loves looking at comic books too, and founded Virgin Comics in 2006 in order to give "a whole generation of young, creative thinkers a voice."

In anyone's book, Richard Branson's achievements, commercially and personally, are remarkable, and he deserves a great deal of respect for having climbed from very ordinary origins to become a multi billionaire in just 40 years. The honours and awards he has received go some way to demonstrating the perceived impact he has had on all walks of life, and the legacy he will leave behind him long after he has gone. Branson was listed on the BBC's 2002 list of 100 Greatest Britons; in 2007 he was included in *Time Magazine*'s Top 100 Most Influential People in the World; and in 2014 he was recognised by *The Sunday Times* as the most admired business person over the last five decades. For business innovation and leadership in Virgin's core businesses, Branson has received the Tony Jannus Award for accomplishments in commercial air transportation; the German Media Prize: the President's Merit Award for services to the music industry, from the National Academy of Recording Arts and Sciences; and the ISTA Prize from the International Space Transport Association for Virgin Galactic's development of suborbital transport systems. Though these gongs are undoubtedly significant, it is probably the awards he has received in the humanitarian field that mean most to Branson. In 2007 UN Secretary General Ban Ki Moon presented Branson with the United Nations Correspondents Association Citizen of the World Award for his support for environmental and humanitarian causes. In 2014 this was followed by the Business for Peace Award, given annually by the Business for Peace Foundation in Norway. When Branson looks back at his life and his achievements, it is these two awards that he will surely value most.

Branson's most famous book, his first biography, is entitled *Losing My Virginity: How I Survived, Had Fun, and Made a Fortune Doing Business My Way,* and in many ways these words sum up completely the man and his approach to business. The lessons we can learn from Branson are all contained therein, and so to conclude this book I'm going to break down that title into its component parts. We learn something important from each of them, and if you remember nothing else from Branson's experiences, take these points to heart.

Losing My Virginity: Every one of us starts out in business like Branson, not knowing what we are going to do or how we are supposed to do it. Don't be put off by your own naivety or inexperience. Recognise your own shortcomings and be prepared to learn quickly, including from your mistakes. If you don't jump into the deep end at some point, you will never learn to swim.

How I survived: In the first few years of your new business, survival is the only thing that matters. You might not hit your targets and make money as quickly as you want, but hang in there through the tough times and eventually you will find the opportunity that makes you a profit. If you always drop out too soon, you will never reach that point.

Had Fun: People buy into Branson and his brands because it looks like he is always enjoying himself. Choose a business you are passionate about and want to get up in the morning to work on. Enthusiasm for your product motivates the team around you and tells customers unequivocally that they want some of what you have.

Made a Fortune: The end game is making money, and you always need to keep this in mind. If something isn't going to work, you have to be prepared to sacrifice it, however emotionally or financially attached you are, in order that something else can fly.

Doing Business My Way: It is your business, so do it your way. If you copy what everyone else is already doing, you will never stand out from the crowd. Branson is a success because he does things differently, and frequently better, than his competitors. Find your niche, or a novel approach, and make it your unique selling point.

You have read the book, you have studied the man, and so now all that remains is to kickstart your own business journey. In the words of Branson himself, "Screw it, let's do it." There's never a better time than now.

50 Life and Business Lessons from Tony Robbins

Introduction

Tony Robbins is a multi-millionaire. He's a best-selling author. He's a TV star. He has the jet set lifestyle and the beautiful blonde wife. He is treated like the Messiah by his millions of loyal followers, people who hang on his every word and will do anything to attend one of his face to face seminars. His rags to riches story embodies the American Dream and has inspired people around the world to buy into his teachings, to learn his techniques, and to try to build better lives for themselves.

This book is a short introduction to Robbins, his life and work. In it we have endeavoured to distil the information into 50 bite-size lessons which you can read and learn from. Whilst we cannot guarantee you too will earn the best part of half a billion dollars (at least not overnight!), by studying Robbins' approach to marketing and self-promotion, you can raise your own profile, negotiate more effectively and, as a result, capitalise on your self-development for financial gain.

Childhood and Education

Tony Robbins' childhood was a recipe for failure, so if you ever think that your impoverished, unhappy background will hold you back, look no further than Robbins for a role model of what anyone with luck and the right mind set can achieve.

Lesson 1: It doesn't matter where you start in life, it is where you end up which counts.

Born as Anthony Mahavoric in Hollywood, California in February 1960, Robbins was the eldest of three children. Unable to support his family financially, Robbins' father walked out when Robbins was just seven years old. His mother, depressed and unable to cope, turned to drink and prescription drugs. Her children were left more or less to fend for themselves, and Robbins took care of his younger siblings. His mother worked her way through a series of husbands, including semi-professional baseball player Jim Robbins, who adopted the children and gave them his name. Robbins describes this period of his life as being characterised by abuse and chaos.

Lesson 2: Poverty and a troubled childhood are no excuses for failure.

Against the odds, Robbins remained in high school in Glendora, California, supporting himself working as a cleaner whilst he studied. He proudly earned $40 a week, and put it towards his first car. Robbins was President of the Student Union in his senior year of high school and may have had the ability to go on to college, but fate took a twist, and it wasn't kind. His mother had another breakdown and chased him from the house with a kitchen knife. Robbins was just 17 years old, and after that he never returned home. He had to work to survive.

Early Career

Even as a teenager, Robbins knew that life had more in store for him than a career as a cleaner, but also that nothing would be handed to him on a plate. He would have to work for it, and hard. He took his inspiration from the rags to riches story of Jim Rohn, arguably the founder of motivational speaking as a discipline in the United States, and when Rohn gave an evening seminar in Robbins' hometown, 18-year old Robbins spent $35 of his $40 weekly earnings to attend. By far the youngest and least experienced person in the room, Robbins sat at his future mentor's feet, enraptured.

Lesson 3: Even when times are tough, you have to invest in your future.

Robbins first proper job was working for Rohn as a sale rep, pitching Rohn's seminars. Robbins took to sales like a duck to water, and made a fortune selling seminars on commission. But as fast as he earned it, he spent it. Grossly immature, and desperate for affection, he threw his money around, hoping it would buy him love, or at least attention. It was a period of tragic self-sabotage, and Robbins was soon once again desperate and broke. Hating himself and at a life-long low, Robbins realised that he had to take responsibility for himself, to be the positive force in his own life. He wrote in his journal everything that he despised, everything that he wanted to change, and set about finding out how to do it.

Lesson 4: You have to be able to self-critique before you can implement lasting changes.

Two of Robbins' earliest discoveries were Neuro-Linguistic Programming (NLP) and Eriksonian hypnosis. He trained with NLP's co-founder, John Grinder, believing that he could train his own mind to operate in its peak state. In a demonstration of self-control, of self-mastery, he learned to fire walk and then began to give seminars about how the mind can be used to conquer one's fears. Robbins was attention grabbing, utilising not only fire walking but also board breaking and skydiving to capture his audiences' attention, and he went head to head with traditional psychiatrists on the radio, curing their patients of long-held phobias. Such behaviour raised his public profile immeasurably, and once again the money started rolling in.

Lesson 5: If you want people to listen to you, you have to do something which will grab their attention.

Neuro-Linguistic Programming (NLP)

NLP cannot be dismissed as just another hustle. Its theoretical underpinnings represent an ambitious attempt to codify and synthesize the insights of linguistics, body language, and the study of communication systems.

Psychology Today

Neuro-Linguistic Programming (NLP) is not a science but a set of guiding principles and techniques which practitioners can use to change, adopt or eliminate certain behaviours in themselves and others. This gives greater control over your mental, emotional, and physical states of well-being, and advocates believe that by having greater control over ourselves and our ability to communicate and interact with those around us, we are better placed to shape what happens to us, now and in the future. NLP is a popular tool amongst business and political leaders, sports stars and film stars, and it has allegedly been used by Bill Clinton and Tony Blair, Bill Gates and Oprah Winfrey, Tiger Woods and J.K. Rowling.

Lesson 6: You can change your behaviour, and that of other people, by controlling your thoughts and emotions.

NLP has three core components:

1.   Subjectivity

We experience the world subjectively through our five senses and language. Before something happens, we create in our heads a subjective representation of the event, what we will see, hear, smell etc., and there is a discernible pattern or structure to this. We can modify behaviour (our own and that of others) by understanding and manipulating these subjective representations.

2.   Consciousness

Human consciousness actually has two parts: the conscious and the unconscious. Subjective representations often occur in the unconscious mind, and so we need to be able to access, and exert some control, over this.

271

3.   Learning

We learn by imitating, or modelling. You can codify and reproduce someone else's behaviour by understanding their subjective representations during a particular activity.

In terms of techniques and processes, NLP has four main stages. These are establishing rapport between the NLP practitioner and the subject; finding out information about goals the subject wants to achieve, or the problems that they are facing and want to overcome; using specific techniques to make interventions; and integrating specific changes into the subject's daily routine. Communication between the NLP practitioner and the subject is both verbal and non-verbal.

Lesson 7: Even complicated concepts can be broken down into manageable chunks which anyone can master.

There are multiple techniques for building rapport between the practitioner and the subject. The practitioner might, for example, mirror the body language of the subject, repeating certain gestures so that the two feel that they know each other well. Maintaining eye contact is very important as it suggests that the practitioner is concentrating on, and cares about, what the subject has to say. The practitioner will insert certain, often emotionally charged, keywords into the conversation to achieve a certain outcome. They will also deliberately alter the pace and tone of their speech, subconsciously encouraging the subject to copy the changes.

Lesson 8: You have to build rapport with someone if you want to influence them.

Finding out information about goals and problems also requires both verbal and non-verbal communication: certain hand gestures, glances or ticks, reveal topics which make the subject feel uncomfortable, or about which they are excited, for example. A set of meta-model questions are typically used by the practitioner, and the subject is encouraged to think about the long-term impact of achieving (or not achieving) their goals, or changing their behaviour. A subject who wants to lose weight, for example, might be encouraged to think about benefits to their health from weight loss, how they might look and feel, and the impact that this might have on their personal relationships. Positive emotions will be tied to positive behavioural changes, reinforcing the incentive to implement them.

Lesson 9: Take time to get to know your subject and to understand them in order to increase your impact.

In order to implement changes, subjects are encouraged by the practitioner to visualise the future, taking advantage of the subjective representations we all already produce. Subjects can mentally rehearse actions and scenes in their head, and through guiding the subject's language, the practitioner can make the subject take ownership of the problem and the strategy for overcoming it, or the means for achieving specific goals. This shifts responsibility for behavioural change from the practitioner to the subject, making it an ideal technique for self-help.

Mastering Neuro-Linguistic Programming

Tony Robbins is not the only self-help guru to have mastered NLP and made it part of his mission to teach others the technique: the likes of Paul McKenna and Derren Brown have also used NLP to great effect, making the technique (and particularly its hypnotic elements) appear like magic. Their 10 steps to mastering NLP successfully can be summarised as follows:

1.   Understand what you are getting into

NLP is complex and mastering it takes time and effort. In fact, gaining control of your mind may turn out to be a life-long endeavour!

2.   Understand what NLP actually is

NLP is a pseudo-science with many detractors. Lots of industries try to adopt aspects of it for their own benefit, without really understanding how it works. You need to find out what NLP is, what it can do for you, and what it cannot do. Only then can you decide whether or not it is worth making the effort to learn.

3.   Understand how NLP works

NLP is about input and output. What we put into our brains, and how we process it, determines what comes out. The process is as simple as that. The hard bit is how we manipulate the data.

4.   Understand how NLP has developed

NLP was first developed by Richard Bandler and John Grinder in the mid-1970s. Since then, it has become a global, multi-million dollar movement. It isn't a static practice: it is changing continually as people learn how to optimise the techniques. Keep abreast of these developments if you want to be able to implement NLP as well as possible.

5.   Learn from the experts in NLP

Robbins is one of the most high-profile practitioners of NLP, but there are many others out there, many of whom are prepared to teach others. Watch them at work, in person or via online videos, and read what they have to say.

6.   Understand that there are many paths to mastering NLP

Although many people will sign up for a course to learn NLP, this is by no means the only way to do it. At least in the early stages, you might be satisfied reading books and online forums, and watching videos on YouTube. Remember that everyone learns differently, and has different reasons for wanting to learn NLP. You need to find the strategy which works best for you.

7.   Experiment with NLP

NLP is not a science, and there is no one 'right' way of practising it. Take time to experiment and find out what works best for you. Once you have mastered the basic techniques, there will be things which occur to you that you want to test out. Go for it. Keep experimenting and keep learning, and you will keep improving.

8.   Interpret NLP in your own way

Our brains are incredibly complex, and NLP is incredibly flexible. It is perfectly acceptable to branch out from the usual techniques and functions of NLP, and reshape the practice as works best for you.

9.   Extend your limits

There is no limit to what the human mind can achieve! Use NLP to unlock your potential. Want to master astrophysics, or memorise every FA Cup winning team since time began? How about learning to *recite The complete Works of Shakespeare*? Whatever your memory, learning or communication objectives, NLP can help you achieve it.

10.   Enjoy NLP

If you enjoy something, you will work harder at it and ultimately therefore be more successful. NLP isn't supposed to be prescriptive and dull: it is supposed to be creative and enjoyable. If you aren't having fun whilst you are learning and experimenting with NLP, look at a new way of learning and practising it.

Infomercials and Videos

Robbins knew that his sales pitch had to be perfect: marketing was as important as the actual treatment, if not more so. The 1980s was a golden age for television and television advertising, and so he jumped on the band wagon and began producing a series of cheesy infomercials to be shown in the ad breaks between late night TV shows.

Lesson 10: You have to find ways to make yourself highly visible in your chosen marketplace.

Robbins gave audiences exactly what they wanted to see: his hair was slicked back, his teeth were sparkling white, and his message was engaging, convincing. The public began to buy into Tony Robbins as a brand, and as his fame spread, the calibre of his clients increased. When Quincy Jones, Andre Agassi and even the White House came calling, it did Robbins' reputation no harm at all.

Lesson 11: You are your brand. You are inseparable from your brand. You must remember that at all times.

Through his infomercials, Robbins sold his seminars and coaching videos. The tapes sold by the hundreds of thousand, and when he spoke at an event, he could pack out an arena like a rock star. Robbins was commercial gold dust, but though his marketing pitch was exemplary, in other areas of business he still wasn't quite so savvy. Leaving his unscrupulous manager to handle his financial affairs, he was unaware that the manager embezzled three-quarters of a million dollars. When it did come to light, Robbins was faced with a dilemma: should he declare bankruptcy, leaving his career in tatters, or find another way? For Robbins, it wasn't really a choice. He was a success. He was a leader. He was determined to show the world what he could do, debts or no debts. Robbins did 275 days straight on the road, speaking anywhere and everywhere, and within a year the debts were repaid in full. What looked to be an impossibility had come to pass. Robbins was back in control.

Lesson 12: Integrity and hard work always pay long-term dividends.

Robbins' Books

Although Robbins' seminars attract hundreds of thousands of people every year, those seminars are the end of his sales funnel: attendees' attention is caught much earlier, online, through articles and advertising, and many of them start their commercial engagement with Robbins by buying one of his books. By promising to educate his readers, to enhance their understanding of themselves, and that they will be able to optimise their lives, achieving wealth and happiness, he draws them in. Buying and reading his books is just one step to unearthing his secrets, which he will benevolently share in their pages.

Lesson 13: Books are a great way of spreading your message to people who you would otherwise be unable to reach.

Unlimited Power

The first of Robbins' books, *Unlimited Power*, was published in 1987 when Robbins was in his mid-20s with a young family at home.

Lesson 14: No one is too busy to write! Make time to promote yourself and your ideas, even when work and family commitments are piling up.

In the book he unveils his seven disciplines for success, which can be summarised as follows:

1.   Do not think of success or of failure, only of outcomes. Use your own power to produce the outcomes you want. To do this is within your capability.

2.   Take charge of your own life and create the world you want to live in.

3.   Always stretch yourself: if you do so, you will be able to achieve more tomorrow than you could today.

4.   Commit to unconscious competence: make a skill become second-nature so that you can perform it even whilst executing another task.

5.   Always act with personal integrity. Your beliefs may change over time – they need not be static – but you must remain true to your values, and adjust your behaviour accordingly.

6.   Communication is not about the communicator, but about the person who receives the message. Their understanding of that message is paramount.

7.   You must be committed to do whatever it takes to succeed.

Unlimited Power was published in 17 different languages and put Robbins on the path to becoming the household name he is today. In it, he discussed his views on health, persuasive communication, building and maintaining relationships, and how you can conquer your fears. The book drew heavily on the concepts of neuro-linguistic programming (see Neuro-Linguistic Programming), though Robbins also added his own thoughts about how we can better utilise our brains.

More than a decade after it was first published, *Unlimited Power* did cause some difficulties for Robbins. He had dedicated the book to his first wife, Rebecca "Becky" Jenkins (see Personal Life) and much of its content focused on how to achieve success in relationships, including marriage. When Robbins and Jenkins' marriage broke down and the couple divorced, this called into question to some extent Robbins' credibility: if his advice didn't even work in his own life, why should it work for anyone else?

Lesson 15: Be aware of the long-term implications of what you say, write and do, and be prepared to be challenged on your ideas at any point during your career.

Although Robbins did inevitably lose some followers during this period of emotional upheaval, the majority of his devotees did stay true to their guru. The extended length of time between the publication of this book and Robbins' divorce may in part account for this: Robbins had moved on in his thinking in the intervening years, published updated titles, and his readers were aware of this and respected it.

Awaken the Giant Within

Robbins' hotly awaited second book, *Awaken the Giant Within*, hit the shelves of bookstores across America in 1991. A lengthy 539 pages, many considered it to be the *Bible* of self-help books.

Lesson 16: A book demands a sequel, a product demands an upgrade! Once you have created a body of customers, keep giving them something new.

In *Awaken the Giant Within*, Robbins returned to his earlier topics of enhancing one's own body and mind to optimise personal and professional relationships, but he expanded the scope of his advice to include taking control of your finances, managing your emotions, and overcoming detrimental habits such as drink and drug addiction, and over-eating. In doing so, he drew attention to common readers' vulnerabilities – things they worried about most – and suggested ways in which they might be able to solve their problems. Robbins' message running throughout the book is that none of our everyday behaviour, good or bad, is beyond our control. There are small, relatively easy changes we can make in our lives which will have a long-term, positive impact. We are, in short, the force which shapes our own destiny.

Lesson 17: Small changes in your behaviour and habits can have a significant, positive impact.

Robbins opens Chapter 1 of *Awaken the Giant Within* with a quote from the 19th century British Prime Minister, Benjamin Disraeli:

"A consistent man believes in destiny, a capricious man in chance."

This may seem a little high-brow for a glorified personal trainer, but that is part of the attraction of Robbins: he encourages his readers to aspire to greater heights, personally, physically and intellectually. Robbins packages such content in a way which is easily accessible, and readers then feel a sense of intellectual superiority when they have grasped the concepts.

Lesson 18: Draw inspiration and tips from greater men and women than yourself.

Throughout the book, Robbins combines inspiration, advice, and personal anecdotes. On the topic of dreaming, of aspiring, for example, he talks of what is required to keep one's dreams in focus, and to realise them. He talks of his own dreams, and tells the story of flying over a building in his helicopter, realising that it is the same building where 12 years earlier he worked as a janitor. This kind of anecdote is prevalent in *Awaken the Giant Within*, and hugely important as it builds rapport between Robbins and his readers. In a few short sentences, he is able to remind readers of his humble origins and earlier struggles, and of his monumental rise. This is inspirational: if Robbins can do it, so can you. All you have to do is to follow his advice. Similarly, by dropping the mention of the helicopter into the story, Robbins dangles the carrot of aspiration: this is what you are working towards. Robbins already has what you want. Again, follow his advice and you can become like Robbins.

Lesson 19: Dreams and aspiration are powerful motivating factors.

From a marketing point of view, *Awaken the Giant Within* is a masterpiece. Right from the very first chapter, Robbins lays a trail of breadcrumbs for his readers to follow: you read my book, you attend my seminar, and then you can become like me. The path is clear and certainly seems easy enough. He talks of the number of people trying to attend his talks – 7,000 on one occasion, when only 2,000 were expected. He points out in the story that the auditorium will only hold 5,000 guests, so not everyone will fit into the room. Still, people have come, crowding onto the helipad waiting for him. All that these people want is a sighting of Robbins, and perhaps the chance to touch him, or to thank him.

In this way, Robbins builds up his image to be like that of a Messiah: he is the chosen one, the teacher. He creates this picture in which people are desperate to be in his presence, to hear his words, and by doing so he creates in his readers a desperate fear that if they do not join the crowd, they will be missing out on something terribly important. If so many people want a piece of Robbins, there must be something amazing about him, right? Robbins is a master at creating his own hype, creating demand for his product. He uses the fervour of the crowd (which he himself has deliberately stimulated) to sell his message, to be his cheerleaders. All he then needs to do is to give them what they want and expect: apparently easy solutions to life's little problems, and the possibility that by fixing the small things in life, bigger problems might also be solved.

Lesson 20: People want to be inspired, and they want to be led. Create for them the leader they dream of, and they will follow you.

Money: Master the Game

Robbins' followers had a long wait for his third major book, *Money: Master the Game*. It wasn't published until 2014, and though it reached the #1 spot on the Amazon best-sellers list, it met with mixed reviews from readers and the press.

Lesson 21: Commercial success does not necessarily equate to universal approval.

Although still within the self-help genre, *Money: Master the Game* took a different format from *Unlimited Power* and *Awaken the Giant Within*. A weighty tome of nearly 700 pages, the insights Robbins gives here are drawn from both his own experiences of making mega bucks, but also those of others: he interviewed more than 50 leading businessmen and financiers, including Warren Buffet, Steve Forbes, and Carl Icahn. He then attempted to distil what these individuals were doing into seven actionable steps which readers could implement in their own lives.

Lesson 22: Never be afraid to draw from, and quote from, the experiences of others.

The seven steps, and a brief explanation of them, are as follows:

1.   Make the Most Important Financial Decision of Your Life

You have to make an active decision to become an investor rather than just a consumer. Commit to saving some of what you earn, even just a small amount, and automate your investments.

2.   Become the Insider: Know the Rules Before You Get in the Game

Find a financial advisor, and do your market research. You shouldn't absolve re-sponsibility for your financial decision making to someone else, but learn about the market, fees, and available investment plans.

3.   Make the Game Winnable

Use realistic financial data and create a plan which is both actionable and achievable. You have to know what your financial goals are, what is required to achieve them, and how you can optimise your return on investment through various means.

4.   Make the Most Important Investment Decision of Your Life

Understand topics such as risk, asset allocation, security, growth and cash flow, and make informed choices.

5.   Create a Lifetime Income Plan

Plan for the long-term. Take advice from those who are already investing suc-cessfully, investigate tax-efficient investment strategies, and insure your income.

6.   Invest Like the .001%

Read the book's core interviews and learn the take-away lessons that the inter-viewees offer. Lessons come from the likes of Charles Schwab, Warren Buffet, and Mary Callahan Erdoes.

7.   Just Do It, Enjoy It, and Share It!

Committing to be wealthy is in itself a gift to yourself, so start now. Think about your expectations and legacy, and make a positive difference in the world.

The criticism of Robbins and *Money: Master the Game* came from multiple quar-ters, and much of it is justified. Cullen Roche of Market Watch, a finance indus-try insider, stated that, "While a lot of it is useful, the self-help guru contradicts himself and confuses readers." For a man who usually prides himself as being clear in his explanations, this is particularly unfortunate.

Lesson 23: You won't please everybody all of the time.

The root of the problem seems to be that although he has a lot of money, finance and financial management is not Robbins' area of expertise: he is a marketing man, not an investor, economist or financial advisor. Though he has taken advice from the right quarters – men and women who really are experts in this field – it's a case of Chinese whispers: what might have started out as a clear and concise message has become addled by the time it reaches the reader. More stringent editing might have helped.

Lesson 24: Stick to what you know, and if you do venture into unfamiliar territory, listen to expert advice.

Robbins rightly stresses the important of getting involved in investing (you can't just expect your money to multiply unless you invest it) and in getting professional advice. The problem is that although this is crucial, Robbins steers his readers right into the arms of his own companies and partners. This is understandable, but means that the book reads not like a genuine self-help tool, but an advertising pamphlet. Readers are coming to Robbins looking for objective, unbiased advice, and they are being sold specific products and companies instead. The fact that Robbins advocates a low-fee approach to investment, but then endorses companies which charge high fees, makes him look hypocritical or, perhaps even worse, that he hasn't bothered to check out the companies he is recommending. Given that his career is built on trust between writer/speaker and reader/audience, this is concerning.

Lesson 25: There is a fine line to be trodden between recommendations and endorsements, and straying onto the wrong side of it might cause people to question your credibility.

Much of what is written in *Money: Master the Game* is confusing for the casual reader at whom it is aimed. The commentary which Robbins gives often contradicts the points made by the interviewees: Robbins advocates using passive index funds, but also recommends asymmetric returns and active strategies; he cites his own market-timing calls as exemplary, ignoring the fact he's lost vast sums on the stock market in the past; and he at once puts some high-fee, active managers on a pedestal, making them look like geniuses, whilst decrying their high fees model. Collectively, such issues undermine Robbins' credibility as a financial commentator and advisor, something which is reflected by the unusually high number of 1* reviews the book receives on Good Reads and other such peer-review sites. *The Guardian* newspaper, in its November 2014 review of the book, points out that, "anyone who listened to him in 2010 would be hurting financially now." It is a rather sobering thought.

Lesson 26: If you make overly-confident assertions about things you can't really be sure about, there is always the risk that you will be caught out. Be cautious in what you say.

On the plus side, it is a positive step forward to get the general public thinking – and talking – about money and how they can take a more active role in their own financial planning. This has to be better than just running up vast debts and advocating responsibility for financial due diligence to the government or financial advisors.

Lesson 27: As a leader you have a social responsibility to educate others and stimulate debate about important issues.

Robbins is also contributing the profits from the sale of *Money: Master the Game* to his charitable organisation, Feeding 100 Million People (see Philanthropy). In the book's final chapter, Robbins outlines what he calls, "The Final Secret": generosity brings happiness and satisfaction to the giver just as much as to the recipient. To some extent, then, the critical reviews of the book matter less than the fact that it is generating sales for Robbins, further raising his public profile, and those in need are benefitting from the sales.

Taking Business Online

Robbins was a businessman of the 1980s and 1990s, and the arrival of the Internet could have spelt the end of his career: why would people keep buying books and videos, and turning up to seminars in person, if they could access the same content, and discuss it, online? Luckily for Robbins, he was quick to identify and exploit the new technology, making the internet version of self-help his own.

Lesson 28: Keep abreast of technological developments so that you can remain ahead of the competition.

Robbins served on the board of directors of a company called DreamLife, a penny stock, and with his input the company grew dramatically, peaking at $18 a share. Robbins drew on his own fame to publicise the offering, and also brought in famous friends such as Tom Brokaw, Andre Agassi and Bob Wright (the President of NBC) to participate. DreamLife crunched, along with many other tech firms, in the dot.com crash, but during its brief lifespan Robbin learned enough about how to exploit the online marketplace.

Lesson 29: Events outside your control can dictate the ultimate outcome of your endeavours.

TonyRobbins.com

Today, Tony Robbins' primary communication and marketing vehicle is his website, www.tonyrobbins.com. Slickly designed and reminiscent in its styling of a law firm's site, the homepage is dominated by Robbins' webcasts. Although he can write effectively – and continues to do so – Robbins realises that the best way to communicate with his audiences is visually. Not everyone can come to one of his seminars in person, either for geographical or financial reasons, but they can glean some of his advice from watching him online, and, importantly, this begins to build rapport (see Neuro-Linguistic Programming). He whets audiences' appetite for his products, and in doing so sets them on the first step of his sales channel.

Lesson 30: Your website is the shop window of your brand. Exploit its full potential.

The webcasts on Robbins' website are offered for free, but viewers must sign up in order to be able to watch them. This is important in marketing terms for two reasons: firstly, viewers have to invest a small amount of effort and time in order to access Robbins' material. Having invested, they are more likely to appreciate it. Secondly, Robbins has been able to capture their contact details. He can therefore send them an ongoing stream of emails and notifications about new content, engaging in an e-conversation and further building rapport so that he people are more likely to buy his products in the future. The basic contact information capture form on the homepage has the same role.

Lesson 31: Capture contact details as early as possible to get potential customers into your sales channel.

What People are Saying

Also on the homepage you see *What People Are Saying*. This newsfeed trawls the internet for stories about Robbins, and displays key quotes. At the time of writing this book, the top feeds state *Tony Robbins ranks as one of the "Top 50 Business Intellectuals in the World."* (Accenture); *Tony Robbins ranks among the "Top 200 Business Gurus."* (Harvard Business School Press); and *Tony Robbins named one of the top 6 advisors to help clients take their business to the next level.* (American Express).

Lesson 32: Use the words of others to endorse you and your products. This increases your credibility in the eyes of potential customers.

Robbins uses such quotes to draw attention to his achievements and the high regard in which he is held by the business community and the press. Of course, he (or rather his marketing team) have chosen these quotes deliberately to project a particular, positive image, to tell a particular story. It is effective, though, because rather than just hearing Robbins extoll his own virtues (which we would consider to be arrogant, and probably just a sales pitch), it appears that other, credible sources rate him highly. As these quotes are taken from authoritative organisations, we are more inclined to believe them, to buy into Robbins' aura of success.

Lesson 33: Tread the line carefully between self-promotion and unattractive immodesty.

The balance of Robbins' website is divided into four key sections: Products; Events; Coaching; and Resources.

Products

The number seven is a recurring theme in Robbins' work: there are seven disciplines for success in *Unlimited Power*; and seven simple steps to financial freedom in *Money: Master the Game*. Perhaps it is a lucky number for Robbins (or at least an effective marketing tool), as he lists seven categories of products on his website too.

Under *Personal Growth and Development* you will find boxed sets of Robbins' motivational and self-help DVDs. The sales copy suggest that more than 50 million people worldwide have already used these DVDs to improve their lives, though that probably does overestimate their impact, given that many of those who purchased such a course will still have it sat on their shelf collecting dust, without ever having played it.

Lesson 34: Hyperbole and exaggeration do have their place in sales when used sparingly.

The DVD sets command top-notch prices, but here too Robbins is a master of marketing. The Ultimate Edge, a three-part course, is advertised as having a value of $649, but there are numerous come-ons to make you buy: you can buy the course for a discounted rate of just $299; it's free for the first 30 days; you can return it and pay no fee within that period if you don't like it; you can pay in instalments; you get bonus material in the form of an audio magazine; you get a free personal profile, supposedly alone worth $250; and there is also a $100 discount voucher which you can use towards any of Robbins' events. Readers are left feeling that the package is such good value, they cannot afford NOT to buy it. What is more, having invested this not insignificant amount of money, they must then use the voucher to buy a further product – a ticket to one of Robbins' events – so that that money is not wasted. Readers have entered Robbins' sales funnel, and are, through their own fear of missing out and/or wasting money, automatically moved on through it. At every step, Robbins makes money. It is genius.

Lesson 35: *Always make customers believe that they are getting value for money when they buy your products.*

Equally interesting is Robbins' approach in *Love and Passion*, the courses he has produced with his second wife, Sage Robbins (see Personal Life). The couple appears in the opening shot of the YouTube video which graces this page of the website, telling the viewer immediately that the course is drawn from personal experience (in theory, therefore, increasing its credibility) and also that by following these steps, viewers can also obtain the marital happiness that Robbins and his wife apparently share.

Lesson 36: *Everyone wants to buy into a love story.*

Love and relationships are sensitive topics, and seen to be key to personal fulfilment. Even someone who is exceptionally successful in business may be unlucky in love, and looking to find a special someone to fill that gap, or need, in their life. Robbins is acutely aware of this, and plays on our insecurities. He uses highly emotive vocabulary – true fulfilment; emotional power; passion – to emphasise what readers are currently missing in their own lives, but also what they might be able to have in the future if they buy the course.

Lesson 37: *Playing on people's emotions is a very effective, if controversial, sales tool.*

Co-authoring the course with his wife is a shrewd marketing move because readers are assured that this will not just give a man's perspective on marriage and relationships: the woman's perspective and advice will be communicated also. As on the homepage, Robbins uses other people's endorsements to give him authority: in this case, a quote from Grammy Award-winning musician

Quincy Jones (a personal friend of Robbins') states, "Witness what the power of love can do in 90 minutes. Tony Robbins is a gift to humanity and most certainly a huge blessing to my family." Covering his tail from a legal perspective, however, Robbins follows the quote with an important caveat: *results obtained vary, and specific outcomes may not occur.* He is, at once, offering visitors to his site everything they have ever wanted, but at the same time promising nothing.

Lesson 38: If you may not be able to deliver what people are hoping to get from your product, ensure caveats protect you from legal action.

Events

Robbins' events are the main opportunity he has for followers to meet him in the flesh. They can read his books, watch his podcasts and DVD courses, and see him interviewed on the television, but still there is a huge attraction to seeing him in person, as if by being in close proximity to him, some of his success might rub off. Like all great orators – Winston Churchill, Adolf Hitler and Enoch Powell among them – Robbins knows full well that it is not just what you say that counts, but how you say it, and with a physical crowd in front of you, you can drum up emotion and manipulate the atmosphere until it reaches fever peak.

Lesson 39: Oratory is a hugely powerful skill to learn, and it can be used for good or ill.

A video trailer of an event appears on the *Events* page, and the opening shot shows Robbins, larger even than life within the screen, reaching down to the outstretched fans of his disciples. The image is deliberately evocative of Jesus preaching to the crowds on the shores of Lake Galilee, or of Mahatma Gandhi, or of Martin Luther King. When we see this picture we immediately think of the great leader and game changers of history, and mentally put Robbins in their camp. We want to be a part of his story, and to hear his message and be changed by it. The only way we can do this is by being one of those people at his feet, arms outstretched towards him. We have to buy a ticket. We have to be at the next event.

Lesson 40: If you have the ability to create a personality cult, do so!

Alongside this video is a continually updating calendar of forthcoming events. The titles – *Dates with Destiny Leadership*; *Business Mastery*; *Unleash the Power Within* – are highly emotive and attention grabbing, but what is most important to note here is the text beneath many of the event entries: *LIMITED AVAILABILITY*; *SOLD OUT*. These two-word phrases are vital marketing tools: they show huge demand for Robbins' events, and make readers terrified that if they don't book their tickets now, they will miss out. Fear on missing out, on being left behind, is a tremendous motivating force which drives sales. No wonder Robbins' events are selling out.

Interestingly, the prices for Robbins' events are not immediately obvious. We are used to loading a website and immediately being told the prices of everything, bombarded with discounts and special offers. Robbins is far more subtle. He isn't selling on price. He is selling on value. He creates demand for his products first. You have to look for information, investing your own time reading about the event and building up an appetite for it. This means that when you do eventually find the price – which may well be upwards of $2,000 – you have already bought into the idea and want it. You aren't put off by the price tag, and the long list of benefits (segregated by ticket type so you can always see what the next level offers, what you are missing out on) and risk-free satisfaction guarantee further convince you that this is acceptable value for money. In fact, Robbins is doing you a favour: he is giving you a bargain. All you have to do is part with the cash.

Lesson 41: It is always better to sell your products and services on their value, not on their price.

Throughout the *Events* section, readers are time and again advised to call Robbins' 800 number to enrol. The same message is repeated over and again. The fact that booking takes place over the phone rather than via a simple online form is significant because it gives Robbins' sales force the opportunity to upsell their products. Engagement with another human – even one working in call centre who we know to be there to sell to us – makes it more likely that the deal will be closed, and the profit for Robbins optimised.

Coaching

As with his video courses, Robbins offers a teaser/taster session of 30 minutes of free life coaching. You can sign up via the website, and one of his consultants will then contact you to schedule an appointment. As usual with Robbins' site, there's a YouTube video and testimonials, and has the initial session is free, users are more inclined to try it out and see if they like it.

The 30-minute life coaching sessions are with what Robbins terms Results Coaches. These are coaches selected and trained by Robbins, in sales as well as in coaching. You don't get time with the man himself, but rather his employees. This is fascinating because Robbins has been able to turn himself and his ideas into a brand. The transformation has been so effective that he can delegate his teaching to others, and clients will still buy into it. They are paying to learn the Robbins method from an intermediary.

Lesson 42: Build a business model which is scalable, i.e. where you can delegate running of the business to others.

Robbins also advertises business coaching through his website, using his nickname "the CEO whisperer" – coined by *Fortune* magazine – to entice his customers. The sales patter describes how Robbins has spent the last 30 years training the world's most successful business executives on the psychology of peak performance and organisational turnaround. The pitch is targeted specifically at CEOs, business owners and sales team leaders, and focuses on their desire to increase sales, empower their teams, and be better leaders.

Again, it is only when you read between the lines, however, that you realise that Robbins isn't actually providing this coaching himself. You will be paying for a professional business coach to work with you, and it will be someone trained by Robbins, but that is not the same as having facetime with the big guy. The sales copy is slightly misleading in this regard, and one wonders what you would actually have to do in order to get a training session with Robbins himself. If President Obama or Yahoo's Marissa Mayer called up and put their cash on the table, would they be granted time face to face with Robbins? I would imagine so, not necessarily because they would be paying a higher fee and thus getting better service, but because Robbins intimately understands the power of celebrity endorsement to ordinary Joes, and would want such individuals on his customer list. Their value in his marketing strategy is what is most important.

Lesson 43: If you create a big and strong enough brand, you can use it to sell others as well as yourself.

Resources/Experiences

The resources section (also labelled *Experiences* in some parts of the site) is probably the most comprehensive section of Robbins' website, and the sales message here is more subtle, though no less effective. Visitors are encouraged to, "Experience the magic of Tony Robbins" as though he is some mystical being with superhuman powers. Well, that is how he wants to be seen.

This section of the website contains a number of free tools that Robbins' fans can use. I say 'free' because you don't pay to use them, but they are there to guide you along the sales channel, buying other Robbins' products recommended to you at the different stages. You have to register and login to access much of the content, giving up your contact details and automatically subscribing to Robbins' mailings as you do so.

Lesson 44: Nothing should ever be totally free. Instead, use freebies to bait customers into entering your sales funnel.

The content is a mixture of general information, activities, and the opportunity to engage with other fans on discussion boards and through the *Crew Community*, a group of volunteers who share their leadership skills and expertise as a means of giving back what they have gained through Robbins' intervention.

This is one of the most effective parts of Robbins' website, for two reasons. Firstly, readers feel that they are being given something of value: there are blogs on business, finance and how to change your life for the better; short workshops you can do for free; and a free eBook. Briefly, you don't feel that you are being sold too, but rather than Robbins has chanced upon, then honed, techniques that have changed his life, and he is willing to share them with you. Once you drill deeper, you realise that this is part of his effective marketing strategy, but there is a moment when you almost believe he is doing it for your good.

Secondly, this part of the site works because it builds a sense of community amongst Robbins' followers. The testimonials on the site are generally from celebrities and hugely successful business leaders, but on the discussion boards you can read and share the dreams, observations and tips of ordinary people just like you. The discussion boards are integrated with Facebook, for ease of sharing content via social media, and this further expands the reach of Robbins' material. He is making use of peer to peer marketing: when you read one of his posts and like or share it on Facebook, you are, in essence, endorsing his views and products to everyone in your social network.

Lesson 45: Creating a sense of community amongst your customers increases their loyalty to your brand.

The *Crew Community* appears to take its inspiration from the evangelical churches in the USA, and as we've discussed before, as Robbins sees himself as a Messianic figure, and exploits this view in his marketing materials, this should come as no surprise. Those individuals who have attended one of Robbins' live events and been inspired by it are encouraged to give back by volunteering at future training sessions. Robbins thus reduces his staffing costs to almost zero and ensures he has a ready-made team of evangelists to proselytise on his behalf. In fact, the interaction with these converts might well be the most useful part of signing up to one of Robbins' live events, as participants will be able to get face time with the volunteers, even if not with Robbins.

Image and Appearance

By any account, Robbins strikes an imposing figure: he is six foot seven, a growth spurt he attributes to a teenage pituitary tumour, and he fully occupies the space around his body, in every dimension. Larger the life, and with endless confidence, his audiences are captivated by his every move. And that's before he opens his mouth.

With such an absorbing presence, Robbins has little need to impress those around him through his clothes. Like Steve Jobs, another inspirational business leader and disruptive thinker, Robbins dresses most often in a black shirt and dark jeans. This keeps the focus on his face, his facial expressions and hand gestures, and his words.

Robbins and the Media

From the very beginning of his career, Robbins has actively courted the media, especially in the United States, because he recognises its power in raising his public visibility, increasing his credibility, and thus driving sales. From television appearances to celebrity endorsements, Robbins is a superb, one-man PR agency.

Lesson 46: Use other people – your customers and the press – to raise your profile and thus do your advertising for you.

As a celebrity in his own right, Robbins has had cameo appearances in a number of films. Most notably, he hypnotised Hal, Jack Black's character, in *Shallow Hal* so that he sees the inner beauty of the women around him; and he also makes a small appearance in *Men in Black*. If you watch the scene of screens showing aliens masquerading as humans, you will probably be able to spot Robbins.

On the small screen, Robbins has had mixed results. The comedians behind *Family Guy* caricatured him in an episode titled "When you wish upon a Weinstein": the cartoon's star, Peter Griffin, goes to one of Robbins' book signings but is then inexplicably swallowed by Robbins. How odd!

Although Robbins had been featured on a number of shows over the years, it was in 2010 that he was given his own billing. On NBC, *Breakthrough with Tony Robbins* followed Robbins in his daily life as he tried to help his audiences overcome their problems. The show mixed self-help with reality TV but it struggled to gain popularity amongst television viewers: in the end, NBC aired just two of the six episodes they filmed, and cancelled the series. OWN Network did, however, re-run the original series in full in 2012, followed immediately by a second series.

Lesson 47: Not everything will work out the way that you want it to the first time. Sometimes you will have to re-work an idea, or sell it in a different way.

Riding on the back of Oprah Winfrey's fame, Robbins returned to the small screen in 2012 as part of a panel of spiritual teachers *in Oprah's Lifeclass: The*

Tour, which also aired on OWN. Robbins was by no means the star of the show – he was just one of a number of contributing guests – but the close association with, and apparent endorsement by, Oprah Winfrey had a significant and positive impact on his product sales. Once again, Robbins demonstrated the importance of celebrity endorsements in increasing one's own profile and credibility in the marketplace.

Controversies

For a figure who courts public exposure so aggressively, and has done so over such an extended period, it is remarkable that Robbins has not become embroiled in more controversies than he has. There have been, it seems, no major fraud scandals, no rape accusations, and no downward spirals into drug and alcohol abuse. He is, on the face of it at least, clear and wholesome.

There are, though, as one expect, some smaller areas where Robbins has strayed into the grey, and for which he has been rightly criticised, and some of these involve financial irregularities. In 1995, Robbins' company, Robbins Research Institute (RRI), was accused of misrepresenting potential returns to franchisees. RRI never admitted guilt, but did settle out of court, committing to pay claimants more than $200,000 in compensation.

Robbins was also forced by a court to pay more than $650,000 in damages to a competing self-help guru, Wade Cook, who alleged that Robbins infringed his copyright and plagiarised his ideas in his seminars. Cook's own book, *Wall Street Money Machine*, had never had the same commercial success as Robbins' titles, but Robbins has foolishly copied some of the proprietary terms used within it.

Lesson 48: When you are in the wrong, for whatever reason, step up to the plate and expect to compensate those who have been hurt.

Under *Books*, we have already discussed the criticism of *Money: Master the Game* by the financial and general press, but this is by no means the only one of his books to have been seriously questioned by other experts. *Unlimited Power* includes a chapter about health and energy, of which The National Council Against Health Fraud (NCAHF) has been especially critical. Writing in NCAHF's journal, Dr. William T. Jarvis explains:

Robbins reveals his ignorance about physiology as he misinforms readers about how the body rids itself of metabolic wastes...

Robbins combines misconception, misinformation, and misguided advice based upon the crackpot theories of Herbert Shelton, a self-styled "nature doctor" who operated a "health school" in Texas...

Robbins recommends the American Natural Hygiene Society, which promotes Shelton's dangerous ideas. He also advances the unfounded notions about diet and crime promulgated by Alexander Schauss, a self-styled expert who promotes himself with dubious credentials.

Given Robbins' very public platform, his huge number of devoted followers and his ability to influence their thoughts and behaviour, such criticism is deeply troubling. It is one thing to endorse and promote ideas which, though ineffective, are not actually harmful, but quite another to give oxygen to ideas which could be damaging to health, and to distribute misinformation. It is, one would think, the responsibility of someone like Robbins to check the credibility of his own sources, to get a second opinion where necessary, and to only write about what is proven to be correct and safe. This would not only protect the individuals following his advice but would also protect Robbins' own reputation, something which he is sure to fiercely defend.

Apart from this, the most valid criticism of Robbins is surely that he manipulates the vulnerabilities of his followers to sell them products. His marketing strategy and sales channel is fine-tuned to be as effective as possible, which in itself is understandable, but there are those who see NLP as a pseudo-science, and his advice as little more than common sense and encouragement. They question how a man with no academic training (Robbins only just graduated from high school, see *Childhood and Education*) should be able to work in this way, calling him a con artist and his methods a scam.

This is a very difficult area to explore, to investigate and, indeed, to defend. The prices Robbins charges for his services are very high, and there are no guaranteed results: disclaimers to that effect pepper his website, as we discussed before. He does not claim to be able to work miracles, and for every detractor, there are at least two or three fans who will come forward and state publicly that following Robbins' advice worked for them, that doing so has changed their life. No one can doubt that Robbins is a master of self-publicity and has built an enviable business empire. This will, of course, make some people jealous. It must also be said that though Robbins is undeniably very convincing in his sales pitches, no one is forcing customers to buy his products. They buy because they want to buy, and Robbins will charge whatever the market will allow. This is the basis of market economy, and what has allowed him to become such a successful businessman. Whether or not you approve of his promotional methods, of his commercialisation of advice and help, is an entirely different issue.

Philanthropic Giving and Outreach

Robbins founded the Antony Robbins Foundation to give back some of his wealth, which is estimated at around $480 million. The foundation claims to feed 4 million people around the world each year, and it also supports programmes in schools, prisons, service organisations and shelters.

Robbins' most high profile philanthropic activity is his partnership with FeedingAmerica.org, a hunger relief charity in the United States. Perhaps due to his personal experiences in poverty as a child, Robbins knows what it is like to be hungry, and that despite everyone talking about the American Dream, poverty and hunger do still exist in the USA.

Launched in December 2014, the 100 Million Meals Challenge is, as one would expect from Robbins, a smart piece of marketing. Robbins pledged to donate 50 million meals, and asked the American public to match his donation so that 100 million meals would be given in total. These would be distributed through Feeding America's 200 food banks over the course of 2015. Robbins' gift was funded by profits made on sales of *Money: Master the Game* (and hence helped to further publicise the book), and also a donation from Robbins' private wealth. The total value of Robbins' gift was in the region of $5 million, a not inconsequential sum.

Lesson 49: If you have been fortunate in life, give back to an organisation who supports issues you care about.

Personal Life

Robbins' lively personal life, the result, perhaps of his own tumultuous childhood, began well before he was famous. Though he has spoken little about his earliest romantic encounters, in his early 20s his then girlfriend, Liz Acosta, became pregnant with his child. Their son, Jairek Robbins, was born in 1984 in Santa Monica, California, and Robbins junior has taken full advantage of his father's fame to launch his own relatively successful career as a coach and motivational speaker. Though no best-seller, he is the author of *LIVE IT!: Achieve Success By Living With Purpose* and has delivered TEDex talks.

Robbins' relationship with Acosta broke down almost immediately after the birth of their son, and within a year Robbins had married another woman, Rebecca Jenkins, who he met at one of his seminars. Jenkins was 11 years Robbins' senior and had three children from former relationships, all of whom Robbins legally adopted. Their marriage lasted 14 years, ending in divorce by mutual consent in 1997. Neither Robbins nor Jenkins spoke publically about the reasons for their divorce at their time, but subsequent interviews with Robbins suggest he had never wanted to marry but did so in order to provide stability for Jenkins' children and his own. The marriage turned bitter in its latter stages, and was drawn out as the couple debated how to divide their considerable assets. Before the divorce was finalised, Robbins met the woman who would ultimately become his second wife, health food store clerk Bonnie Humphrey, and there are allegations that her affection for Robbins was a major contributing factor in her own marriage breakdown.

Robbins and Humphrey (now known as Sage Robbins) married in Palm Beach, Florida in October 2001. Together the couple has written *Love & Passion: The Ultimate Relationship Program* and they also write a blog of the same name. Marriage has clearly been a profitable enterprise: at its peak their collective wealth was estimated to be in excess of $480m. They own fast cars, boats, planes and private islands. Put simply, Robbins is living the dream.

Lesson 50: Your personal life and your professional life go hand in hand. True success requires finding happiness in your personal life, and fulfilment and wealth in your professional life too.

Conclusions

When journalists write about Tony Robbins, they usually call him a self-help guru. Yes, that is how he projects himself, and that is the brand which his followers have bought into, but in actual fact, that is not what is at the core of his identity. It is not what has made him a success.

Robbins has not made his money from self-help. He has made his money, and his career, from marketing and continual, effective self-promotion. He could have made his fortune selling cars, newspapers, religion, or a political ideology. The same techniques, the same strategies, and the same approaches would work in all of these fields. Robbins just happens to have chosen self-help and business coaching as the industry through which to demonstrate his considerable marketing skills.

If you want to have a lifestyle like Tony Robbins, if you want to earn just a fraction of his wealth, or to stand on a pale imitation of his pedestal, learn to sell. Learn to sell yourself, and learn to sell your products.

Start by identifying your target market, what they want to buy, and how they can be sold to. Identify their interests, their vulnerabilities, and what you can do to inspire them. How can you convince them that you, and what you have to sell, is the answer that they have been looking for? Only when you know this can you decide what product it is you need to sell, how you can package it, and what your sales pitch should be.

Robbins teaches us that these skills, though naturally more developed in some people than in others, can be learned and honed over time. Whether you choose to study NLP or other similar psychological techniques, you can improve your memory, your visualisation, and your communication skills. You can become more effective at relationship building. You can become more persuasive in your language and in your non-verbal communication. It is worth investing time and effort in these skills, practising them on others, and observing the impact that they have. Deployed in the right circumstances, you can use such skills to be a better negotiator, a better lover, and a better leader.

From Robbins we can also learn that once you have built a brand, you can use that brand to sell anything. Robbins sells DVDs. He sells books. He sells seminars. He sells coaching sessions. And he doesn't even have to deliver these himself. It may even be that his books are ghost written for him too. But that is the power of his branding. These things don't matter. Robbins is associated with these products. He has endorsed them, and that is why his followers want to buy them. They want to buy a little piece of Robbins, to get close to him and how he thinks, in the hope that some of his success, personal and financial, will rub off on them too.

The Life and Business Lessons of Warren Buffett

Wizard Of Omaha

This book offers an introduction to Buffett, his business success and the lessons that we can learn from him. This is not a text book nor a biography, but more of a cheat sheet for reading on the bus or in the bathroom, so that you can pick out the most significant points without having to carry around a bag of weighty tomes. You can read it all in one sitting, or look up specific case studies as and when you are looking for inspiration or direction. You will learn the most significant skills and qualities that made him the most successful investor ever, plus some of his greatest investing tips.

"Never give up searching for the job that you're passionate about. Try to find the job you'd have if you were independently rich. Forget about the pay. When you're associating with the people that you love, doing what you love, it doesn't get any better than that." — Warren Buffet

What is it that sets a successful man apart from others? Is it his willingness to take risks? Is it his ability to see opportunity when others only see adversity? Is it his creative drive and determination to make the world a better place not only for himself and his family and friends, but for for his fellow human beings as a whole? Are certain people simply predestined to be more successful than others because of breeding? Or is it a combination of experience, education, and a simple willingness to take risks that others aren't willing to take? Or is it that a successful person is simply more passionate and driven than their peers?

The next question you have to ask is, can financial and personal success be something that can be taught and passed down to others? The answer, of course, is yes if you have the willingness to go beyond what is expected of you. To strive every day to be a better person and and take personal responsibility for all of your decisions whether they are good or bad, or successes or failures, and to not view your failures as such, but rather as lessons you learn and profit from.

"What we learn from history is that people don't learn from history."

In the case of the "Wizard of Omaha", the great Warren Buffett, had a great many benefits that most people are not as lucky to have. He came from a longline of financial experts who made their fortunes buying and selling businesses and stocks, which in-turn afforded Buffett the chance to learn at the feet of great financial minds, as well as attend top notch schools that   opened doors to prestigious investment firms and the ability to grow his family fortune.

But other than being a child of wealth and privilege, there is something about Buffett that sets him apart. Something that is beyond breeding, education, and business connections. It is not something that can be taught and must be discovered, and that is living his passion. In his iconic rise in the American financial scene, Buffett has proven time and again that passion breeds ingenuity, determination, and ultimately, massive profits.

"There comes a time when you ought to start doing what you want. Take a job that you love. You will jump out of bed in the morning. I think you are out of your mind if you keep taking jobs that you don't like because you think it will look good on your resume. Isn't that a little like saving up sex for your old age?"

Most people believe that they will never be able to live out their passion and spend their days toiling away working jobs they hate and never taking the time to discover their true path in life. Because, simply put, discovering your passion is a journey unto itself, and is something that isn't easily obtained. Which is why we look to people like Buffett for inspiration, because maybe some of what drives and motivates him will somehow rub off on us.

But along with taking inspiration Buffett's amazing accomplishments, we need to take a look at his life and how's he lived it. We need to take a look at not only his successes—such as Buffett's legendary holding company, Berkshire Hathaway—but also his financial missteps such as his involvement with insurance giant AIG and Gen Re and the Solomon Brothers scandal of the late 1990's and how he overcame those missteps; of how he dealt with adversity and came out the other end not only a better, wiser businessman, but a better person. Because the fact is, when you're discussing passion, you can't only judge someone on their success, but on their failures as well.

Throughout his long career, Buffett has faced many challenges and has met each with humility and affability. Never backing down when faced with road blocks big and small, Buffett is a true American success story who has more than a few important lessons to pass onto investors and non-investors alike. In the forthcoming text, we will take an in-depth look into the life of Warren Buffett to see would helped become one of the wealthiest and most innovative businessmen of the 20th century and beyond.

We'll look at his upbringing and his early forays into the business world. We will take a look at both his education and the friends and teachers who helped mold him, and we will take an extended look at his vast financial accomplishments through his early holding companies Buffett Associates and Buffett Partners Ltd, and, of course, the monolithic and iconic Berkshire Hathaway. (If you're not familiar with Berkshire Hathaway it is a holding company whose shares trade on the New York Stock Exchange at close to $50,000 a share and is the partial or whole owner of such retail and food giants such as Coca-Cola, Wrigley's, Nestle, See's Candies, and many, many more.)

Also, we'll take the experiences from Buffett's amazing life and try applying Buffett's principles to our own.

The Education Of A Passionate Life

"Rule No. 1 : Never lose money. Rule No. 2 : Never forget Rule No. 1."

Born in Omaha, Nebraska in August of 1930. Buffett was the middle child and only son of three children of four-term congress man and stock broker, Howard Buffett, and his wife Leila. From an early age, Buffett showed an exceptional aptitude in numbers and a desire to make money. Starting at the age of six, Buffett entered the business world by purchasing six packs of Coke (a drink, by the way, Buffett consumes ceaselessly)from his grandfather's grocery store for 25 cents a six pack, and then re-sold them to his childhood friends for five cents per bottle, which was a five cent profit per six pack.

While most of Buffett's friends spent their days playing football and other games, he was learning the ins-and-outs of investing from his father and beginning to discover his passion for saving money and investment. Throughout his childhood, Buffett worked at his grandfather's grocery store, saving money and re-investing it in his small businesses which included selling magazines door-to-door and candy and gum to his classmates.

Five years after his first forays into business, Buffett took his first tottering steps into the world of investment. At age eleven, he purchased three shares of Cities Service Preferred at $38 a share for both himself and his sister. Not long after buying the stock, it plummeted to $27 a share. Ever resilient, Buffett held onto his shares until they rebounded and increased to $40 a share, at which time he promptly sold them. The transaction ended up being a huge mistake for the fledgling stock broker, because the price of Cities Service Preferred skyrocketed to $200 a share.

This first step—and a serious misstep—into the world of high finance would make a lasting, lifelong impression on Buffett and would teach him that when it comes to investing—as in life—patience is a virtue.

"No matter how great the talent or efforts, some things just take time. You can't produce a baby in one month by getting nine women pregnant."

Perhaps the biggest mistake that most fledgling investors make when they first begin buying and selling stocks is that panicking over losses, which is a huge determinate to building a strong and long lasting portfolio. We all work hard for our money, and we want to see it grow and work hard for us. We want our money and our investments to help us provide for our retirements, our children's educations, for the ability to provide us with a certain level of comfort and security. But what most beginning and more than a few veteran investors don't understand is that the stock market is a risk, and that with risk, you sometimes take losses. For many investors, taking a loss induces panic and they toss out the offending stock like spoiled milk.

Perhaps the biggest lesson we can take away from Buffett's first experience in trading stock is that just because an investment is falling in price doesn't mean you have to immediately abandon it. For instance, take amazon.com, when the massive online retailers stock was first offered in 1997 it traded for just a little over $20 a share and was considered by many investment analysts to be an extremely risky investment.

Throughout its opening year on the NASDAQ index, Amazon's stock fluctuated wildly with the stock trading sometimes as high as $58 a share-to-as low as $18 a share. Now imagine an 11-year-old Warren Buffett—or imagine yourself— buying three shares of Amazon for himself and his sister instead of Cities Service Preferred. Chances are he would've panicked just as he did when his shares of Cities Service Preferred tanked and would've waited just as patiently for the stock to recover some of its value and then dumping it. Can you say you would blame him? Would you blame yourself? Of course not, financial preservation is a natural instinct because absolutely no one enjoys losing money.

We use Amazon as an example in comparison to Cities Service Preferred because Amazon's stock did exactly the same thing. In 1997, Amazon was considered a foolish investment due to what many considered to be the instability of the internet as an overall business model and Amazon's ability to deliver purchased items in a timely manner. A good number of investors failed to see the longterm usefulness of the internet—and many, oddly, still do—and dumped the stock the minute it began to fluctuate.

"The critical investment factor is determining the intrinsic value of a business and paying a fair or bargain price."

But if we look at Amazon stock now, it's currently trading at $310 a share. And if most investors had held onto the stock for even a year longer, they would've seen their initial $20 invest jump to $200 a share a year after it's first offering. The point is, as an investor, we should embrace short term loss and the idea of longterm growth. If we take a look at Buffett's legendary holding company, Berkshire Hathaway, and the purchases led and made by Buffett for the company, a good deal of investors would have questioned the usefulness of some of his investment decisions. Coca-a-Cola, GEICO,

Wrigley's chewing gum, on paper—at lease to the short term thinker—these businesses would've looked like sure fire losers when Buffett originally acquired them.

But the true genius of Buffett—and the lesson he learned from his first investment in Cities Service Preferred—is that he recognizes what people both need, want, and use, and what they will want, need, and use five, ten, twenty years in the future, and that in order to make that judgement, you have to be patient as an investor and analyze the intrinsic value of a business and its longterm value in the market place overall. Yes, this can be a frightening way to invest, particularly for those investors who are betting their life savings on how well a handful of companies will do in the long run. But if one is patient and rides the ups-and-downs of a stock, you could have a sure fire winner that will set you up for life.

Long story short, take a lesson from what 11-year-old Warren Buffett did wrong and be patient and persistent when it comes to not only your stock portfolio but to personal investments as well.

"The best education you can get is investing in yourself. But this doesn't always mean college or university."

In 1947 at 17-years-old, Buffett graduated from Woodrow Wilson High School in Washington D.C. (Buffett's father, Howard, was serving as a U.S. congressman) Upon graduation, Buffett originally had no intention of going to college and further pursuing his education. At this early age, Buffett had already made $5,000 delivering newspapers and buying 3 pinball machines and placing them in different businesses throughout the Washington D.C. area, (Buffett eventual sold his pinball business to a veteran of World War II for $1,200) which was the equivalent of around $50,000 in 2015 money. Although Buffett's education oriented parents had other plans, and pressured their only son to attend the Wharton Business School at the University of Pennsylvania.

Buffett attended reluctantly and stuck out Wharton for two years, and often complained that he knew more about business and investing than most of his professors. When Buffett's father was defeated in his 1948 congressional re-election bid, Buffett returned to Omaha and transferred to the University of Nebraska-Lincoln. While attending university, Buffett worked full-time at his father's investment brokerage and managed to graduate in only three years time.

Buffett approached his graduate studies with the same stubbornness as he did when he first entered college. But once again he was pressured by his parents to apply to Harvard Business School. However, Harvard rejected—a decision they are sure to regret to this day—Buffett, who was then only 20 years-old, on the basis that he was too young to attend. Stinging from the rejection, Buffett applied to the Columbia School of Business, where renowned investor and future mentor and business partner Ben Graham was teach. Buffett's time at Columbia under the wing of Ben Graham would prove to be one of the most formative of Buffett's life.

Mentors & Collaborators: Ben Graham & Charlie Munger

"If I hadn't read that (Ben Graham classic investment text, *The Intelligent Investor*) *book in 1949, I'd have had a different future."*

Throughout Buffett's long storied career as a business man and investor, he has always emphasized and promoted the need for continuing education—whether it be through conventional means such as college, or more unconventional as surrounding yourself with people that you admire—and for elders to pass along their knowledge to forthcoming generations.

The need for a mentor in business—or in any endeavor, really—is vital. Business and investing can be an intimidating labyrinth, and with the beginning investor or business owner, sometimes a helping, wise hand to guide that person along can be the single greatest assist a business can have. Although as investors and independent business owners, we don't always have the benefit of having a nurturing college professor or a veteran business owner to help guide us down the right path. But for most, a mentor does not have to be someone we actually know.

For the investor, business owner, or even to the construction worker or waitress, a mentor can simply be someone whose ideas you identify with on a personal or professional level through articles, books, and television programs. Sometimes inspiration drawn from these distant, abstract relationships can drive you forward in setting and accomplishing the goals you create for yourself.

However, for Warren Buffett, he benefitted from having sage advice from two of the most brilliant business minds of the 20th century, investor and GEICO insurance chairman, Ben Graham, and his long time partner in Berkshire Hathaway, Charlie Munger.

Ben Graham

In the 1920's stock broker Ben Graham had become extremely well know through out many business circles as a shrewd, calculated, and aggressive investor. During the period when most investors were approaching the stock market as something of a giant crap shoot, Graham sought out stocks that were so radically undervalued that they were consider practically devoid of risk or, in the eyes of most investors at the time, any real investment growth.

One of Graham's best known investments was the Northern Pipe Line, a oil transportation company managed by the Rockefeller family. Shares of Northern Pipe Line were trading at around $60 a share, but after careful analyzing an annual balance sheet, Graham realized that Northern Pipe Line had bond holdings worth $95 for each share of the stock. Graham attempted and failed to convince Northern Pipe Line management to sell the portfolio, but they ultimately refused. Soon after Graham waged a proxy war and secured a spot on the Board of Directors. The company sold its bonds and paid a dividend in the amount of $70 per share.

At the age of 40, Ben Graham published what is widely considered one the cornerstones of modern investment literature, *Security Analysis.* At the time of its publication, investing in the stock market was consider extremely risky and investing in equities futures had become something of a joke with the Dow Jones having plummeted to record lows over the course of four short years after the stock market crash of 1929.

It was during this period that Graham introduced the principle of intrinsic business value, which is a means of measuring the true value of a business that was completely and totally independent of its stock offering. Using intrinsic value, investors could decide what a company was worth and make investment decisions accordingly. His subsequent book, *The Intelligent Investor*, a book Buffett characterized as the greatest book on investing ever written.

"It's better to hang out with people better than you. Pick out associates whose behavior is better than yours and you'll drift in that direction."

Through his simple investment principles, Ben Graham became a hero to the then twenty-one year old Warren Buffett. Before Buffett became a student of Graham's, he was reading an old edition of the publication *Who's Who*, and he discovered Graham was the chairman of a small, unknown insurance company at the time named GEICO. Upon learning this, Buffett rushed to Washington D.C. one Saturday morning to find the headquarters and in hope of actually meeting Graham. However, upon at arriving at GEICO's headquarters, the doors to the business were locked and closed for the weekend.

"There seems to be some perverse human characteristic that likes to make easy things difficult."

Not to be deterred, Buffett pounded on the doors of GEICO until a janitor opened them. Buffett asked if there was associated with GEICO in the building. As luck would have it, there was someone working on the sixth floor of the GEICO offices. Warren was escorted up to meet the diligent worker and upon entering the office, Buffett immediately began asking him questions about the company and its business practices. The conversation went on for over four hours, and the man who tolerated Buffett's seemingly unending string of questions was none other than GEICO's Vice President of Finance, Lorimer Davidson. The conversation with Davidson would be an experience that stuck with Buffett for the rest of his life and fostered his belief in seeking out education and guidance in unlikely places and taking bold personal chances.

During his studies at the Columbia School of Business, Buffett was the only student ever to earn an A+ in one of Graham's classes. After graduation, Buffett was set on becoming a full time stock broker on Wall Street, but both Graham and Buffett's father advised him against the move. However, Buffett was so determine to work on Wall Street, he offered to work for Graham's investment firm for free. However, Graham turned him down. Obviously, not being able to work for his friend and mentor was crushing and Buffett returned home to Nebraska to once again work at his father's firm.

It would be another ten plus years before Buffett would meet the man who would become his life long business partner and right hand man at Berkshire Hathaway, the enigmatic Charlie Munger.

Charlie Munger

Like Buffett, Munger was originally from Omaha, Nebraska. After brief period of studies in mathematics at the University of Michigan, Munger dropped out of college to serve in the U.S. Army Air Corps as a meteorologist during World War II. After the war, Munger began studying law at Caltech before entering Harvard Law School without an undergraduate degree and was a member of the Harvard Legal Aid Bureau, which at the time was practically unheard of, but that was the brilliance of Charlie Munger. Munger graduated from Harvard in 1948 with a Juris Doctor (professional doctorate) magna cum laude, he moved with his family to California where he began practicing law with the firm Wright & Garrett

In 1962, Munger moved back to his childhood home of Omaha from California where he had been practicing law. Originally introduced by mutual friends, initially Buffett found Munger to be somewhat snobbish and a bit off-putting, he soon came to recognize Munger's financial and legal brilliance, and the two drew closer together and became fast friends and quickly formed a bond and became trusted partners and advisors for over forty years.

Along with co-chairing Berkshire Hathaway, Munger was previously the chairman of Wesco Financial Corporation, which is now a wholly owned subsidiary of Berkshire Hathaway (Both Munger and Buffett faced the scrutiny of the SEC in the first attempted merger of Wesco and Berkshire Hathaway) The Pasadena, California based Wesco began as a savings and loan association, but eventually grew to control Precision Steel Corp., CORT Furniture Leasing, Kansas Bankers Surety Company, and among many other ventures. Wesco Financial also held a concentrated equity portfolio of over $1.5 billion and holds vast investments in companies such as Coca-Cola, Wells Fargo, Procter & Gamble, Kraft Foods, US Bancorp, and Goldman Sachs.

"Our favorite holding period is forever."

In an article written by investor and author, Guy Spier, *5 lessons from my $650,000 lunch with Warren Buffett*, he writes:

"The lunch made me realize that I had previously undervalued the power of making sure that I am around people who are better than me, and around whom I can improve. These days I am lucky enough to think nothing of buying a transatlantic plane ticket and enduring the resulting jet-lag, if it means being able to spend quality time with someone whom I admire and from whom I can learn."

You should take these words to heart above all else, because it is true that the people you chose to have around you help you form your opinions and general attitudes about the world at large. If the people you surround yourself with are generally negative people, than there is a better chance than not that your attitudes will also be negative. However, if you chose to surround yourself with people who have a far more positive outlook, their attitudes will rub off on you. Success typically comes to people who project confidence and a positive outlook, so you should ask yourself, what kind of person do you attract?

In Buffett's case, he attracted Graham and Munger because of his overall drive and ambition, and they in turn recognized in him a twin spirit and someone who was not only interested in voicing his opinion and thoughts, but also a willingness to learn and a genuine openness to new and different ideas that he may not have gained on his own without their guidance and friendship.

The point is that when it comes to friendships and mentorships, you give what you get. If you project an overall negative outlook on the world, better chances than not you will receive negative in kind. But if you act and react positively and project kindness and intelligence, this will be visited back on you.

True enough, you can't always control the people you have in your life, this is particularly true of family and co-workers. But, you can improve on the overall dynamic of these forced relationships by taking charge of these relationships by not getting sucked into negative conflicts and feelings and avoiding these types of situations if you're able to.

Project a willingness to listen and learn from your peers and you will attract quality people who you can learn and benefit from.

Omaha-to-New York & Back Again: Buffett Associates, Ltd & Buffett Partnerships

After taking a job at his father's brokerage firm, Buffett began seeing Susie Thompson. Within a few years, their relationship turned serious and in April of 1952, Buffett and Thompson were married. The young couple rented out a three-room apartment for $65 a month. The apartment was run down and served as home to several mice. It was here their daughter, also named Susie, was born. In order to save money, they made a bed for her in a dresser drawer.

During these initial years, Buffett's investments were predominately limited to a gas station and unfruitful real estate investments. Unfortunately none of his personal financial ventures during this early period of his marriage were successful. However, It was during this time that Buffet began teaching night courses at the University of Omaha, a feat that would not have been possible for the naturally shy and humble Buffett if it were not for a public speaking course he took at Dale Carnegie University, a degree that Buffett still credits as being the most beneficial to his professional life.

"Wall Street is the only place that people ride to in a Rolls-Royce to get advice from those who take the subway."

Despite the financial obstacles of Buffett's post-graduate school career, things began to look up when he received a call from his old mentor, Ben Graham. Graham finally invited the young stock broker to join his New York brokerage firm, an opportunity Buffett had long sought was now finally coming to fruition. Buffett and Susie purchased a home in the suburbs of New York. Buffett spent his days analyzing Standards & Poors reports seeking out investment opportunities. It was during this early period at Graham Partnerships that the differences between Buffett and Graham's financial philosophies began to surface.

"Investors making purchases in an overheated market need to recognize that it may often take an extended period for the value of even an outstanding company to catch up with the price they paid."

Buffett became interested in how companies worked. More specifically, what made certain companies superior to their competitors. Graham simply wanted cold, hard numbers, whereas Buffett was far more interested in a company's management style and work force as a major factor of when deciding to invest. Graham looked only at balance sheets and income statements and could care less about corporate management and leadership.

During Buffett's time at Graham Partnerships between 1950-to-1956, Buffett built his personal capital up to $140,000 from an initial $9,800 in personal assets. With this massive personal fortune, Buffett decided to leave Graham Partnerships and return to Omaha and plan his next big financial move.

On May 01, 1956, shortly after returning to Omaha, Buffett recruited seven limited partners which included his oldest Sister and his Aunt and raised an extra $100,000 in capital. With only $100 he put in himself, he officially creating Buffett Associates, Ltd.

Within the year, he was managing over $300,000 in capital. Small, to say the least, but he had much bigger plans for that pool of money. In the same year, he and Susie Buffett purchased a home and affectionately nicknamed "Buffett's Folly". (a house that Buffett and his longtime companion, Astrid, still occupy, at least part time, to this day) He managed the partnership originally from the master bedroom, but later moved the operation to a small office. Buffett's life in Omaha was finally beginning to take shape. He was married to a beautiful woman, he had three adoring children, and was running his first very successful holding company.

"You only have to do a very few things right in your life so long as you don't do too many things wrong."

Over the next five years, Buffett Associates generated an impressive 250% profit per year. What made it even more impressive was that the Dow was uncharacteristically low during this period, and yet Buffett Associates was seeing massive returns. Buffett was seemingly made of solid gold and was becoming somewhat of a celebrity around Omaha because of his success. By 1962, Buffett Partnership had capital in excess of $7.5 million, $1 million of which was Buffett's personal stake in the fund, which in turn made Buffett a majority owner.

During this period, he also made more than 90 limited partners available to investors across the United States. In one decisive move, he grouped the partnerships into a single entity and renamed the company Buffett Partnerships Ltd., and increased the minimum investment in the holding company to $100,000, and opened an office in Kiewit Plaza on Farnam street in Omaha.

A decade after its founding, Buffett Partnerships was seeing record breaking profits with it assets generating over a 1000% return over the course of a decade. By 1967, Buffett Partnerships had grown to an amazing $45 million dollars, with Buffett's personal stake being around $7 million. By 1968, Buffett closed the partnership to new accounts and saw its largest gain, recording a nearly 60% increase in profits even as the Dow fluctuated wildly due to the Vietnam war. Because of these massive gains, Buffett's personal fortune swelled to over $100 million is assets.

Let's touch on the importance of partnerships and investors in regards to creating your own business before we move on. With Buffett, because of his connections and his family's renown, he was able to easily find investors and partners in his early ventures. Without these partners, however, chances are Buffett would have never been able to get Buffett Associates or Buffett Ltd off the ground. True, he could have simply invested his own capital, but this would have limited his overall investment dollars and only he would've benefited as opposed to creating vast amounts of wealth for his investors.

Creating a business, particularly in a still struggling economy, can seem like an almost impossible feat. But if you have an idea, the know how, and the willingness to work hard, creating your own business isn't as unachievable as you would think it is.

"You're neither right nor wrong because other people agree with you. You're right because your facts are right and your reasoning is right – that's the only thing that makes you right. And if your facts and reasoning are right, you don't have to worry about anybody else."

But when you have a good idea and a solid business plan in place, you would be surprised by the number of people who are willing to get in on the ground floor. Particularly family members and friend's. If you look at Buffett Associates, his two biggest contributors to the original partnership were his oldest sister and his aunt. Buffett most likely approached his family members first with the idea of creating a partnership because chances are they knew him best, and also knew that he had the education and the know how to make their initial money grow into the fortune that it eventually became.

So does this mean you should hit mom and dad up for a loan to open up your first business? Absolutely not! Because you won't be asking for a loan, you will be asking your loved ones to make an investment so that they can share in the profits of your idea. To many, your idea may seem risky (and chances are it may even seem risky to you) and they may seem reluctant to enter into a business venture where they may lose their initial investment, or not see a return on it for many years.

Which is why it is absolutely vital that you create a solid business plan before you actually approach anyone about investing in a business opportunity. Even if you go the more conventional route of approaching a bank for a small business loan, they are going to want to see solid documentation that will convince them that your idea will make money and that they will be paid back in a timely manner.

So if you have what you think is a zero failure (but what idea or plan is really zero failure?) idea, plan ahead. In fact, plan very far ahead—as much as a decade if you can project that far ahead—because this will be very effective in convincing investors of how serious you are in pursuing your passion. Also let potential investors know that you are willing to risk just as much capital as they are by trying to match their initial investment. For most people, this will take a bit of saving—because if you're trying to entice potential investors, you don't also want the responsibility of paying back a bank loan as well—but if you have the passion, drive, and ambition, you obviously will have no problem with cutting a few financial corners to help you save for your seed money.

But most importantly, don't give up! If you are truly passionate about your business plan, you will find a way to make it happen, even if you have to work three jobs and operate on zero sleep to do so.

A Giant In Our Midst: The Creation of Berkshire Hathaway

"Look at market fluctuations as your friend rather than your enemy; profit from folly rather than participate in it."

In 1969 at the peak of the Vietnam War, a period which saw the Dow ballooned and stock prizes rise to unprecedented highs, Buffett began to liquidate the partnership. In May of the same year, he informed his partners that he was "unable to find any bargains in the current market" and he spent the remainder of the year liquidating the portfolio, with the exception of two companies: Berkshire and Diversified Retailing.

Shares of Berkshire were distributed among the partners with a letter from Warren informing them that he would in some capacity be involved with Berkshire, but was under no obligation to them in the future. Warren was clear in his intention to hold onto his own stake in the company—he was a majority owner of Berkshire Hathaway owning a 29% stake in the company—but he did not reveal his intentions with the company or with what role he would be playing in it.

"Somebody once said that in looking for people to hire, you look for three qualities: integrity, intelligence, and energy. And if you don't have the first, the other two will kill you. You think about it; it's true. If you hire somebody without [integrity], you really want them to be dumb and lazy."

Buffett's role at Berkshire Hathaway had actually been defined years earlier. In 1965 after accumulating 49% of the common stock in Berkshire Hathaway, Buffett named himself Director. Poor management had run the company nearly into the ground, and he was certain with a bit of tweaking, it could be run better and begin generating a profit for the flagging holding company. Buffett made Ken Chace President of Berkshire Hathaway, giving him complete autonomy over the organization. Although he refused to award stock options on the basis that he considered it unfair to shareholders, though he did agree to co-sign for a loan of nearly $20,000 so that Chace could to purchase 1,000 shares of tBerkshire Hathaway stock.

Two years later in 1967, Buffett met with Berkshire Hathaway controlling shareholder, Jack Ringwalt, and asked what he thought the company was worth? Ringwalt told Buffett at least $50 per share, which was at a $17 premium above its then-trading price of $33. Warren offered to buy the whole company on the spot, a move that cost him $8.6 million dollars. That same year, Berkshire paid out a dividend of 10 cents on its outstanding stock, something that would never happened again. Years later, Buffett joked that he must have been in the bathroom when the dividend was declared.

In 1970, Buffett named himself Chairman of the Board of Berkshire Hathaway and for the first time, wrote the letter to the shareholders, a responsibility that had been Ken Chace's in the past. That same year, Buffett's capital allocation began to display his prudence; textile profits were a pitiful $45,000, while insurance and banking each brought in $2.1 and $2.6 million dollars. The paltry cash brought in from the struggling looms in New Bedford, Massachusetts had provided the stream of capital necessary to start building Berkshire Hathaway.

A year or so later, Warren Buffett was offered the chance to buy a California based company called See's Candy. See's was a gourmet chocolate maker sold its own brand of candies to its customers at a premium. The balance sheet reflected what Californians already knew, they were more than willing to pay a bit more for the special See's taste. Buffett decided Berkshire would be willing to purchase the company for $25 million in cash. See's owners were holding out for $30 million, but quickly conceded. It was the largest acquisition Berkshire or Buffett had ever made.

After the successful See's Candy acquisition, Buffett attempted to merge Berkshire Hathaway with industrial giant, Wesco which prompt an SEC investigation that ultimately caused a corporate merger between Berkshire Hathaway and Wesco to fail. Buffett and Charlie Munger offered to buy the stock of Wesco stock at a highly inflated price simply because they thought it was "the right thing to do". Unsurprisingly, the government didn't believe them and the merger was denied.

Buffett began to see Berkshire Hathaway's net worth climb. From 1965- to-1975, the company's value rose from $20 per share to close to $100. It was also during this period that Warren made his final purchases of Berkshire stock—when the partnership dolled out the shares, he owned 29%. Years later, he had invested more than $15.4 million dollars into the company at an average cost of $32.45 per share—which brought his ownership of to over 43% of the stock with Susie holding another 3%. His entire net worth was placed into Berkshire Hathaway. With no personal holdings, the company had become his sole investment vehicle.

"Diversification is a protection against ignorance. It makes very little sense for those who know what they're doing."

In 1976, Buffett once again became involved with GEICO insurance company. The company had recently reported amazingly high losses and its stock was trading at only $2 per share. Buffett wisely realized that the basic business was still intact and that most of the problems GEIGO was facing was caused by an inept management. Over the next several years, Berkshire built up its position in this ailing insurer and reaped millions in profits. Benjamin Graham, who still held his fortune in the company, died in in September of the same year, shortly before the turnaround. Years later, the insurance giant would become a fully owned subsidiary of Berkshire.

By the late 70s, the Buffett's reputation had grown to the point that if there was even a rumor Warren Buffett was buying a stock, it was enough to shoot the stocks price up 10%. Berkshire Hathaway's stock was trading at more than $290 a share, and Buffett's personal wealth was almost $140 million. The irony was that he never sold a single share of Berkshire Hathaway, meaning his entire available cash was the $50,000 salary he received as Chairman. At the time, he made a offhanded comment to a broker, "Everything I got is tied up in Berkshire. I'd like a few nickels outside."

This prompted Warren to start investing for his personal life. According to Roger Lowenstein's biography "Buffett", Buffett was far more speculative with his own investments. At one point he bought copper futures which was unadulterated speculation and was viewed in the investment world as being entirely a crap shoot. But, in a brief 9 month period, he had made $3 million dollars. When prompted to invest in real estate by a friend, he responded "Why should I buy real estate when the stock market is so easy?"

For all the fine businesses Berkshire Hathaway had managed collect, one of its best and most profitable was about to come under its stable. In 1983, Warren Buffett walked into Nebraska Furniture Mart, the multi-million dollar furniture retailer built from the ground up by Rose Blumpkin. Speaking to Mrs. Blumpkin, Buffett asked if she would be interested in selling the store to Berkshire Hathaway. Blumpkin's answer was a simple yes, to which she responded she would part for $60 million. The deal was sealed on a handshake and a single page contract was drawn up. Blumpkin, a Russian-born immigrant, merely folded the check without looking at it when she received it days later in the mail.

Scott & Fetzer was another great addition to the Berkshire family. The company itself had been the target of a hostile takeover when an LPO was launched by Ralph Schey, the Chairman of Scott & Fetzer. The year was 1984 and Ivan Boesky, the maker of Kirby vacuum cleaners and World Book encyclopedia, soon launched a counter offer for $60 a share—the original tender offer stood at $50 a share which was $5 above market value. Scott & Fetzer, needless to say,was panicking. Buffett, who owned a quarter of a million shares, sent a message to the company asking them to call if they were interested in a merger.

The phone rang almost immediately. Berkshire offered $60 per share in cold, hard, cash. When the deal was wrapped up less than a week later, Berkshire Hathaway had a new $315 million dollar cash-generating powerhouse to add to its collection. The small stream of cash that was taken out of the struggling textile mill had built one of the most powerful companies in the world. Far more impressive things were to be done in the next decade. Berkshire would see its share price climb from $2,600 to as high as $80,000 in the 1990's.

In 1986, Buffett bought a used Falcon aircraft for $850,000. As he had become increasingly recognizable, it was no longer comfortable for him to fly commercially. The idea of the luxury was hard for him to adjust to, but he loved the jet immensely. The passion for jets eventually led him to purchase Executive Jet in the mid-1990's.

The 80's went on with Berkshire Hathaway continued increase in value. All for except for one noisy, destructive bump in the road: The stock market the crash of 1987, Black Monday. Buffett, wasn't upset about the market correction, calmly checked the price of his company and went back to work. It was representative of how he viewed stocks and businesses in general. This was one of the stock market's temporary aberrations, albeit, it was quite a strong one—nearly a quarter of Berkshire's market capital was wiped out. Seemingly unfazed by the losses, Buffett and Berkshire Hathaway powered through the devastation of Black Monday.

"Why not invest your assets in the companies you really like? As Mae West said, 'Too much of a good thing can be wonderful."

A year later, in 1988, Buffett started buying up Coca-Cola stock. The President of Coca-Cola noticed someone was loading up on shares and became concerned. After researching the transactions, he noticed the trades were being placed from the Mid-west. He immediately thought of Buffett, whom he called. Buffett confessed to being the culprit and requested they didn't speak of it until he was legally required to disclose his holdings at the 5% threshold. Within a few months, Berkshire owned 7% of the company or $1.02 billion dollars worth of the stock. Within three years, Buffett's Coca-Cola stock would be worth more than the entire value of Berkshire when he made the investment.

By 1989, Berkshire Hathaway was trading at $8,000 a share. Buffett was now personally worth more than $3.8 billion dollars. Within the next ten years, he would be worth ten times that amount.

During the remainder of the 1990's, Berkshire Hathaway's stock catapulted as high as $80,000 per share. Even with this astronomical feat, as the dot-com frenzy began to take hold, Warren Buffett was accused of "losing his touch". In 1999, when Berkshire reported a net increase of 0.5% per share, several newspapers ran stories about the demise of the Oracle.

Confident that the technology bubble would burst, Buffett continued to do what he did best: allocate capital into great businesses that were selling below intrinsic value. His efforts did not go unrewarded. When the markets finally did come to their senses, Warren Buffett was once again a star. Berkshire's stock recovered to its previous levels after falling to around $45,000 per share, but then rebounding to around $75,000 a share, and Buffett was once again held with as high of regard as before the tech bubble burst.

"Our approach is very much profiting from lack of change rather than from change. With Wrigley chewing gum, it's the lack of change that appeals to me. I don't think it is going to be hurt by the Internet. That's the kind of business I like."

After the turn of the millennium, Buffett continued to purchase companies that he liked because of long standing and successful business models and because of their long histories within the American scene. Most notably, he purchased controlling shares for Berkshire Hathaway of Wrigley's, Nestle, and the Heinz ketchup company. His reasoning behind each of the purchases was simple enough, he liked the taste of the products. Certainly there were other factors involved with the purchasing of these companies such as solid and consistent returns, but obviously keeping his response so whimsical made for far better copy.

"Most people get interested in stocks when everyone else is. The time to get interested is when no one else is. You can't buy what is popular and do well."

The most important thing Buffett took away from his education with Ben Graham was the concept of intrinsic value, and that the value of a company and an investment is far greater than what you see on a spreadsheet, and is in fact every aspect of a company. From its executive and management teams, down to its lowest level employee. Where as Ben Graham was very much a dollar and cents kind of investor, who needed to only to see that a business or stock had longterm potential because of past consistent performance, Buffett is the type of investor who actually needs to see how the business operates and how its employees interact and enjoy their work.

Buffett knows that a business is only as good as the people who run it and operate it. For him, a solid reputation in the world, and just not on paper, makes all the difference. This belief has served Buffett and his business decisions for well over sixty-years

Making The World A Better Place

"I don't measure my life by the money I've made. Other people might, but I certainly don't."

In 1981, the decade of greed, Berkshire announced a new charity plan which was thought up by Charlie Munger and approved by Buffett.

The plan called for each shareholder to designate charities which would receive $2 for each Berkshire share the stockholder owned. This was in response to a common practice on Wall Street of the CEO choosing who received the company's hand-outs—often they would go to the executive's schools, churches, and organizations—the plan was a huge success and over the years the amount was upped for each share.

At its peak, Berkshire shareholders were giving millions of dollars away each year, all to their own causes. The program was eventually discontinued after associates at one of Berkshire's subsidiaries, The Pampered Chef, experienced discrimination because of the controversial pro choice charities Buffett chose to allocate his pro-rated portion of the charitable contribution pool.

"If you're in the luckiest one per cent of humanity, you owe it to the rest of humanity to think about the other 99 per cent."

In 2006, Buffet pledged the bulk of his fortune the Bill and Melinda Gates foundation, which in turn sparked the Giving Pledge. The foundation started by Buffet and Gates in recruiting the wealthiest 1% of Americans to give away at least half of their personal fortunes upon their deaths or before.

What is most amazing about Buffett is despite being one of the wealthiest men in the world, he is also one of its most generous. When there are so many wealthy people in the world who think they are going to be able to take their riches with them when they die, Buffett has taken the exact opposite road and has decided to make the world a better place in his lifetime. Every day he strives to set the example among his peers and he has been doing so for over thirty years.

Even with his children, Buffett has stipulated in his will that he will only give them and his grand children enough so that they can discover their own passions, but the rest of it is to be entirely willed to the Bill and Melinda Gates Foundation, so they can put it towards any cause they see fit. This level of generosity and forethought is truly inspiring and it cannot help but get you thinking about how you will leave the world when you die.

What kind of mark have you made upon the planet and on your fellow human beings? What do you do right now that effects those around you?

No, most of us will never be able to create and leave behind the kind of legacy Warren Buffett has, but we can take his cue start attempting to change the world in small ways. Probably the most effective way is by simply volunteering our time to causes that we believe in. Give an hour or two of time a month to volunteering at homeless shelters or at local area schools, or anywhere where actual human resources are needed but are in short supply. Yes, it may seem like an effort because all of us lead busy lives. In between work and family, there doesn't even seem to be enough time in the day to properly eat and rest.

But if you really take a look at your schedule, chances are there is time for you to go out and help your community in some way. If you really think about it, how much time do you waste through out the day doing things like watching television or spending time on the internet? Chances are you spend days doing nothing but relaxing.

"It is not necessary to do extraordinary things to get extraordinary results."

And volunteering doesn't always have to focus on those who are less fortunate. If you look at your community, how many different activities are available to children in it? Are there sports leagues that are in need of coaches? Are there adult education classes that need tutors for individuals who are struggling to learn a new skill? These are all things that you can give a bare amount of time to and it actually changes the world because of the effort you put in. No, volunteering to be a soccer coach isn't as dramatic as donating billions that will go towards curing diseases or building new schools. But what it will do is create positive change to the individuals you're helping, and this, hopefully, in turn will hopefully inspire those people you've reach out to, and they'll want to help others as well.

But if all of this seems like it is too much for your plate, look to your own home instead. Are there even more smaller ways you can effect change right from your couch at the end of the day? Chances are , the answer is yes, and they're probably sitting right in front of you or right besides you. Look to your family, your children, your spouse, and think about what you do that effects them in a positive manner? What lessons are you teaching them that will help them better the world? Will they go onto greater things than you have accomplished? Are you acting as a positive role model in their upbringing to ensure their success in the world?

Yes, these are all small things and by no means grandiose and scale, but these small things could very well lead to a far brighter future for everyone if we simply show an effort and try to change the world.

In Every Life, Some Rain Must Fall

Despite Buffett's idyllic life, like the rest of us, he has faced his fair share of personal and business crisis'. What sets Buffett apart from others when faced with a personal or professional criss is his ability to logically asses various situations and not allow it to physically and emotionally shock him and disrupt his day-to-day existence. This is by no means saying that he isn't upset or distraught, the man is human after all, but it's the way he conducts himself when he is faced with the inevitable pitfalls of high finance and the stresses of every day life that sets Buffett apart from others when dealing with a criss.

And although most of Warren Buffett's life has been blessed with more than his fair share of good fortune and success. But as with every success story, there has to be periods where a person is tested to almost beyond their physical and emotional limits, and Buffett is not the exception and has faced levels of adversity that would break most people.

The Separation and Death of Susie Buffett

In 1977 at the age of 45, Susan Buffett left her husband. Although she remained married to him, Susie wished to pursue a career as a singer and moved herself to an apartment in San Francisco to do so. Needless to say, Buffett was devastated by the loss of his marriage. Throughout his life, he had often described Susie as being "the sunshine and rain in my garden".

Despite the separation, Buffett and Susie remained close, speaking every day, taking their annual two-week New York trip, and meeting the kids at their California Beach house for Christmas get-togethers. The transition was hard—as it would be for anyone in similar circumstances— for Buffett, but he eventually grew somewhat accustomed to the new arrangement. Susie called several women in the Omaha area and insisted they go to dinner and a movie with her husband. Eventually, Susie introduced Buffett to a waitress named Astrid Menks. Within the year, Astrid moved in with Buffett into "Buffett's Folly" and the two have been together ever since, and all with Susie's blessing.

In 2003, Susie was diagnosed with oral cancer and underwent surgery, radiation treatments, and facial reconstruction due to bone loss. Buffett made it a point to fly out to Susie's home every weekend during this long, painful period. Just as it looked as if Susie would fully recover from the cancer, she suffered a cerebral hemorrhage and died at the age of 82, Buffett was by her side when she passed and was so devastated by her loss that he was unable to attend her memorial service.

The Solomon Brothers Scandal

"It takes 20 years to build a reputation and five minutes to ruin it. If you think about that, you'll do things differently."

In 1991, U.S. Treasury Deputy Assistant Secretary Mike Basham learned that Salomon trader Paul Mozer had been submitting false bids in an attempt to purchase more Treasury bonds than permitted by one buyer during the period between December 1990 and May 1991. Salomon was fined $290 million for this infraction, the largest fine ever levied on an investment bank at the time. It was just after this period that Buffett was brought in and took control of the day-to-day operations of Solomon Brothers— a firm which Berkshire Hathaway held a partial stake in and that Buffett held a personal, yet entirely passive, investment in as well— in order to strip the brokerage firm of its untoward elements and to find a buyer for the struggling firm.

Buffett described the period in which he was running Solomon Brothers to be one of the most stressful periods in his long career because of the external pressures of SEC investigators, and the internal strife and disorganization of Solomon's management team, as well as issues it faced in its public offering of MCI Communications.

Within a year, Buffett found a buyer for the embattled firm. The Travelers Group was the one to buy Solomon and Solomon Brothers CEO was forced out of the company in August 1991 and a U.S. Securities and Exchange Commission (SEC) settlement resulted in a fine of $100,000 and his being barred from serving as a chief executive of a brokerage firm. The scandal was then documented in the 1993 book Nightmare on Wall Street.

After the acquisition, the parent company (Travelers Group, and later Citigroup) proved culturally averse to the volatile profits and losses caused by proprietary trading, instead preferring slower and more steady growth. Salomon suffered a $100 million loss when it incorrectly positioned itself for the merger of MCI Communications with British Telecom which never occurred. Subsequently, most of its proprietary trading business was disbanded.

The combined investment banking operations became known as Salomon Smith Barney and was renamed Citigroup Global Markets Inc. after the reorganization.

Gen Re & AIG

In October of 2000, some Wall Street analysts and SEC investigators questioned the decline in American International Group (AIG) loss reserves. In an effort to quell these concerns, AIG entered into two sham reinsurance transactions with Cologne Re Dublin, a subsidiary of General Reinsurance, that had no economic substance but were designed to add $500 million in phony loss reserves to AIG's balance sheet in the fourth quarter of 2000 and first quarter of 2001.

In 2005, New York Attorney General Eliot Spitzer began an investigation into the two reinsurance transactions. Soon afterwards, AIG came under market pressure, and admitted it had undertaken what could be construed as securities fraud. The staff admitted that the two reinsurance transactions had inflated AIG's balance sheet and propped up AIG's stock price. In the resultant stock crash, investors lost $500 million in investments.

General Reinsurance, or more commonly known as Gen Re, was a wholly owned subsidiary of Berkshire Hathaway, and Buffett was called to a New York grand jury and in front of congress to detail his involvement with both Gen Re and AIG. Buffett had faced federal scrutiny before as well as investigations from the SEC, but he had never been involved in a scandal as far reaching as this one.

Through out the various hearings, Buffett kept his cool and affable demeanor, answering every question thrown at him with his trademark intelligence and good humor despite the seriousness of the allegations and the overall threat to the stability of Berkshire Hathaway. By the end of the hearings, Buffett and Berkshire Hathaway walked away fairly unscathed, but the hearings themselves were far reaching and many new protections were put into place to make sure that business firms can not create such oversights in the future.

"The most important thing to do if you find yourself in a hole is to stop digging."

How do you react when you are faced with adversity? Do you run and hide from it, emotionally shut yourself down in hopes that it will just disappear if you're are quiet and meek enough? Or do you face it head on and take responsibility for your actions?

In certain circumstances, adversity and strife are unavoidable. When faced with the longterm illness or death or a loved one such as a parent, a spouse, a child, this kind of adversity is unavoidable and beyond painful, and all we can really do is live through the pain.

But what about other types of adversity such as work assignments or the occasional fights you have with your spouse or friends? Do you often times find yourself feeling overwhelmed and cowering from confrontation or extra responsibility? Or do you try to shift blame on to others or simply shirk the idea of putting extra effort into your various endeavors?

In the adverse situations Buffett faced, he remained clear headed and rational when confronted with them. He knew that if he did not face his and Berkshire Hathaway's issues head on, that chances were that they would come back to haunt him and ultimately hurt his business.

Although the chances of you having to appear in front of a senate subcommittee are slim, how do you think you would react in similar situation? Would you crumble? Would you run? (Because let's face it, if you're being called in front of congress, chances are you would have the assets to run) Or would you stay and face the music and let the chips fall where they may? You can, of course,

How we face adversity and turmoil is the best measurement of a person. The best of us will rise to any challenge whether it is positive or negative, and the worst will simply fade into the background and never make an impact of any sort.

A Quiet Life

"I insist on a lot of time being spent, almost every day, to just sit and think. That is very uncommon in American business. I read and think. So I do more reading and thinking, and make less impulse decisions than most people in business. I do it because I like this kind of life."

What has set Buffett apart from most investors is his willingness to soldier on in his work no matter the amount of adversity or personal issues he faces. For Buffett, work was his solace, his escape. Where many of us retreat and run for our problems, Buffett has tackled his challenges head on and has always seemed to profit from his straight forward approach to business and life.

With the housing crash and great recession of 2008, Buffett and Berkshire Hathaway went through the same amount of turmoil as most investment firms and holding companies did. Although because of the sound, proven investments within Berkshire Hathaway portfolio, and Buffett's complete lack of interest in real estate, real estate holding companies, and mortgage futures, Berkshire Hathaway and Buffett came out of the Great Recession fairly unscathed. Of course, like most stocks and stock portfolio's, Berkshire Hathaway did suffer a devaluation. But at that point in Buffett's long life and career, the loss of capital was a minor one, and one which he saw as simply another fluctuation in a long history of schizophrenic fluctuations within the stock market.

On Feb. 15, 2011 Warren Buffett was awarded with the "Medal of Freedom" (the highest civilian honour) by President Barack Obama. Buffet on his side has been a huge supporter of Obama's campaign in 2008.

At age 82, Buffett now mostly concerns himself with the Giving Pledge charity he established with Bill Gates and various speaking engagements at colleges and corporations around the world, and although he still chairs the annual Berkshire Hathaway investors meeting, he now allows others to pilot the day-to-day operations of the iconic holding company.

What Warren Buffett's life has taught us, more than anything else, is that a life of passion is also a life of obsession, and that the two walk hand-in-hand.

When you are living a life of passion and obsession, there are no limits. There are no time clocks or time off, no vacations, no bosses breathing down your neck to perform, because with obsession, there is no boss, there is only you. There is only your obsession and wanting to work on it day after day as a means of perfecting it and making it fully your own. This kind of passion and obsession does not happen over night. Yes, there are some people, like Buffett, like Picasso, like Einstein, who simply seem to be born with a clear idea of what they want and how to accomplish it. But for most, it takes time for passion to emerge and set you down your chosen path.

If this is you, if you have found your passion, the very thing that makes you jump out of bed every day eager for it to start and disappointed when it comes to a close because you feel you still have so much more to do, count yourself lucky, because you are a true rarity. Although living a life of passion at times may feel like a burden because of various roadblocks and limitations. But if you stay true to yourself and your passion, eventually you will find yourself doing exactly what you want to be doing if you remain persistent and true to your vision of your future and career.

For those of you who have yet to discover what drives you, don't give up. Never stop looking and stay curious and focused. Read, give yourself time to sit and think, experience life, and constantly pursue your education whether it is in a classroom, or in the classroom of experience. If you remain curious, there's a better chance than not you will eventually discover your passion. But if for some reason you don't stumble upon what makes you tick, don't feel disheartened. Sometimes passion only emerges from effort. Effort at your job, effort as a spouse and a parent, effort in your hobbies and interests. The point is to constantly strive to make yourself a better person who cares deeply and passionately about family, friends, work, life and to eventually achieve all of your goals no matter what they are. And by doing this, living for every moment as if it was your last, you will be living the Warren Buffett way.

Thank you for purchasing and reading my book! I know you could have picked from dozens of books about successful people, but you took a chance with mine and I appreciate it. If you believe that this book is worth sharing, would you take a few seconds to let your friends know about it? If it turns out to help them achieve their goals and live a happier life, they will be forever thankful to you. As I will be.

52399169R00190

Made in the USA
Lexington, KY
28 May 2016